NATURALISM IN MATHEMATICS

Our much-valued mathematical knowledge rests on two supports: the logic of proof and the axioms from which those proofs begin. *Naturalism in Mathematics* investigates the status of the latter, the fundamental assumptions of mathematics. These were once held to be self-evident, but progress in work on the foundations of mathematics, especially in set theory, has rendered that comforting notion obsolete. Given that candidates for axiomatic status cannot be proved, what sorts of considerations can be offered for or against them? That is the central question addressed in this book.

One answer is that mathematics aims to describe an objective world of mathematical objects, and that axiom candidates should be judged by their truth or falsity in that world. This promising view—realism—is assessed and finally rejected in favour of another—naturalism—which attends less to metaphysical considerations of objective truth and falsity, and more to practical considerations drawn from within mathematics itself. Penelope Maddy defines this naturalism, explains the motivations for it, and shows how it can be helpfully applied in the assessment of candidates for axiomatic status in set theory.

Maddy's clear, original treatment of this fundamental issue is informed by current work in both philosophy and mathematics, and will be accessible and enlightening to readers from both disciplines.

NATURALISM IN MATHEMATICS

PENELOPE MADDY

CLARENDON PRESS · OXFORD

OXFORD

Great Clarendon Street, Oxford OX2 6DP

Oxford University Press is a department of the University of Oxford
It furthers the University's objective of excellence in research, scholarship,
and education by publishing worldwide in

Oxford New York

Athens Auckland Bangkok Bogotá Buenos Aires Calcutta
Cape Town Chennai Dar es Salaam Delhi Florence Hong Kong Istanbul
Karachi Kuala Lumpur Madrid Melbourne Mexico City Mumbai
Nairobi Paris São Paulo Singapore Taipei Tokyo Toronto Warsaw

with associated companies in Berlin Ibadan

Oxford is a registered trade mark of Oxford University Press
in the UK and in certain other countries

Published in the United States
by Oxford University Press Inc., New York

© Penelope Maddy 1997

The moral rights of the author have been asserted

Database right Oxford University Press (maker)

First published 1997

First issued in paperback 2000

British Library Cataloguing in Publication Data

Data available

Library of Congress Cataloging in Publication Data
Maddy, Penelope.
Naturalism in Mathematics / by Penelope Maddy.
Includes bibliographical references.
I. Mathematics—Philosophy. 2. Naturalism. I. Title.
QA8.4.M328 1997 510'.1—dc21 97–12665
ISBN 0–19–823573–9
ISBN 0–19–825075–4 (pbk.)

Printed in Great Britain
on acid-free paper by
Biddles Ltd.,
Guildford & King's Lynn

For
Sue, Jenny, Annie, and Unc

PREFACE

As the title suggests, this book is in some ways a sequel to *Realism in Mathematics* (1990a). Though the presentation is self-contained, the central problem is a version of the issue raised in chapter 4 of the earlier work as the most pressing open problem for the set theoretic realist: how are set theoretic axioms to be judged? I now think that set theoretic realism founders (in part) on this problem, and that set theoretic naturalism provides a more promising approach. Spelling this out is the burden of what follows.

My profound and continuing debt to the writings of Quine and Gödel will be obvious from a glance at the Table of Contents; John Burgess, Tony Martin, and John Steel have also made irreplaceable contributions along the way. Jeff Barrett, Sarah Resnikoff, Jamie Tappenden, and Mark Wilson helped with conversations and correspondence, and George Boolos, Bill Harper, and Ruth Marcus with timely encouragement. Mark Balaguer, Jeff Barrett, Gary Bell, Lara Denis, Don Fallis, Tony Martin, Michael Resnik, and Jamie Tappenden read all or part of the manuscript at various stages and made valuable suggestions. My heartfelt thanks go to all these people, and to Peter Momtchiloff and Angela Blackburn for their support and guidance.

Most of this book is based on a series of articles ((1988), (1992), (1993a), (1993b), (1994), (1995), (1996b), (199?a), (199?b), (199?c), (199?d), and (199?e)); there is hardly a section that doesn't trace an ancestor in at least one of these papers. II. 4. ii and II. 6. ii contain substantial verbatim borrowings from (1993a), § 2, and (1994), 385–95, respectively. III. 6. i and ii present an expanded version of (199?d), §§ 3 and 4. Smaller extracts (from a phrase to a paragraph) appear elsewhere: I've been able to keep track of bits of (1988), § 1, in I. 3; of (199?a) in II. 6. ii; of (1996b), § 2, in III. 2; of (199?c), §§ II and III, in III. 4. iii and III. 4. iv, respectively; and of (199?d) in III. 5. My thanks to the original publishers—especially the Association for Symbolic Logic, North Holland

Publishers, and Springer Verlag—for their permissions to reprint. Despite the close connection between the treatments here and in the ancestral papers, there are also departures, large and small, so the reader should not expect everything I say here to square perfectly with what she may happen to have read there.

As my work on several of the original articles was supported by the National Science Foundation, I would like once again to express my deep gratitude to them. I am also indebted to the University of California at Irvine for a sabbatical leave that allowed me to complete the final manuscript. And finally, let me extend special thanks to the set theoretic community, for its kind generosity to a prying philosopher, over a period of many years.

P. M.

Irvine, California
February 1997

CONTENTS

THE PROBLEM

The truths of mathematics hold a place of honour in our collective web of belief. While our fondest empirical beliefs—that the earth is round, that plants grow from seeds, that heavy objects fall—are all supported by definitive accumulations of good empirical evidence from observation, experiment, and theory, in the mathematical case, we reach a cherished evidential ideal: we have proofs. Granted, these proofs often rest on premisses or background assumptions, but perhaps such assumptions can themselves be proved. Indeed, they often are proved, in the literature of the field, in its canonical textbooks or its folklore; sometimes, the unproved assumptions are considered so trivial that the informed reader is supposed to be capable of sketching for herself whatever further argumentation is desired. But this process of appeal to further and further proofs can't go on for ever; eventually, we must reach fundamental assumptions.

In fact, it is these fundamental assumptions that often define a branch of mathematics, as the Peano axioms define arithmetic, or axioms for complete ordered fields define the real numbers at the basis of the calculus and higher analysis. The astounding achievement of the foundational studies of the late nineteenth and early twentieth centuries was the discovery that these fundamental assumptions could themselves be proved from a standpoint more fundamental still, that of the theory of sets. The idea is simple: the objects of any branch of classical mathematics—numbers, functions, spaces, algebraic structures—can be modelled as sets, and resulting versions of the standard theorems can be proved in set theory. So the most fundamental of the fundamental assumptions of mathematics, the only such assumptions that truly cannot be proved, are the axioms of the theory of sets itself.

In this sense, then, our much-valued mathematical knowledge rests on two supports: inexorable deductive logic, the stuff of proof, and the set theoretic axioms. The question of what grounds our faith in logical inference is a vital and profound one, but the subject of this book is the second question: what justifies the axioms of set theory? Though it might seem that the only justificatory method of mathematics is proof, our question points to something more, to a brand of mathematical evidence that has received much less attention.

Questions of justification are always of interest to philosophers, but it should be noted that this particular question of justification is of considerable importance to contemporary set theorists as well. Though the current axioms of set theory are strong enough to found all of classical mathematics, they cannot settle some of the most basic questions of set theory itself, and as set theoretical considerations have reached into other branches of mathematics, the current axioms have also been unable to settle natural questions of algebra, topology, and so on. This situation has led to a search for additional axioms, for new fundamental assumptions, at which point the question of how such assumptions are to be justified takes on a fully practical application. My fondest hope is to provide a philosophically useful account that is also sensitive to (or better yet: relevant to) this pressing methodological concern of contemporary set theory.

My goal in Part I is to give a more complete characterization of this problem in contemporary set theoretic axiomatics. Much of this material will, of necessity, be familiar to the specialist, who is cordially invited to skip or skim. (Those most concerned with the philosophical issues surrounding realism and naturalism might prefer to do the same, returning to Part I as need or curiosity arise.) I begin (in I. 1) with a sketch of the origins of set theory and end (in I. 6) with a discussion of the particular new axiom candidate that will serve as a recurrent case study in Parts II and III. Along the way, I look more closely at the nature of set theory's foundational role (in I. 2), summarize the arguments given in defence of the standard axioms (in I. 3), describe a sampling of the independent questions left open by those axioms (in I. 4), and survey the various styles of available new axiom candidates (in I. 5).

1

The Origins of Set Theory

Set theory, as we now know it, resulted from a confluence of two distinct historical developments, one beginning from the work of Gottlob Frege from the 1870s to the early 1900s, the other beginning from the work of Georg Cantor during roughly the same period. That Frege's initial motivations were at least partly philosophical, while Cantor's were at first largely mathematical, only serves to highlight the rich conceptual roots from which the theory arose. I'll begin here with the Fregean line of development (in (i)), then turn to the Cantorian (in (ii)), and conclude (in (iii)) with a glance at the confluence.

(i) In his *Begriffsschrift* of 1879, Frege invented modern mathematical logic, but his motivating concern at that time was a project in the foundations of arithmetic: he hoped to show that Kant was wrong about arithmetic, that it is analytic, rather than synthetic, as Kant had claimed. On Kant's definitions of the relevant terms, analyticity is a feature of the content of a judgement: the concept of the predicate is contained in the concept of the subject. Frege criticized this definition as too narrow,[1] as applying only to universal affirmative statements like 'all bodies are extended', and proposed to correct this flaw, 'to state accurately what earlier writers, Kant in particular, meant by'[2] the terms analytic and synthetic; but in doing so, he shifted focus from the content of a judgement to its ultimate justification:

This means that the question is removed from the sphere of psychology, and assigned, if the truth concerned is a mathematical one, to the sphere of mathematics. The problem becomes, in fact, that of finding the proof of the proposition, and of following it up right back to the primitive truths. If, in carrying out this process, we come only on general logical laws and on definitions, then the truth is an analytic one. (Frege (1884), § 3)

---

[1] See Frege (1884), § 88.
[2] See ibid. § 3.

This process of tracing the grounds for a statement of arithmetic turned out to be very difficult:

To prevent anything intuitive from penetrating here unnoticed, I had to bend every effort to keep the chain of inferences free from gaps. In attempting to comply with this requirement in the strictest possible way I found the inadequacy of language to be an obstacle; no matter how unwieldy the expressions I was ready to accept, I was less and less able, as relations became more and more complex, to attain the precision that my purpose required. (Frege (1879), 5–6)

It was to overcome this difficulty that Frege devised the formal language of the *Begriffsschrift*.

The main philosophical and mathematical outlines of the demonstration that arithmetic is analytic appear in the *Grundlagen* of 1884. The plan is to define numbers as logical objects, and to prove the basic propositions about numbers (something like the Peano Axioms)[3] from fundamental logical laws. The logic involved, from the *Begriffsschrift*, is higher order: in addition to objects, it includes first-order concepts, under which objects do or don't fall, second-order concepts, under which first-order concepts do or don't fall, third-order concepts, under which second-order concepts do or don't fall, and so on.[4]

Frege's first step is to analyse statements of number: what is claimed, for example, when we say that there are two decks of cards on the table? Some might be tempted to say we are ascribing a property to a physical thing, but Frege points out that the very same physical thing is one deck, four suits, fifty-two cards, and ever-so-many-more molecules. A physical thing by itself, as a mere aggregate of stuff, could have any number whatsoever, if the units were appropriately specified. In Frege's parlance, what settles the unit is the concept involved; the statement that there are two decks of cards on the table is a statement about a concept—the con-

---

[3] The Peano Axioms (actually due to Dedekind (1888)) state that (1) every natural number has a unique successor, (2) natural numbers with the same successor are the same, (3) there is a natural number 0, which is not the successor of any natural number, and (4) mathematical induction. See Wright (1983) for an explicit derivation, and Heck (1993) for a more recent account.

[4] The more common logic today is first-order logic, which quantifies only over individuals (objects). The Peano Axioms are actually second order, because mathematical induction (if a set of natural numbers contains 0 and is closed under successor, then it is the set of all natural numbers) quantifies over sets of natural numbers (the modern counterpart to Frege's first-order concepts) as well as natural numbers themselves. The same is true of the axioms for complete ordered fields that characterize the real numbers, because they include the continuity axiom (every non-empty set of reals with an upper bound has a least upper bound).

cept 'deck on the table'—to the effect that there are distinct things x and y that fall under it and no other things fall under it. As noted, we would be inclined to say something quite different about the concept 'card on the table' or the concept 'molecule on the table'.

Given this analysis of numerical statements, Frege moves on to the notion of sameness of number: what is claimed, for example, when we say that there are as many forks on the table as there are spoons? Here Frege borrows a familiar answer from Hume: we claim that there is a one-to-one correspondence between the forks on the table and the spoons on the table.[5] Such a correspondence could be displayed by moving the forks and spoons into pairs, so that each fork is paired with a single spoon and vice versa, but the correspondence itself is a relation, a two-place concept, that links forks to spoons regardless of their location in space or time. The result of this analysis is what's now called 'Hume's Principle': for any concepts F and G, the number of Fs = the number of Gs if and only if there is a one-to-one correspondence between the things falling under F and the things falling under G.

Hume's Principle is enough to identify or distinguish numbers when they are presented to us in the form 'the number of Fs', but it will not settle more general questions like those raised in Frege's famous complaint, 'we can never—to take a crude example—decide by means of our definitions whether any concept has the number Julius Caesar belonging to it, or whether that same familiar conqueror of Gaul is a number or is not' (Frege (1884), § 56). To solve this problem, Frege requires explicit definitions of the numbers, and he proposes his well-known solution: the number of Fs = the extension of the concept 'equinumerous with F' (where two concepts are equinumerous if and only if there is a one-to-one correspondence between the things falling under them).[6] The notion of extension he does not explain, taking it to be a previously-understood notion of logic; roughly, the extension of a concept F can be understood as the collection of things falling under F. So the number of decks of

---

[5] That is, we claim there is a relation R between forks and spoons on the table such that (1) for any fork f, there is a unique spoon s, such that R holds of f and s (more fully: for any f, there is an s such that R holds of f and s, and for any s', if R holds of f and s', then $s = s'$), and (2) for any spoon s, there is a unique fork f, such that R holds of f and s. Notice that, despite the appearance of the word 'one' in the expression 'one-to-one correspondence', this notion is defined without presupposing any notion of number.

[6] The reader may wonder how we know that Julius Caesar is not an extension, given that we don't know he isn't a number, or why extensions are logical objects and numbers are not. For a recent statement of these and related perplexities, see Heck (1993).

cards on the table is the collection of all concepts equinumerous with the concept 'deck of cards on the table'; in our example, this would be the collection of all concepts under which two things fall (that is, under which fall an x and a distinct y and no z distinct from both of them). Then $0 =$ the collection of all concepts equinumerous with 'not equal to itself'; $1 =$ the collection of all concepts equinumerous with 'equal to 0'; $2 =$ the collection of all concepts equinumerous with 'equal to 0 or 1'; and so on.

In this way, numbers are defined as logical objects. The next step is to use this definition, along with the fundamental principles of logic, to prove the basic propositions of arithmetic. This Frege did, sketchily in the *Grundlagen*, in detail in the *Grundgesetze* (vol. i in 1893; vol. ii in 1903). One among the logical laws from which arithmetic is there derived is the crucial Basic Law V: for all concepts F and G, the extension of F equals the extension of G if and only if the same things fall under F and G, or, in symbols, $\hat{x}Fx = \hat{x}Gx$ iff[7] $\forall x(Fx \equiv Gx)$. In the preface to the first volume of the *Grundgesetze*, Frege expressed some discomfort over this assumption:

A dispute can arise, so far as I can see, only with regard to my Basic Law . . . V, which logicians perhaps have not yet expressly enunciated, and yet is what people have in mind, for example, where they speak of the extensions of concepts. I hold that it is a law of pure logic. In any event the place is pointed out where the decision must be made. (Frege (1893), 3–4)

This old worry recurred to Frege some years later, in 1902, when vol. ii was in press and he received an admiring letter from a British student of his work, Bertrand Russell. Along the way, Russell remarks that 'there is just one point where I have encountered a difficulty' ((1902), 124), and he goes on to derive what is now known as Russell's paradox.

The proof is easy.[8] First, define a new relation, membership, symbolized '$\in$' as follows: y is a member of z iff z is the extension of some concept that y falls under, or, in symbols, $y \in z$ iff $\exists F(z = \hat{x}Fx \land Fy)$. Then it is easy to show that for any y, $y \in \hat{x}Fx$ iff Fy.[9] Now consider $x \in x$. This says that x is the extension of a concept under which x falls; an ex-

---

[7] 'Iff' abbreviates 'if and only if'.

[8] Perhaps not quite so easy as the familiar version in set theoretic (rather than Fregean) notation: consider $R = \{x \mid x \notin x\}$. Then $R \in R$ iff $R \notin R$.

[9] If $y \in \hat{x}Fx$, then by definition of '$\in$', there is a concept G such that $\hat{x}Fx = \hat{x}Gx$ and Gy. Then by Basic Law V, $\forall x(Fx \equiv Gx)$, so in particular, $Fy \equiv Gy$, and thus, Fy. Conversely, if Fy, then $\hat{x}Fx = \hat{x}Fx$ and Fy, so by definition of '$\in$', $y \in \hat{x}Fx$.

ample would be the extension of the concept 'z is infinite', because (presumably) there are infinitely many infinite extensions (so that $\hat{z}(z$ is infinite) is the extension of a concept—'z is infinite'—under which $\hat{z}(z$ is infinite) falls). On the other hand, consider $x \notin x$. This says that x is the extension of a concept under which x does not fall; an example would be the extension of 'z is red', because (presumably) no extension is coloured at all, let alone coloured red. So $\hat{x}(x \notin x)$ contains some extensions and not others. The paradox arises when we ask if it contains itself. If $\hat{x}(x \notin x) \in \hat{x}(x \notin x)$, then $\hat{x}(x \notin x) \notin \hat{x}(x \notin x)$, and vice versa.

Frege was deeply shaken by Russell's letter:

> Your discovery of the contradiction caused me the greatest surprise and, I would almost say, consternation, since it has shaken the basis on which I intended to build arithmetic. . . . with the loss of my [Basic Law] V, not only the foundations of my arithmetic, but also the sole possible foundations of arithmetic, seem to vanish. (Frege (1902), 127–8)

It is a tribute to the man that he was able to add, 'In any case, your discovery is very remarkable and will perhaps result in a great advance in logic, unwelcome as it may seem at first glance' (ibid. 128). It seems that Russell, whose fascination with antinomies traced back to his studies of Kant and Hegel, became convinced of the lasting importance of his latest paradox only when faced with Frege's profound dismay.[10] Frege himself rushed to add an appendix to vol. ii of the *Grundgesetze* that begins: 'Hardly anything more unfortunate can befall a scientific writer than to have one of the foundations of his edifice shaken after the work is finished' (Frege (1903), 234). He goes on to suggest a hurried amendment to the system, but this was later shown to be inconsistent, assuming there are at least two things.[11] Toward the end of his life, Frege gave up the idea of founding arithmetic on logic and sought to base it on geometry instead.[12]

Recent commentators have noted that Frege's versions of the basic propositions of arithmetic can be derived from Hume's Principle alone,[13] that the fatal Law V is only needed to derive Hume's Principle itself from the definition of number. Still more recent commentators have argued that Frege himself was aware of this fact, that Frege himself provided

---

[10] See Moore (1988) for a history of Russell's efforts.

[11] For discussion, see Quine (1955a) and Geach (1956).

[12] See Frege (1924/5).

[13] Heck (1993) credits Parsons (1965) with the first observation that arithmetic follows from Hume's Principle; actual derivations appear in Wright (1983).

the derivation of arithmetic from Hume's Principle, a result aptly dubbed 'Frege's Theorem'.[14] These observations raise a wealth of fascinating and important questions: why did Frege find it unacceptable to adopt Hume's Principle in place of Basic Law V as a 'primitive truth'? What is the real force of the Julius Caesar problem? Why do extensions, but not numbers, count as logical objects? These questions and their close relatives form a vital part of contemporary Fregean scholarship.

Historically, however, the failure of Frege's project led to a careful examination of Russell's paradox, in the hope that it might be circumvented. And Russell's wasn't the only paradox up for consideration at the time. An example with a different flavour is Berry's paradox: as there are only finitely many descriptions of numbers in fewer than eighteen syllables, there must be a least number not nameable in fewer than eighteen syllables; but this number has just been named in seventeen. Russell himself progressed through several diagnoses of the root cause of these and other paradoxes, but he finally settled on the notion of a vicious circle.[15] Such circles are forbidden by the Vicious Circle Principle (VCP) on which the system of *Principia Mathematica* is based. In this daunting three-volume work (published between 1910 and 1913), Russell and Whitehead set out to provide a foundation for all of classical mathematics.

The VCP, as stated in the introduction to the *Principia*, takes two forms: the first rules out any collection with members that 'involve' or 'presuppose' the collection as a whole; the second rules out those with members that 'can only be defined by means of' the collection as a whole.[16] So, for example, 'the least number nameable in fewer than eighteen syllables' presupposes a collection of names, but that collection contains a name—'the least number nameable in fewer than eighteen syllables'—that can only be defined in terms of the collection. According to the VCP, such a collection of names cannot exist.[17] Another way to phrase this restriction is to forbid an object to be defined by making reference to a collection of which that object is a member. Such definitions are called 'impredicative'. Consider, for example, Russell's paradox, stated this time in more generic terms: we define Russell's collection— 'the collection of all collections that are not members of themselves'—

[14] See Burgess (1984), Hodes (1984), Boolos (1987; 1990), and Heck (1993).
[15] A similar diagnosis appears in Poincaré (1913), chs. IV and V.
[16] See Russell and Whitehead (1910), 37.
[17] See ibid. 63–4.

then ask if it is a member of itself. But the very definition of Russell's collection makes reference to 'all collections', a collection to which Russell's collection itself is supposed to belong.[18] So the paradox rests on an impredicative definition, which is ruled out by the VCP.

These elementary applications of the VCP depend only on the second version—that a collection cannot contain members definable only in terms of that collection—but the development of the full logical system of *Principia* requires appeal to the first version as well, plus some auxiliary assumptions about the nature of propositional functions and quantifiers.[19] To see how this works, consider the proposition 'Socrates is wise'. A propositional function is generated when one of the terms of the proposition is replaced by a variable, as in 'x is wise' or 'Socrates is x'.[20] Russell holds that a propositional function presupposes or involves its values, that is, that 'x is wise' presupposes or involves 'Socrates is wise', 'Plato is wise', 'Trollope is wise', and so on. From this auxiliary supposition, and the VCP in its first form, it follows that a propositional function cannot appear in one of its own values; if it did, the collection of its values would include a member that involves or presupposes the entire collection. Thus, '"x is wise" is wise', 'the extension of "x is wise" is wise' and the like, must all be rejected as meaningless.[21] (Notice that 'x is wise' is not defined in terms of the collection of its values, so it isn't the second version of the VCP that's being used here.)

The second auxiliary assumption concerns quantification. This time, consider the claim 'Plato has all the virtues of Socrates'. From this and 'Socrates is wise', it should follow that 'Plato is wise'. The quantifier 'all' seems to range over all properties of individuals; among these, any that are virtues possessed by Socrates must also be possessed by Plato. But notice, 'x has all the virtues of Socrates' is itself a property of individuals; in particular, it is a property of individuals that refers to all properties of individuals. If we add the assumption that a proposition with a

---

[18] The account of Russell's paradox given ibid. 62–3, is more subtle than this one, depending, as it does, on an additional doctrine of the *Principia*, the no-class theory (see III. 2).

[19] See Gödel (1944) for a penetrating and influential study of Russell's views.

[20] If a proposition is some sort of metaphysical existent, rather than a sentence, it makes little sense to speak of substituting a variable into it. In fact, an ambiguity between these two readings runs through the *Principia*, to dire effect. For discussion, see Quine (1941) or (1967). (Metaphysics is the study of what things are like in themselves, independently of our knowledge or cognition; in contrast, epistemology is the theory of knowledge.)

[21] See Russell and Whitehead (1910), 39.

quantifier involves or presupposes everything in the range of that quantifier—this is Russell's second auxiliary assumption—then 'x has all the
virtues of Socrates' is a property of individuals that involves or presupposes all properties of individuals; in other words, it is a property of individuals that involves or presupposes a collection to which it itself
belongs. This is ruled out by the first version of the VCP. If 'x has all the
virtues of Socrates' is to be meaningful, the 'all' cannot range over all
properties of individuals; the range of 'all' must be restricted in such a
way as to exclude 'x has all the virtues of Socrates'.

To accommodate these two restrictions—on the values of propositional functions and on the ranges of their quantifiers—Russell and
Whitehead devised the theory of ramified types. The picture comes in
three steps. Begin with a simple hierarchy of propositional functions
without any quantifiers: (0) individuals, like Socrates; (1) quantifier-free
propositional functions of individuals, like 'x is wise'; (2) quantifier-free
propositional functions of things in (1) and possibly (0), like 'Socrates is
x' or 'y is x'; (3) quantifier-free propositional functions of things in (2)
and possibly (1) and (0); and so on. We now allow the variables in these
quantifier-free propositional functions to be quantified. Order 0 consists
of individuals; order 1 consists of propositional functions generated
by adding quantifiers to propositional functions in (1) above; order 2
consists of propositional functions generated by adding quantifiers to
propositions functions in (2) above, and so on. Within these orders, we
distinguish types,[22] depending on the nature of the quantifications, so
e.g. 'y has all the virtues of Socrates' and 'if x is a virtue of Socrates, then
everybody has x' are both of order 2, because they are both generated
from 'if x is a virtue of Socrates, then y has x', which is in (2) above, but
they are of different types within that order, because one uses quantification over items of order 1 (virtues of persons) and the other uses quantification over items of order 0 (persons).[23]

Consider now the propositional functions that take individuals as arguments. Some of these—like 'x is wise'—are of order 1, the smallest
order compatible with their having items of order 0 as arguments. But
others—like 'x has all the virtues of Socrates'—are of order 2, because
they use quantifiers over items of order 1. Propositional functions of the

---

[22] The reader is warned that Russell's use of the terms 'order' and 'type' do not coincide with the now-standard uses in simple type theory, discussed below.

[23] Strictly speaking, quantification is only over a type, rather than a full order, so even
the description given here is too loose, but the finer details are not crucial for this overview.

first sort, those of the smallest order compatible with their arguments, Russell calls 'predicative'; the others he calls 'impredicative'. The connection with the non-technical use of these terms should be obvious: an impredicative propositional function Fx of individuals uses a quantifier over (some) propositional functions of individuals (though the VCP requires that the quantifier range over a type of propositional functions of individuals to which Fx itself does not belong).

The theory of ramified types is obviously quite complex; in fact, most commentators would agree that Russell's presentation is so imprecise as to leave some crucial matters obscure.[24] But there can be no doubt that the ramification inspired by the VCP ultimately undermines the derivation of classical mathematics in the system. This can be seen in a number of ways, the most dramatic of which concerns a fundamental theorem of analysis:[25] the real numbers are complete, that is, whenever the reals are divided into two disjoint,[26] non-empty sets A and B, with each member of A smaller than each member of B, then there is a real number r that is the greatest member of A or the least member of B. The trouble with the proof is that r is defined in terms of 'all reals'; in ramified type theory, if A and B are of order n, then r is of order $n + 1$, and the reals of order n have not been proved complete. Without this theorem, classical analysis is crippled.[27]

To circumvent this difficulty, Russell and Whitehead introduce the Axiom of Reducibility, which states that every propositional function is extensionally equivalent[28] to some predicative proposition function. To

---

[24] For example, Gödel writes, 'It is to be regretted that this first comprehensive and thorough-going presentation of a mathematical logic and the derivation of mathematics from it [is] so greatly lacking in formal precision in the foundations . . . that it presents in this respect a considerable step backward as compared with Frege' ((1944), 120). A particularly serious defect is the use/mention confusion diagnosed by Quine (1941; 1967).

[25] In fact, the difficulties in deriving mathematics from the theory of ramified types actually arise before analysis, in the theory of natural numbers. The standard Fregean definition of 'natural number' is 'x is a natural number iff x has every inductive property that 0 has' (where a property P is inductive if and only if the successor of n has P whenever n does). From this, mathematical induction is derived: if 0 has property P and P is inductive, then every natural number has P. But if the properties quantified over must be restricted to a single order, it isn't clear that all the usual derivations go through. In fact, Myhill has shown that they do not; see Parsons (1990), 111, for discussion and references.

[26] That is, A and B have no elements in common.

[27] The study of what can be obtained under predicative restrictions, without the Axiom of Reducibility, begins with Weyl (1918). For a more recent discussion, see Feferman (1964).

[28] Fx and Gx are extensionally equivalent iff they are true of exactly the same arguments.

see how this helps, suppose we define the real numbers for the first time at order n, and set out to show that these reals are complete. We suppose they are divided into sets A and B, as above, and we define our r of order $n + 1$. But r is of an order greater than its argument requires—it's a real like those of order n, so its arguments are of the same type as theirs, yet it contains a quantifier over reals of order n—that is, it is impredicative. The Axiom of Reducibility then provides a predicative real r', extensionally equivalent to r, which is to say, a real r' of order n that acts exactly like r. So the reals of order n are complete after all.

Though the Axiom of Reducibility allows the derivation of classical real number theory, and the rest of classical mathematics, to go through, ramified type theory with the Axiom cannot ultimately be accepted. The trouble is that the Axiom undermines the motivation behind the ramification of types; in Quine's words,

If for every propositional function there is a coextensive predicative one, then the symbols for propositional functions could have been construed from the start as referring outright just to the corresponding predicative ones. In short, the types of propositional functions could have been described in the first place as depending simply on the types of the arguments. The axiom of reducibility is self-effacing: if it is true, the ramification it is meant to cope with was pointless to begin with. (Quine (1967), 152)

Furthermore, the very success of the system of ramified types with the Axiom of Reducibility, that is, its success in implying a classical theory of real numbers, shows that it does not satisfy the VCP in its second form; in Gödel's words,

It is demonstrable that the formalism of classical mathematics does not satisfy the vicious circle principle in its [second] form, since the axioms imply the existence of real numbers definable in this formalism only by reference to all real numbers. Since classical mathematics can be built up on the basis of *Principia* (including the axiom of reducibility), it follows that even *Principia* . . . does not satisfy the vicious circle principle in its [second] form. (Gödel (1944), 127)

In sum, the needs of classical mathematics require the addition of the Axiom of Reducibility to the theory of ramified types, which essentially collapses the ramification and produces a theory of simple types (that is, one in which the type of a propositional function depends only on the types of its arguments). And the VCP in its strongest form is thereby jettisoned.

Does this mean that the paradoxes are reinstated? The answer seems to be yes and no. Paradoxes like Russell's are avoided by simple type theory: because a propositional function is of a higher type than its arguments, it makes no sense to ask whether it applies to itself, but Russell's paradox requires just this; when we ask if a set is self-membered, which we do in defining the Russell set, we are, in the context of the *Principia*, asking if the propositional function that defines the set applies to itself. Matters are not so simple with paradoxes like our second example, that of the smallest number not definable in fewer than eighteen syllables. Here the notion of 'definability', with its implied quantifier over 'all definitions', plays a key role, and simple type theory alone promises no cure.

At this point, commentators make two crucial points. First, there is Ramsey's observation that paradoxes like Russell's are those 'which, were no provision made against them, would occur in a logical or mathematical system itself. They involve only logical or mathematical terms such as class and number, and show that there must be something wrong with our logic or mathematics' (Ramsey (1925), 20). Paradoxes like Berry's, on the other hand, 'are not purely logical, and cannot be stated in logical terms alone; for they all contain some reference to thought, language, or symbolism, which are not formal but empirical terms. So they may be due not to faulty logic or mathematics, but to faulty ideas concerning thought and language' (ibid. 20–1).[29] Given that our goal is to found of mathematics, paradoxes of the second variety can be safely ignored. The second observation, more tangential to our purposes, is that the shortcomings of the ramified theory render its purported solutions to the Berry-like paradoxes problematic, anyway.[30] Under the circumstances, it seems reasonable to leave the ramified theory and concentrate instead on the simple theory of types.[31]

On the simple theory, type 0 consists of individuals, type 1 of properties (or collections) of individuals, type 2 of properties (or collections) of items in type 1, and so on. Here, as in the ramified theory, two additional assumptions are needed:[32] the Axiom of Infinity (there are infinitely many individuals) and the Axiom of Choice (to be considered in

---

[29] Ramsey credits Peano with a similar analysis of the second group of paradoxes.

[30] See Quine (1967), 152.

[31] In Quine's memorable phrase, 'The whole ramification, with the axiom of reducibility, calls simply for amputation' ((1941), 25).

[32] Notice that the presence of these additional assumptions, in any version of type theory, raises the question of whether or not the system is properly characterized as purely logical, and hence the question of whether or not mathematics is being founded on pure logic, as Frege originally intended.

some detail later) for objects of each type. On the basis of this theory, classical mathematics can be derived, though with some infelicities and inconveniences.[33] Even these can be eliminated if mixed types are allowed, e.g. if collections of type 2 are allowed to include items of type 0 as well as items of type 1. The theory with mixed types is called the theory of cumulative types; are there good reasons to prefer simple type theory, despite the advantages of cumulative type theory?

Notice, first of all, that the VCP alone[34] does not adjudicate between the two: in both simple and cumulative type theory, an item of type n collects only items of earlier type, so there is no danger of vicious circles. In the *Principia*, Russell presents another, essentially Fregean, argument for the simple, as opposed to cumulative, aspect of his theory. For Frege, a concept (or function) differs from an object in being 'unsaturated', that is, it stands in need of supplementation. For example, if it is a first-level concept, it needs supplementation by an object, as Socrates supplements 'x is wise' to form the 'saturated' proposition 'Socrates is wise'. A higher-level concept, like 'Plato and Socrates have P in common' is also unsaturated, but it needs a first-level concept, like 'x is wise', with an appropriate unsaturatedness of its own, to become saturated, as in 'Plato and Socrates have wisdom in common' (or 'Plato and Socrates both satisfy "x is wise"'). It wouldn't make sense to substitute an individual, that is, an item of type 0, for x in 'Plato and Socrates have x in common', because the x place in this concept is designed for a first-level concept, and the individual would not have the appropriate sort of unsaturatedness.[35] In Gödel's analysis, 'a function cannot replace an individual in a proposition, because the latter has no ambiguity to be removed, and . . . functions with different kinds of arguments (i.e. different ambiguities) cannot replace each other; which is the essence of the theory of simple types' (Gödel (1944), 136–7). This is often called the 'direction inspection' argument for the simple theory of types.[36]

---

[33] See Fraenkel, Levy, and Bar-Hillel (1973), 158–61, 191, for a concise discussion.

[34] Meaning, of course, the first version, the only one that remains viable when we insist on a classical theory of real numbers.

[35] Formally, let 'x is wise' be Wx and 's' stand for Socrates. Then 'Socrates is wise' becomes Ws, and the unsaturatedness of 'x is wise' has been filled by 's'. Furthermore, if 'Plato and Socrates have P in common' is symbolized $Pp \land Ps$, then the unsaturatedness of the variable P can be filled by 'Wx' to form $Wp \land Ws$. But if we attempt to substitute 's' for 'P', we get $sp \land ss$, which makes no sense at all, since neither s nor p has an unsaturated place that allows it to combine with itself or the other.

[36] See Russell and Whitehead (1910), 47–8.

Unless we buy the direction inspection argument, we are free to embrace the cumulative theory. I leave the matter here for now. Both simple type theory and cumulative type theory provide adequate foundations for classical mathematics, though cumulative type theory is the more workable of the two.

(ii) The second line of development contributing to the modern theory of sets stems from Cantor's mathematical work in the 1870s.[37] Cantor's initial goal was to describe the behaviour of infinite trigonometric series in terms of their sets of 'exceptional points'. He began by showing that a function given by a trigonometric series that converges at every point is uniquely represented by that series; he then generalized this result to series that converge at all but a finite number of points—these are the 'exceptional points'—then to series that converge at all but an infinite number of points, as long as those points accumulate at a single point,[38] and from there to series with more and more complicated sets of exceptional points. This detailed analysis required a precise account of the real numbers—rational and irrational—which Cantor also provided, more or less concurrently with various equivalent formulations, most notably Dedekind's.[39]

The problem solved by Cantor's theorem on trigonometric series and the pattern of its generalizations all followed a familiar line of mathematical development, growing out of natural questions in mathematical analysis, but Cantor soon pushed the enquiry in ground-breaking directions of his own. To see how, consider the elaboration of those sets of exceptional points: first an infinite set with one accumulation point; then an infinite set with finitely many accumulation points; then an infinite set with infinitely many accumulation points, but whose set of accumulation points has only one accumulation point; and so on. This thinking leads naturally to the notion of a 'derived set': the derived set of A is the set of its accumulation points. In general, if A is a point set, let

$$A_0 = A$$

---

[37] For a full discussion of the development of Cantor's thought, see Dauben (1979).

[38] That is, there is a single point x with exceptional points arbitrarily close to it.

[39] Cantor understood the real numbers in terms of Cauchy sequences of rationals; Dedekind used 'cuts' in the rationals instead. (See Enderton (1977), ch. 5, for a readable exposition.) Both treatments involved regarding infinite items (sequences or sets) as completed and subject to further manipulation, which brings the completed infinite into mathematics unambiguously for the first time (see I. 3. v).

A_1 = the derived set of A_0

.

.

.

A_{n+1} = the derived set of A_n

.

.

.

If the original set A is rich enough (e.g. if it is the set of reals itself), then all the A_ns will be non-empty, and there is room for

A_ω = the intersection of the A_ns

We can then form

$A_{\omega+1}$ = the derived set of A_ω

and so on.

Two separate themes are emerging here, both of which inspired Cantor to bold conceptual innovations. The first begins from the realization that infinite sets of reals can be quite subtle and complex, but nevertheless be 'small' enough not to disrupt the uniqueness theorem. This thought led Cantor to ponder the relationships between these sets of reals and the natural numbers, and between these sets of reals and the entire set of reals; the breakthrough was to think in terms of cardinality comparisons. So, for example, Cantor asked: are there more real numbers than natural numbers? He had already shown that, despite appearances, there are no more rational numbers than natural numbers, in the sense that the rationals can be put into one-to-one correspondence with the naturals,[40] but the answer to this further question was not immediately forthcoming. He first proved the answer to be yes—there are more reals than naturals—in 1873, and of all Cantor's accomplishments, this—along with the later (1891) generalization that the power set[41] of any set is larger than that set—is the one now dubbed 'Cantor's Theorem'.[42] The stunning discovery that infinity comes in different degrees led to the

---

[40] See Enderton (1977), 130.
[41] The power set of a set A, written $\wp(A)$, is the set of its subsets; e.g. the power set of the set of natural numbers is the set of all sets of natural numbers.
[42] See Enderton (1977), 132.

theory of infinite cardinal numbers,[43] the heart of contemporary set theory.

The second theme Cantor gleaned from his early work on derived sets came some years later, when he focused not on the sets of reals involved, but on the subscripts used in the definition, especially the infinite ordinal numbers:[44] ω, $\omega + 1$, $\omega + 2$, and so on.[45] In cardinal terms, these are all 'countable'—that is, capable of being brought into one-to-one correspondence with ω itself—but the set of all such countable ordinals, the next ordinal after all the countable ordinals, is itself uncountable.[46] This process leads to ever-increasing infinite ordinals, each of the next highest cardinality: $\aleph_0$ = the cardinality of ω, the set of all finite ordinals; $\aleph_1$ = the cardinality of ω_1, the set of all countable ordinals; $\aleph_2$ = the cardinality of ω_2, the set of all ordinals of size $\aleph_1$; and so on.[47] Cantor's first innovation was to treat cardinality as strictly a matter of one-to-one correspondence, so that the question of whether two infinite sets are or aren't of the same size suddenly makes sense; his second innovation was to extend the sequence of ordinal numbers into the transfinite, forming a handy scale for measuring infinite cardinalities. And all this began as a study of point sets, the study of ordinary sets of real numbers.

For the record, we should note that despite Cantor's boldness in bringing the transfinite within the purview of mathematical treatment, he drew the line at another kind of infinity, which he called the Absolute. By the mid-1890s, Cantor was aware that there could be no set of all sets, as its cardinal number would have to be the largest cardinal number, while his own theorem shows that for any cardinal there is a larger. Similarly, there could be no set of all ordinals, because it would then itself be the largest ordinal, and hence a member of itself, and hence smaller than itself. Nor could there be a set of all cardinal numbers, as this set would be equinumerous with the (non-existent) set of all ordinals. But Cantor was not disturbed by these results; rather, he took them to show that, in addition to the mathematically accessible transfinites, there is also an

---

[43] Cardinal numbers tell 'how many'—one, two, three . . . —as opposed to ordinal numbers, which tell 'how many-ith'—first, second, third, . . .

[44] See previous note.

[45] Following contemporary practice, think of ω as the set of all natural numbers (that is, the set of all finite ordinals).

[46] That is, not countable. For example, Cantor's Theorem says that the real numbers are uncountable.

[47] In contemporary set theory, a cardinal number is identified with the first ordinal of its size, so that $\aleph_0 = \omega$, $\aleph_1 = \omega_1$, $\aleph_2 = \omega_2$, etc.

Absolute Infinite, which cannot be treated mathematically. This Absolute Infinite Cantor associated with God. The merely transfinite is limited—for each there is a larger—and hence within the reach of mathematical methods; these transfinite numbers lead directly to the Absolute Infinite, which is limitless and beyond human understanding.[48]

But to return to Cantor's mathematical (as opposed to theological) development, the leading question concerned the cardinality of the continuum. Fairly simple cardinal arithmetic established that it is $2^{\aleph_0}$, and Cantor's Theorem establishes that it is greater than the cardinality of ω, that is, greater than $\aleph_0$. Cantor believed that it was, in fact, $\aleph_1$—this is the famous Continuum Hypothesis[49]—but he couldn't prove it. In fact, he couldn't even prove that $2^{\aleph_0}$ must be one of the alephs (that is, one of $\aleph_0$, $\aleph_1$, $\aleph_2$, . . .). To show this, he needed to show that the reals can be well-ordered;[50] in fact, he believed that every set can be well-ordered, but again, this was something he could not prove.

The Well-Ordering Theorem was eventually proved, not by Cantor, but by Zermelo, in his (1904). The proof bases the theorem squarely on a new fundamental assumption, now known as the Axiom of Choice: if $\mathfrak{S}$ is a family of disjoint, non-empty sets, then there is a set C (the choice set for $\mathfrak{S}$) that contains exactly one element of each set in $\mathfrak{S}$.[51] Various forms of this axiom had been used unconsciously by many early set theorists, but Zermelo's use of the full axiom to prove a controversial result provoked a barrage of criticism from the international mathematical community.[52] In response, Zermelo published two further articles: one

---

[48] Dauben (1979) tells the fascinating story of Cantor's dealings with the Catholic theologians. The concrete existence of the transfinites seemed to bring God (the infinite) into the world, and thus threatened to lead to pantheism, but Cantor's delineation of the Absolute infinite, which is not in this world, defused this doctrinal worry. Constantin Guberlet went so far as to use Cantor's theory as the basis for a Berkeley-style argument for the existence of God: the entire sequence of transfinite numbers exists in the mind of God (see Dauben (1979), 143).

[49] The Generalized Continuum Hypothesis says that for all ordinals α, $2^{\aleph_\alpha} = \aleph_\alpha$.

[50] A well-ordering of a set A is a relation, R, on A that is reflexive (for all $a \in A$, Raa), transitive (for all $a,b,c \in A$, if Rab and Rbc, then Rac), antisymmetric (for all $a,b \in A$, if Rab and Rba, then $a = b$), and well-founded (for any $A' \subseteq A$, if $A' \neq \emptyset$, then there is an R-least element of A, i.e. there is an $a \in A'$ such that for all $b \in A'$, Rab). Intuitively, after any initial segment of such an ordering, there is a 'next' element, namely, the R-least member of the remaining elements.

[51] As noted earlier, a well-ordering requires that there always be a 'next' element among those remaining; the axiom of choice can be used to make such a selection. For a proof of the Well-Ordering Theorem along these lines, see e.g. Levy (1979), 160–1.

[52] For some discussion, see I. 1. 3, below. Moore (1982) gives a wonderful history of this controversy and its resolution.

contains a more careful and explicit proof of the Well-Ordering Theorem (Zermelo (1908a)); the other presents the first axiomatization of set theory and develops the theory of cardinal numbers through Cantor's Theorem on the basis of those axioms (Zermelo (1908b)). Zermelo's goal in both these papers is to put set theory in general, and his proof of the Well-Ordering Theorem in particular, on a sound foundation. To the extent that the paradoxes jeopardize this goal, he is concerned with the paradoxes[53]—he pauses, for example, to show that the usual derivations of the paradoxes are not possible in his system— but he concentrates his attention on the project of selecting a simple, efficient, and powerful set of axioms from among the jumble of controversial and mutually exclusive set theoretic principles being debated at the time. In this effort, he is guided, quite pragmatically, by the needs of his proof, and more broadly, by the need to reproduce the central theorems of the theory of sets. His list of axioms, with some adjustments and additions, forms the bulk of the Zermelo–Fraenkel set theory (ZFC) we use today (see I. 3).

This, then, was the source of the first explicit axiomatization of set theory. Its goals were practical—find a short, simple list of acceptable set theoretic statements which will allow the derivation of all important results of informal set theory, but will not allow the derivation of the known paradoxes—and its approach was pragmatic. Some years later, presenting a second version of his axiomatization, Zermelo took a deeper, more theoretical look at the structure of the world of sets.[54] This time, inspired by a new axiom, the Axiom of Foundation (see I. 3. ix), Zermelo described the models of his theory in a systematic way, as arranged in the series of stages: the first stage, V_0, is the set of all non-sets, that is, the set of ordinary objects, which Zermelo calls 'urelements'; the second stage, V_1, includes all objects and all sets of objects, in other words, $V_0 \cup \wp(V_0)$,[55] where $\wp(V_0)$ is the power set of the first stage; the third stage consists of objects, sets of objects, and sets of objects and sets of objects, in other words, $V_1 \cup \wp(V_1)$, and so on. In general, for any ordinal α, $V_{\alpha+1}$ is $V_\alpha \cup \wp(V_\alpha)$, and if λ is a limit ordinal,[56] then V_λ is the union of

---

[53] Actually, Zermelo discovered Russell's paradox two years before Russell did, but he did not consider it a serious threat to the theory of sets. See Moore (1982), 89, 159.

[54] See Zermelo (1930).

[55] $V_0 \cup \wp(V_0)$ is the union of V_0 and $\wp(V_0)$; the union of two sets A and B is the set whose members are the members of A and the members of B.

[56] A limit ordinal is an ordinal with no immediate predecessor, like ω.

the V_αs for $\alpha < \lambda$. This picture of sets as arrayed in a series of stages is often called 'the cumulative hierarchy'.

(iii) Now recall that the simple theory of types begins with a type of individuals, presumably the same things as the ordinary objects of Zermelo's V_0. If the vaguely described 'collections' of type 1 are taken to be sets, then type 1 consists of $\wp(V_0)$, type 2 of $\wp(\wp(V_0))$, and so on. The only difference, for example, between type 2 and V_2 is that V_2 includes both V_1 and V_0. In other words, Zermelo's cumulative hierarchy is essentially what we previously described in the theory of cumulative types; and even in the context of type theory, the cumulative theory is preferable.[57] This, then, is the confluence of the two sources of modern set theory; both lines of thought lead us to the idea of cumulative stages, which is brought to mathematical precision in the cumulative hierarchy.[58]

Finally, one more point of convergence. We've seen that Frege's initial motivation was philosophical while Cantor's was mathematical; Frege wanted to show that arithmetic is analytic while Cantor wanted to prove theorems about trigonometric series. But it must be admitted that Frege's motivations included a mathematical one: he hoped to complete the mathematical project of rigorization that began with Berkeley's criticisms of the calculus, continued through the work of Cauchy and Weierstrass on continuity and convergence, and led up to Cantor and Dedekind's accounts of real numbers.[59] Frege writes:

The concepts of function, of continuity, of limit and of infinity have been shown to stand in need of sharper definition. Negative and irrational numbers, which had long since been admitted into science, have had to submit to a closer scrutiny of their credentials. . . . In all directions these same ideals can be seen at work— rigour of proof, precise delimitation of extent of validity, and as a means to this, sharp definition of concepts. . . . Proceeding along these lines, we are bound eventually to come to the concept of Number and to . . . the foundation of the whole of arithmetic. (Frege (1884), §§ 1–2)

Frege's goal was to show that those foundations lay in pure logic, and Russell continued on this path.

Meanwhile, Cantor's narrowly mathematical goal of proving theo-

---

[57] Assuming we remain unmoved by the direct inspection argument.
[58] Cf. Gödel (1933), 45–9.
[59] See Demopoulos (1994) for discussion.

rems about trigonometric series was soon overshadowed by the larger project as he moved into the general theory of sets. By 1884, the very year Frege broached the foundations of arithmetic in his *Grundlagen*, we find Cantor writing: 'pure mathematics . . . according to my conception is nothing other than pure set theory' (Cantor (1884a), 84). Here set theory, not pure logic, is cast as the ultimate foundation for mathematics, but given the eventual convergence of ontologies noted above,[60] this difference seems less significant. This perspective continues in Zermelo's thinking: 'Set theory is that branch of mathematics whose task is to investigate mathematically the fundamental notions "number", "order", and "function", taking them in their pristine, simple form, and to develop thereby the logical foundations of all of arithmetic and analysis' (Zermelo (1908b), 200). So the two strands of set theoretic development also share the goal of providing a comprehensive foundation for mathematics. Let's now pause to reflect on what this goal does and doesn't involve.

[60] Ontology is the philosophical study of what there is; one's ontology is the sum of what one considers to exist. (Thus, 'ontology' is a subheading under 'metaphysics'.) My point is that the ontology that resulted from the Frege–Russell line of development—cumulative type theory—and the ontology that resulted from the Cantor–Zermelo line of development—the cumulative hierarchy of sets—are, in the end, practically indistinguishable.

2

Set Theory as a Foundation

The view of set theory as a foundation for mathematics emerged early in the thinking of the originators of the theory and is now a pillar of contemporary orthodoxy. As such, it is enshrined in the opening pages of most recent textbooks; to take a few illustrative examples:

All branches of mathematics are developed, consciously or unconsciously, in set theory. (Levy (1979), 3)

Set theory is the foundation of mathematics. All mathematical concepts are defined in terms of the primitive notions of set and membership . . . From [the] axioms, all known mathematics may be derived. (Kunen (1980), xi)

[M]athematical objects (such as numbers and differentiable functions) can be defined to be certain sets. And the theorems of mathematics (such as the fundamental theorem of calculus) then can be viewed as statements about sets. Furthermore, these theorems will be provable from our axioms. Hence, our axioms provide a sufficient collection of assumptions for the development of the whole of mathematics—a remarkable fact. (Enderton (1977), 10–11)

From its Cantorian beginnings through its modern flowerings, set theory has also raised problems of its own, like any other branch of mathematics, but its larger, foundational role has been and remains conspicuous and distinctive.[1]

The initial stages of this foundational project have already been sketched: The finite ordinals begin with the empty set, $\varnothing$, and continue at each stage by taking the set of previous ordinals, so that $\varnothing$ is followed by $\{\varnothing\}$, $\{\varnothing,\{\varnothing\}\}$, $\{\varnothing,\{\varnothing\},\{\varnothing,\{\varnothing\}\}\}$, and so on. (The first infinite ordinal, ω, is again the set of all smaller ordinals.) We can define an operation—'S' for successor—on these finite ordinals by $Sn = n \cup \{n\}$, a binary relation—'$<$' for less than—by $n < m$ iff $n \in m$, and all the usual facts about the natural numbers, successor and less than will be provable. We can identify $\varnothing$ as 0, $\{\varnothing\}$ as 1, $\{\varnothing,\{\varnothing\}\}$ as 2, and so on, and define

---

[1] There are those who propose category theory as an alternative to set theoretic foundations, but at least for now, this has not changed the fact that set theory is so viewed.

binary operations $+$ and $\times$ by recursion,[2] and again all the usual facts about these particular numbers and these arithmetic operations become theorems of set theory. Even mathematical induction becomes a theorem.[3]

Given these set theoretic versions of the natural numbers, integers can be identified as ordered pairs, the various operations and relations on integers defined in terms of the prior relations on natural numbers, and again all the usual theorems proved.[4] Similarly, ordered pairs of integers can serve as rational numbers or ratios.[5] The real numbers are more difficult, but here Dedekind cuts do the job.[6] From there, curves, complex numbers, algebraic structures, geometric and topological spaces, functions, functionals, functors, and all the vast menagerie of modern mathematics can be represented within set theory, and its standard theorems proved from ZFC.

This is a truly 'remarkable fact', but mathematicians and philosophers have long debated precisely what it shows. The strongest reading of Frege's project would see him as discovering or uncovering the true identity of the natural numbers; from this point of view, the current set theoretic versions of numbers, functions, spaces, etc. would show us what numbers, functions, spaces, etc. really are.[7] Benacerraf (1965) has argued that this interpretation is implausible, beginning with the set theoretic account of natural numbers, because many different identifications seem equally good. For example, von Neumann (1923) made the identification

---

[2] That is, $n + 0 = n$ and $n + Sm = S(n + m)$ for addition, $n \times 0 = 0$ and $n \times Sm = (n \times m) + n$ for multiplication.

[3] For details, see Enderton (1977), ch. 4. This formulation is preferable to Frege's because the system in which it is framed, ZFC, is not prone to Russell's (or any other known) paradox. In the cumulative hierarchy corresponding to ZFC, Frege's candidates for the numbers do not exist. This is because, for example, there are new three-element sets formed at every stage of the hierarchy, so there is no stage of the hierarchy at which the set of all three-element sets could be formed.

[4] The integers are the positive and negative whole numbers. The underlying idea is to let $\langle n,m \rangle$, where n and m are natural numbers, represent the integer $n - m$. So e.g. the integer $\langle n,m \rangle$ is less than the integer $\langle n',m' \rangle$ iff $n + m'$ is less than $n' + m$ as natural numbers. See Enderton (1977), 90–101, for the niceties.

[5] Here the idea is to let $\langle a,b \rangle$, where a and b are integers, represent the fraction a/b. For details, see Enderton (1977), 101–11.

[6] See Dedekind (1872). A Dedekind cut is a pair (A,B) of sets of rationals such that A and B are non-empty and disjoint, every element of A is less than every element of B, and every rational is in either A or B. So, for example, if A is the set of all negative rationals and all positive rationals whose square is less than 2, and B is the rest of the rationals, then (A,B) is the cut corresponding to $\sqrt{2}$. For more, see Enderton (1977), 111–20.

[7] This would be a metaphysical reading, as it purports to reveal the true nature of numbers, etc.

described above—0 with $\varnothing$, 1 with $\{\varnothing\}$, 2 with $\{\varnothing,\{\varnothing\}\}$, and so on—and it works perfectly well, while Zermelo, in fact, made another identification—0 with $\varnothing$, 1 with $\{\varnothing\}$, 2 with $\{\{\varnothing\}\}$, and so on—that works just as well.[8] Once this is noted, we realize that many other identifications would also work, in fact infinitely many. There may be technical reasons to prefer one to another,[9] but nothing deep enough to motivate a metaphysical argument that one rather than the other uncovers the true identity of the natural numbers. And the other identifications, of integers, rationals, reals, functions, etc., all share this type of arbitrariness.[10]

In fact, one (admittedly controversial) reading of the Fregean text suggests that even Frege did not take himself to be discovering the underlying nature of the natural numbers themselves. In a much-discussed footnote to his definition of 'the number of Fs' as 'the extension of the concept "equinumerous with F"', he writes, 'I believe that for "extension of the concept" we could write simply "concept"' (Frege (1884), § 68). He raises some potential objections to this move, remarks that he thinks they could be met, then sets them aside because they 'would take us too far afield for present purposes' (ibid.). Now if our 'present purpose' is revealing the true nature of the natural numbers, then the choice between these two answers—an extension and a concept—is central, surely not an expendable detour. Later, in his summary, Frege writes:

In this definition the sense of 'extension of a concept' is assumed to be known. This way of getting around the difficulty [the Julius Caesar problem] cannot be expected to meet with universal approval, and many will prefer other methods of removing the doubt in question. I attach no decisive importance even to bringing in the extensions of concepts at all. (Ibid. § 107)

It's clear that Frege wants very much to find some logical surrogate for the natural numbers, but perhaps he is not concerned to find a unique such surrogate. If so, he could hardly have taken his task to be the discovery of precisely which logical objects the numbers are.[11]

In any case, from this point of view, the job of set theoretic founda-

---

[8] See Zermelo (1908b). On this account, other adjustments must also be made; e.g. the successor of n is $\{n\}$, not $n \cup \{n\}$.

[9] Von Neumann's version is in fact preferred because it carries over directly to the transfinite ordinals.

[10] We noted earlier that Cantor and Dedekind gave distinct but equally workable accounts of the real numbers.

[11] See Benacerraf (1981) for this interpretation of Frege, and Burge (1984) for the other side of the story. Wilson (1992) comes at the issue from another angle.

tions is not to reveal the true identities of the various mathematical objects. Another possibility, championed by Quine,[12] is that the set theoretic versions of various mathematicalia provide an 'ontological reduction', that is, they show us that we can legitimately replace a world view that countenances both natural numbers, integers, rationals, reals, etc., etc. on the one hand, and sets on the other, with a more streamlined world view that countenances only the sets. The motivation for such a replacement is twofold: first, the observation that natural science is generally chary of new entities,[13] and secondly, the conviction that abstracta tend to generate philosophical problems, for example problems of identity and (perhaps) epistemology.[14] Under the circumstances, a scientifically-minded philosopher would naturally prefer a more austere ontology, and the set theoretic reduction of mathematics is one way of achieving this.

But whatever the merits of ontological reduction, I think this is not what is at issue in mathematical discussions of set theoretic foundations. Consider Moschovakis, in another recent textbook; he begins by considering the relation between geometric objects and their numerical counterparts in analytic geometry:

A typical example of the method we will adopt is the 'identification' of the . . . geometric line . . . with the set . . . of real numbers. . . . What is the precise meaning of this 'identification'? *Certainly not that points are real numbers*. . . . What we mean by the 'identification' . . . is that the correspondence . . . gives a **faithful representation** of [the line] in [the reals] which allows us to give arithmetic definitions for all the useful geometric notions and to study the mathematical properties of [the line] **as if points were real numbers**. (Moschovakis (1994), 33–4)[15]

Such 'identifications' occur on a much broader scale in set theoretic foundations:

In the same way, we will discover within the universe of sets *faithful representations* of all the mathematical objects we need, and we will study set theory on the

---

[12] See Quine (1964) and (1969a).

[13] I come back to this issue in Part II.

[14] See, for example, Quine (1948) or (1960), ch. VII. Without a set theoretic reduction, we would 'face the old abstract objects . . . in all their primeval disorder' ((1960), 267).

[15] Here a point on the line corresponds to the real number that measures the distance to that point from an arbitrarily chosen origin using an arbitrarily chosen unit of length. For plane geometry, a point corresponds to an ordered pair of numbers determined in the familiar style of Cartesian coordinates.

basis of the lean axiomatic system of Zermelo **as if all mathematical objects were sets**. The delicate problem in specific cases is to formulate precisely the correct definition of 'faithful representation' and to prove that one such exists. (Ibid. 34)

So the job of set theoretic foundations is to isolate the mathematically relevant features of a mathematical object and to find a set theoretic surrogate with those features.

Notice that both our earlier notions of set theoretic reduction are explicitly rejected on this account. The identification of the natural numbers with, say, the finite von Neumann ordinals is not claimed to reveal their true nature, but simply to provide a satisfactory set theoretic surrogate; thus, no problem arises from the observation that more than one satisfactory set theoretic surrogate can be found. Likewise, the identification is not understood as a prelude to the repudiation or elimination of the original mathematical objects; though they may well drift off into irrelevancy for the most part, no such strong ontological conclusion is drawn. But if neither metaphysical insight nor ontological economy is forthcoming, what is gained by the exercise?

The answer to this question lies in mathematical rather than philosophical benefits. The force of set theoretic foundations is to bring (surrogates for) all mathematical objects and (instantiations of) all mathematical structures into one arena—the universe of sets—which allows the relations and interactions between them to be clearly displayed and investigated. Furthermore, the set theoretic axioms developed in this process are so broad and fundamental that they do more than reproduce the existing mathematics; they have strong consequences for existing fields and produce a mathematical theory that is immensely fruitful in its own right. Finally, perhaps most fundamentally, this single, unified arena for mathematics provides a court of final appeal for questions of mathematical existence and proof: if you want to know if there is a mathematical object of a certain sort, you ask (ultimately) if there is a set theoretic surrogate of that sort; if you want to know if a given statement is provable or disprovable, you mean (ultimately), from the axioms of the theory of sets.

Moschovakis's example—the identification of geometric points with real numbers—was among the first and most dramatic examples of the power of set theoretic foundations. We saw (in I. 1) how Cantor's work on trigonometric series eventually required a precise account of the real numbers, but the need went much deeper than this. The Greeks were first to worry over the paradoxes of continuous structures: the Pythagoreans discovered that the points on a line were too numerous to be labelled by rational numbers,[16] and Zeno's familiar paradoxes raised further worries about the coherence of our understanding of space and time. For centuries, these troubles were avoided by a deliberate separation between geometry and arithmetic, until Descartes introduced analytic geometry and Newton and Leibniz developed the calculus (in the late seventeenth century). This spectacularly successful method was nevertheless beset by unclarities and outright contradictions; many of these shortcomings were brought out with devastating *élan* by Bishop Berkeley, who ridiculed infinitesimals as 'the Ghosts of departed Quantities' (Berkeley (1734), 199). Only after the work of Cauchy, Weierstrass, and others in the late nineteenth century were infinitesimals eliminated in favour of the notion of a limit, and even then the fundamental theorems about limits could not be proved because the reals themselves were not well understood.[17]

What mathematicians had, throughout this long development, was an intuitive idea of continuity, of the structure of a geometric line; this was enough to tell them that the rational points on the line left gaps, and that gaps of any kind were inconsistent with the notion that the line is continuous. What they lacked was a clear and consistent characterization of continuous structure. And this, finally, is what the set theoretic reductions of Cantor and Dedekind provided: each described a set with an ordering that contained no gaps. In this case, set theory provided a clear and compelling surrogate for what had heretofore been a troubling source of fundamental confusion and concern. These set theoretic reals are constructed out of rational numbers, which are constructed out of pairs of integers, which are constructed out of pairs of natural numbers; Frege saw himself as completing the process of foundation by providing an account of the natural numbers themselves. And, as we've seen, that account now also takes the form of a set theoretic surrogate. In this way, set theoretic foundations ended centuries of mathematical disarray.

Since then, the set theoretic point of view has allowed existence questions to be clearly posed and answered. For example, Lebesgue analysed

---

[16] e.g. by erecting an isosceles right triangle on the unit length of a line, then using a compass to lay out the length of the hypotenuse onto the line, we can generate a point that corresponds to no rational number. (If it did, i.e. if a/b is in lowest terms and $(a/b)^2 = 2$, then $a^2 = 2b^2$, so a is even. But then $a = 2c$, for some c, so $b^2 = 2c^2$, and b is also even. This contradicts the assumption that a/b is in lowest terms.)

[17] See Boyer (1949) for more.

the idea of the 'length' of a point set and produced his notion of Lebesgue measure; then the question—is there a point set with no determinate length?—could be well posed, and in the context of ZFC, it could be answered, 'Yes, there is'. Such conclusive resolutions can be found in various branches of mathematics, including algebra, topology, and analysis. Other cases turn out to be beyond the reach of our current axioms; such examples are the subject of I. 4 below. In these cases, the set theoretic perspective at least puts a stop to doomed efforts at proof. Beyond that, further investigation often uncovers the sensitivity of such existence questions to experimental hypotheses of higher set theory, that is, to new axiom candidates, which allows still deeper interconnections to be drawn and holds out the promise of solution if and when a final consensus is reached on these hypotheses. How such a consensus might be rationally achieved is the central theme of this book.

In sum, then, despite the lack of metaphysical or ontological payoff, I think it is fair to attribute considerable mathematical success to set theoretic foundations of the sort Moschovakis describes: mathematical objects and structures are identified with or instantiated by set theoretic surrogates and the classical theorems about them proved from the axioms of set theory. Mathematics is profoundly unified by this approach; the interconnections between its branches are highlighted; classical theorems are traced to a single source; effective methods can be transferred from one branch to another; the full power of the most basic set theoretic principles can be brought to play on heretofore unsolvable problems; new conjectures can be evaluated for feasibility of proof; and ever stronger axiomatic systems hold the promise of ever more fruitful consequences. As the desired mathematical payoffs can be achieved by this modest version of set theoretic foundations, I will assume no more than this in what follows.

So far, we've seen that the mathematical fruits of set theoretic foundations can be achieved without the various metaphysical and ontological claims that have worried many commentators. So far, so good. But we have yet to touch on the various related epistemological themes. Once again, I think the mathematical benefits can be preserved without any strong (and controversial) additional theses; to suggest why this is so, let me examine a few of the characteristic concerns.

Given that Zermelo introduced axiomatic set theory in part to avoid the nagging paradoxes, it is not surprising that set theoretic foundations are sometimes understood as the project of installing mathematics on a consistent basis. Zermelo himself, before presenting his axioms, laments:

I have not yet even been able to prove rigorously that my axioms are consistent, though this is certainly very essential; instead I have had to confine myself to pointing out now and then that the antinomies discovered so far vanish one and all if the principles here proposed are adopted as a basis. (Zermelo (1908b), 200–1)

Poincaré makes the same point in the form of an objection: 'We have put a fence around the herd to protect it from the wolves but we do not know whether some wolves were not already within the fence' (quoted in Kline (1972), 1186). If our axiomatization is to protect us from contradiction, we must be sure that it harbours no inconsistencies of its own.

The trouble, it later turned out, was not simply that Zermelo and others were unable to provide a consistency proof, but that a meaningful consistency proof is not possible. In his (1931), Gödel showed that any consistent theory strong enough to reproduce arithmetic—and we've seen that ZFC can do this—cannot prove its own consistency. So, if classical mathematics is identified with set theory—as set theoretic foundations would have it—then the consistency of set theory cannot be proved by any method of classical mathematics. The modern form of this objection, making explicit use of Gödel's second incompleteness theorem,[18] can be found in the writings of MacLane, a prominent contemporary critic of set theoretic foundations:

Now in one sense a foundation is a security blanket: If you meticulously follow the rules laid down, no paradoxes or contradictions will arise. In reality there is now no guarantee of this sort of security; we have at hand no proof that the axioms ZFC for set theory will never yield a contradiction, while Gödel's second theorem tells us that such a consistency proof cannot be conducted within ZFC. (MacLane (1986), 406)

Since Gödel, as MacLane notes, Zermelo's hope of establishing the consistency of his axioms has been effectively dashed.

So, if founding mathematics on set theory is supposed to provide it with a foundation in MacLane's sense of a 'security' blanket, keeping us secure from Poincaré's 'wolves', that is, from contradiction, then Gödel's second theorem presents a formidable objection.[19] Much as we might

---

[18] Gödel's first incompleteness theorem says that for any sufficiently strong theory, there is a sentence it cannot prove or disprove. The second incompleteness theorem, cited here, follows from the first. See Enderton (1972) for a textbook treatment.

[19] Detlefsen (in his (1986)) defends Hilbert's programme for establishing the consistency of classical mathematics by arguing that a criticism based on Gödel's second theorem need not be viewed as conclusive. So far as I know, no one has succeeded in exploiting the loopholes Detlefsen identifies.

like to have a guarantee of consistency, we now know this is not forth-coming; the question is whether or not a 'foundation' can provide any-thing of value without this. Here I think our previous discussion points to a positive answer: the mathematical benefits provided by set theoretic foundations do not depend on set theory being provably consistent. We can admit that freedom from contradiction is an obvious desideratum for any mathematical theory, especially one destined for a role as central as the one we've proposed for set theory; we can admit that new axiom can-didates should be viewed with suspicion (at least) to the extent that they seem likely to introduce contradictions; but for all this, we can still hold that the unification provided by set theoretic foundations is mathemati-cally valuable despite the lack of a consistency proof.

Suppose, then, that we adopt a version of set theoretic foundations that does not claim to make mathematics safe from contradiction. We might still wonder about the relative certainty of set theory and the mathematical theories represented in it. Founding arithmetic, for ex-ample, on set theory is sometimes thought to base the relatively certain on the relatively uncertain, or, in Quine's phrase, 'a case of *obscurum per obscurius*'.[20] But again, this criticism only has force if our foundation aims at establishing what it founds with a higher degree of certainty. And again, the mathematical achievements of set theoretic foundations sur-vive without this.

In fact, the idea that to found a theory is to base it on something more certain was rejected early on, by Russell himself:

There is an apparent absurdity in proceeding, as one does in the logical theory of arithmetic, through many rather recondite propositions of symbolic logic, to the 'proof' of such truisms as 2 + 2 = 4: for it is plain that the conclusion is more certain than the premises, and the supposed proof therefore seems futile. (Russell (1907), 272)

But this absurdity is only apparent, Russell argues. When we examine various inferences we discover that

[t]he word 'premise' has two quite different senses: there is what we may call the 'empirical premise', which is the proposition or propositions from which we ac-tually are led to believe the proposition in question; and there is what we will call the 'logical premise', which is some logically simpler proposition or propositions from which, by a valid deduction, the proposition in question can be obtained. (Ibid. 272–3)

---

[20] Quine (1969a), 43. For this and related objections, see Steiner (1975a), ch. 2.

So, for example, we might come to believe the 2 + 2 = 4 on the basis of various observations involving stones, sheep, or ginger snaps, various observations that support the proposition inductively; these are the empirical premisses from which the proposition can be inferred. On the other hand, when we prove 2+2=4 from the axioms of pure logic, these axioms are logically simpler propositions, involving fewer notions; they are logical premisses. Of course, what is simple in one context may be complex in another; the logical premiss of one argument may be proved from premisses still simpler in another argument.

The mistake philosophers make, according to Russell, is supposing that the scale of logical simplicity coincides with the scale of obviousness or certainty:

The propositions that are easiest to apprehend are somewhere in the middle [of the logical scale], neither very simple nor very complex. Generally speaking, they become simpler as civilization advances. Thus *we* probably find it easier to think of fishing than of trout-fishing or salmon-fishing; but I am told that savages are apt to have a verb for trout-fishing and another for salmon-fishing, but no verb for fishing. (Ibid. 273)

So, in our example, the observations that two stones plus two stones make four stones, and that two sheep plus two sheep make four sheep, etc.— these observations are less simple than 2 + 2 = 4, and 2 + 2 = 4 is itself less simple than the axioms of pure logic.

The proposition 2 + 2 = 4 itself strikes us now as obvious; and if we were asked to prove that 2 sheep + 2 sheep = 4 sheep, we should be inclined to deduce it from 2 + 2 = 4. But the proposition '2 sheep + 2 sheep = 4 sheep' was probably known to shepherds thousands of years before the proposition 2 + 2 = 4 was discovered; and when 2 + 2 = 4 was first discovered, it was probably inferred from the case of sheep and other concrete cases. (Ibid. 272)

So the highest degree of obviousness occurs toward the centre of the scale of logical simplicity, and its position can vary with time.

Now when a mathematician proves a theorem, the proposition proved is generally so complex that the premisses of the argument are both more obvious and more logically simple. 'Thus in mathematics, except in the earliest parts, the propositions from which a given proposition is deduced generally give the reason why we believe the given proposition' (i.e. logical and empirical premisses coincide: ibid. 273). But the cases that concern us, cases like the proof that 2 + 2 = 4, are different:

in dealing with the principles of mathematics, this relation is reversed. Our propositions [e.g. the principles of pure logic] are too simple to be easy, and thus their consequences [like $2 + 2 = 4$] are generally easier than they are. Hence we tend to believe the premises because we can see that their consequences are true, instead of believing the consequences because we know the premises to be true. (Ibid. 273–4)

In other words, the more certain is derived from the less certain, thus boosting our confidence in the latter.

Similar approaches to axiomatics appear in the work of Zermelo, Gödel, and many of their successors, as we will see, but they are not without their critics. For example, Tiles argues that to defend an axiom in terms of its consequences is inappropriate

to the conception of set theory as providing a logical *foundation* for mathematics. To claim this status for set theory it is necessary to claim an independent and intrinsic justification for the assertion of set-theoretic axioms. It would be circular indeed to justify the logical foundations by appeal to their logical consequences, i.e. by appeal to the propositions for which they are going to provide the foundation. (Tiles (1989), 208)

But, as we've seen, this style of objection only applies to a foundation in the epistemic sense, one intended to provide a 'secure given starting point' (ibid.). Set theoretic foundations need not be so intended, and their mathematical benefits remain even if such epistemic benefits are foresworn.

This, of course, is what Russell does; he explicitly renounces the epistemic goal of founding mathematics on something more certain than the statements of mid-level mathematics. Having done so, he must see some other goal as sufficiently attractive to motivate the project, and he does:

The advantage of obtaining simple logical premises in place of empirical premises is partly that it gives a greater chance of isolating a possible pervading element of falsehood, partly that it organises our knowledge, and partly that the logical premises have, as a rule, many more consequences than the empirical premises, and thus lead to the discovery of many things which could not otherwise be known. The law of gravitation, for example, leads to many consequences which could not be discovered merely from the apparent motions of the heavenly bodies, which are our empirical premises. And so in arithmetic, taking the ordinary propositions of arithmetic as our empirical premises, we are led to a set of logical premises from which we can deduce Cantor's theory of the transfinite. (Russell (1907), 275)

Of course, Russell's claim to have deduced Cantor's theory from pure logic is subject to dispute—the axioms of Infinity, Choice, and Reducibility used in *Principia Mathematica* do not seem, on the face of them, to be logical—but the general tone of this passage agrees with our assessment: the true benefits of set theoretic foundations are not epistemic but mathematical (e.g. uncovering inconsistencies, organizing knowledge, leading to theories of greater power and fruitfulness).

Before leaving the subject of set theoretic foundations, I would like to consider one last, generally epistemological objection, an objection less precise than those of Poincaré or Tiles, but one that I think is deeply felt by many of the mathematicians who count themselves as strong opponents. The most explicit statement of this objection that I've been able to find occurs in a debate between MacLane, as the opponent, and Mathias, as the defender.[21] In this passage, Mathias describes what he takes to be the concern underlying MacLane's unease:

Set theory is so rich a theory that it has been claimed for much of this century to be the foundation of mathematics. In ontological terms this claim is not unreasonable; but MacLane resists. I would guess that his reason is not so much that he objects to the ontology of set theory but that he finds the set-theoretic cast of mind oppressive and feels that other modes of thought are more appropriate to the mathematics he wishes to do. (Mathias (1992), 115)

I think it cannot be denied that mathematicians from various branches of the subject—algebraists, analysts, number theorists, geometers—have different characteristic modes of thought, and that the subject would be crippled if this variety were somehow curtailed. Mathias appreciates this:

One of the remarkable things about mathematics is that I can formulate a problem, be unable to solve it, pass it to you; you solve it; and then I can make use of your solution. There is a unity here: we benefit from each other's efforts. . . . But if I pause to ask *why* you have succeeded where I have failed to solve a problem, I find myself faced with the baffling fact that you have thought of the problem in a very different way from me: and if I look around the whole spectrum of mathematical activity the huge variety of styles of thought becomes even more evident.

Is it desirable to press mathematicians all to think in the same way? I say not . . . Uniformity is not desirable, and an attempt to attain it, by (say) manipulating the funding agencies, will have unhealthy consequences. (Ibid. 113)

If set theoretic foundations were understood to entail that all mathematics is set theory, in the sense that all mathematicians might as well be set theorists, restricting themselves to the methods characteristic of set

---

[21] See MacLane (1992) and Mathias (1992).

theory, then it would surely represent an unhealthy push towards uniformity. This, Mathias suggests, is (part of) what's bothering MacLane, and we should admit, along with Mathias, that this would be something worth denouncing.

But set theoretic foundations need not be so understood. For the sake of comparison, consider the claim that everything studied in natural science is physical; it doesn't follow from this that botanists, geologists, and astronomers should all become physicists, should all restrict their methods to those characteristic of physics. Again, to say that all objects of mathematical study have set theoretic surrogates is not to say that they should all be studied using only set theoretic methods. Mathias makes this same point in reply to MacLane: 'The purpose of foundational work in mathematics is to promote the unity [as opposed to the uniformity] of mathematics; the larger hope is to establish an ontology within which all can work in their different ways' (ibid. 114). So, once again, set theoretic foundations can do their job without insisting that all legitimate methods are included in the usual methods of set theory.

In what follows, then, I will assume that set theory provides a foundation for mathematics in the modest sense delimited here: for all mathematical objects and structures, there are set theoretic surrogates and instantiations, and the set theoretic versions of all classical mathematical theorems can be proved from the standard axioms for the theory of sets (ZFC).[22] This includes no claim about the real identity of mathematical objects, no claim to have reduced ontology, no claim to have founded mathematics on something provably free from contradiction or more certain, and no claim that all mathematical methods can be replaced by set theoretic methods.[23] For all that, set theoretic foundations still play a strong unifying role: vague structures are made more precise, old theorems are given new proofs and unified with other theorems that previously seemed quite distinct, similar hypotheses are traced at the basis of disparate mathematical fields,[24] existence questions are given explicit

---

[22] Even MacLane allows this much: 'The rich multiplicity of Mathematical objects and the proofs of theorems about them can be set out formally with absolute precision on a remarkably parsimonious base' ((1986), 358). He is referring to ZFC.

[23] It needn't even include the claim that set theory is the only theory that could serve as this sort of foundation.

[24] A striking example: forms of the Axiom of Choice turn up in the fundamental assumptions of algebra, topology, analysis, and logic, as well as set theory. See Moore (1982) for a description of how these interconnections were discovered, and their impact on the various fields.

meaning, unprovable conjectures can be identified, new hypotheses can settle old open questions, and so on. That set theory plays this role is central to modern mathematics, that it is able to play this role is perhaps the most remarkable outcome of the search for foundations. No metaphysics, ontology, or epistemology is needed to sweeten this pot!

3

The Standard Axioms

Having surveyed the background to contemporary set theory and investi-gated its claims to a foundational role, let's now return to our central question: how are the axioms to be justified? As a first step in the direc-tion of answering this question, I propose to look at the actual arguments that have been offered for the axioms now standard and accepted in the field, that is, for the axioms of Zermelo–Fraenkel or ZFC. At this point, I make no attempt to distinguish good arguments from bad, or to say what makes such an argument good or bad. What I present for now is raw data.

Let's begin with those among the standard axioms that trace most directly to Zermelo's first paper of 1908 (Zermelo (1908b)). Zermelo's own defence of these axioms is simple and straightforward. In the wake of the paradoxes, he describes the situation like this:

At present . . . the very existence of this discipline [set theory] seems to be threat-ened by certain contradictions. . . . In particular, in view of the 'Russell anti-nomy' . . . it no longer seems admissible today to assign to an arbitrary logically definable notion a set . . . as its extension. Cantor's original definition of set . . . certainly requires some restriction; it has not, however, been successfully replaced by one that is just as simple and does not give rise to such reservations. (Zermelo (1908b), 200)

The trouble is that the original notion that every property has an exten-sion cannot be maintained, and that no comparably simple conception of set has been found to replace it.

Zermelo concludes that 'Under these circumstances there is at this point nothing left for us to do but to proceed in the opposite direction and, starting from set theory as it is historically given, to seek out the principles required for establishing the foundations of this mathematical discipline' (ibid.). His goal is to isolate a small group of principles—ax-ioms—that are restricted enough 'to exclude all contradictions', but strong enough 'to retain all that is valuable in this theory' (ibid.). This last is the touchstone; the axioms are chosen with an eye to the existing theory: 'principles must be judged from the point of view of science, and not science from the point of view of principles fixed once and for all.' (Zermelo (1908a), 189). The defence of his axioms, then, is that they are 'necessary for science' (ibid. 187), that they allow us to recover 'the entire theory created by Cantor and Dedekind' ((1908b), 200), without (so far as we can tell) the paradoxes.

Notice that this general defence is not phrased in terms of self-evidence or intuition or conforming to some underlying concept of set or anything else along such lines.[1] Instead, the axioms are evaluated in terms of their consequences, or more broadly, in terms of the type of theory they produce. In what follows, I draw a rough-and-ready distinction between justifications[2] of the former variety—intrinsic justifications—and those of the latter variety—extrinsic justifications. Traditionally, some observers have held that the only legitimate justifications are intrinsic; for example, recall Tiles's point in the previous section. Ultimately, I argue that this is incorrect, but for now my goal is merely descriptive; I merely note the extrinsic arguments that have, in fact, been offered.

(i) *Extensionality*. The Axiom of Extensionality is the claim that two sets are equal if and only if they have exactly the same members (in symbols, $\forall x \forall y (\forall z (z \in x \equiv z \in y) \to x = y)$). The contrast is with intensional entities like properties: two properties can apply to exactly the same things and still be different, like the property of being Aristotle's most famous teacher and the property of being the author of *Symposium*. The axiom asserts that sets, unlike properties, are extensional.

This characterization of sets goes back to Dedekind ((1888), 45), and Zermelo puts the axiom first on his list without comment. Some contemporary authors count Extensionality as part of an analysis of the concept of set (e.g. see Shoenfield (1977), 322, 325) or as a part of the definition of the word 'set' (see Wang (1974), 533). Boolos takes a similar line, though with greater care:

The axiom of extensionality enjoys a special epistemological status shared by none of the other axioms . . . if someone were to say 'there are distinct sets with

---

[1] Zermelo does mention self-evidence, which he considers 'a necessary source of mathematical principles', but he regards it as subjective. '[T]he question that can be objectively decided', he writes, is 'whether the principle is *necessary for science*' ((1908a), 187). Under 'science', here and above, Zermelo means to include mathematics.

[2] Here, in I. 3, I will use the word 'justification' simply to mean 'argument for accepting', without any implication that the argument is a good one.

the same members,' he would thereby justify us in thinking his usage nonstandard far more than someone who asserted the denial of some other axiom. Because of this difference, one might be tempted to call the axiom of extensionality 'analytic', true by virtue of the meanings of the words contained in it, but not to consider the other axioms analytic. (Boolos (1971), 501)

Analyticity, as we've seen, is a notion tracing back to Kant, with a detour through Frege, but the contemporary version is as Boolos has it: a statement is analytic if and only if it is true by virtue of the meanings of the words involved. This and the other justifications considered so far clearly count as intrinsic.

But Boolos's characterization is hedged; he doesn't claim that the Axiom of Extensionality is analytic, but that 'one might be tempted to call [it] analytic'. The reason for this hedge is that analyticity is currently a suspect notion. After Frege, in its new meaning-based formulation, analyticity played a central role in the thinking of Carnap and the logical positivists during the 1920s and 1930s; Carnap's student Quine then launched a staggering attack on the notion, beginning with his 'Two Dogmas of Empiricism' in 1951.

The Carnap/Quine debates come up again later (see II. 2 and III. 3), but for now, a hint of their flavour is revealed in this comment of Quine's on the Carnapian doctrine that logical truth is analytic:

true sentences generally depend for their truth on the traits of their language in addition to the traits of their subject matter; and [Carnap holds that] logical truths then fit neatly in as the limiting case where the dependence on traits of the subject matter is nil. Consider, however, the logical truth 'Everything is self-identical' or '$\forall x(x = x)$'. We *can* say that it depends for its truth on traits of the language (specifically on the usage of '$=$'), and not on traits of its subject matter; but we can also say, alternatively, that it depends on an obvious trait, viz., self-identity, of its subject matter, viz., everything. . . . I have been using the vaguely psychological word 'obvious' non-technically, assigning to it no explanatory value. My suggestion is merely that the linguistic doctrine of elementary logical truth likewise leaves explanation unbegun. I do not suggest that the linguistic doctrine is false and some doctrine of ultimate and inexplicable insight into the obvious traits of reality is true, but only that there is no real difference between these two pseudodoctrines. (Quine (1954), 359–60)

In our case, the point could be put this way: yes, if someone denies the Axiom of Extensionality, we might be inclined to say that she is using the word 'set' differently from the rest of us. But we might draw this conclusion as easily from our supposition that reasonable people do not miss obvious facts, like the axiom, as we could from the supposition that the axiom is analytic. From this point of view, the only upshot of Boolos's observation about our reaction to the person who denies this axiom as opposed to others is that Extensionality is more obvious than the rest.

Given this problem, Boolos puts his more considered point like this:

It seems probable . . . that whatever justification for accepting the axiom of extensionality there may be, it is more likely to resemble the justification for accepting most of the classical examples of analytic sentences, such as 'all bachelors are unmarried' or 'siblings have siblings' than is the justification for accepting the other axioms of set theory. (Boolos (1971), 501)

Whatever such a justification might look like, I suspect that it would not be extrinsic, for example, that it would not proceed by consideration of the consequences of the axiom.

Fraenkel, Bar-Hillel, and Levy take a different approach. They seem not to think that the Axiom is analytic in any sense, for they speak unaffectedly of an intensional notion of set: 'from an intensional point of view the set of all non-negative real numbers and the set of all squares of real numbers are not necessarily identical, even though they have the same extension' (Fraenkel, Bar-Hillel, and Levy (1973), 27–8). In fact, they envision a range of intensional notions of set, depending on the criterion of identity adopted; for example, the (intensional) set of things that are red or blue may or may not be considered identical to the (intensional) set of things that are blue or red, depending on whether or not 'red or blue' describes the same property as 'blue or red'. (Presumably both are distinct from the property described by 'of a colour in the US flag, but not white'.) From this point of view, the question 'why should we adopt the Axiom of Extensionality?' becomes 'why should we study extensional rather than intensional sets?'

Fraenkel, Bar-Hillel, and Levy address precisely this question, and they give a three-part answer.

First, the extensional notion of set is simpler and clearer than any possible intensional notion of set. (Ibid. 28)

In other words, the notion of co-extensionality—having the same members—is easier than any notion of co-intensionality—being determined by the same property—at least partly because our understanding of membership is firmer than our understanding of what it is to be the same property.

Second, whereas there is just one extensional notion of set, there may be many intensional notions of set, depending on the purpose for which those sets are needed; so if we wanted to base set theory on some intensional notion of set, we would have to choose among various intensional notions of set in a way which is bound to be at least somewhat arbitrary. (Ibid.)

Still, if the various intensional notions do different jobs, it might seem best to have at least one of them available, despite the clarity consideration in the first argument. In response to this line of thought, the authors point out:

Third . . . starting with the simple notion of extensional set we shall . . . be able to construct intensional notions of set within our system. (Ibid.)

The idea is that, given a set A, we can construct (in ZFC) the sets $A \times \{0\}$ and $A \times \{1\}$, which function as distinct copies of A.[3] If A were the singleton set containing Plato, $A \times \{0\}$ might be used to represent the set of most famous teachers of Aristotle, and $A \times \{1\}$ to represent the set of authors of the *Symposium*, and all three would be distinct.

What's worth noting for our purposes is that these three considerations are broadly extrinsic. The argument is that the extensional notion of set generates a simpler theory, and thus a theory that is easier to use, that it avoids a kind of arbitrariness, and that it is powerful enough to replicate any virtues of its rivals. So even Extensionality, for which intrinsic justifications seem so attractive, has also been defended on extrinsic grounds.

(ii) *Empty Set*. As we've seen, Zermelo realized that the paradoxes require us to reject the principle underlying Frege's system, the so-called Principle of Unlimited Comprehension: every property has an extension. Instead, Zermelo hopes to provide principles for generating new sets from old that will produce all the sets needed to recapture Cantorian/Dedekindian set theory, but won't produce the paradoxical sets. For this to work, he must begin somewhere; the principles of generation must have something on which to work. That starting-point is the empty set; the Empty Set Axiom asserts the existence of a set with no members.

This assumption appears as part of Zermelo's Axiom of Elementary

---

[3] If A and B are sets, $A \times B$ is the set of all ordered pairs whose first element comes from A and whose second element comes from B. The ordered pair of a and b is usually identified with the set $\{\{a\},\{a,b\}\}$ (the Kuratowski ordered pair). For discussion, see Enderton (1977), 35–8.

Sets, which also includes the Pairing Axiom (see (iii)).[4] Zermelo describes the empty set as a 'fictitious' set, but does not explain this odd remark (Zermelo (1908b), 202). Perhaps his reason can be found in the commonplace notion that a set is a collection, and that a collection must collect something; in Russell's words, 'a class which has no terms fails to be anything at all: what is merely and solely a collection of terms cannot subsist when all the terms are removed' (Russell (1903), 74). But even Russell is reluctant to ban the empty set simply because his philosophy suggests that it does not exist:

By symbolic logicians, who have experienced the utility of the [empty set], this will be felt as a reactionary view. But I am not at present discussing what should be done in the logical calculus, where the established practice [use of the empty set] appears to me the best, but what is the philosophical truth concerning the [empty set]. (Ibid.)

Gödel, in his discussion of Russell, shrugs off the purported 'philosophical truth' and isolates the extrinsic justification for admitting the empty set: '[I]t seems to me that these arguments could, if anything, at most prove that [the empty set is a] fiction . . . (introduced to simplify the calculus like the points at infinity in geometry)' (Gödel (1944), 131). This may well have been Zermelo's view: that the empty set is a fictitious entity added for convenience. This would be a typically extrinsic justification of the Empty Set Axiom: it leads to a more workable theory.[5]

Fraenkel, Bar-Hillel, and Levy fill in an argument along these lines. They first argue, as suggested above, that an individual—that is, a thing with no members—is needed to get the construction of sets started. They call this justification 'philosophical', but in our terms, it is extrinsic, that is, the individual is being adopted in the interest of getting the construction off the ground. To this, they add 'practical reasons' for positing such an individual: we want the intersection of two sets always to be defined, even when they have no element in common—this is a reason to posit an individual—and we want the intersections of disjoint sets A and B and disjoint sets A' and B' to be the same—this is a reason to posit a unique individual for this job. They conclude: 'Therefore we

---

[4] Zermelo's axiom also asserts the existence of the singleton $\{A\}$ for any object A, but this is a consequence of Pairing (see (I. 3. iii)).

[5] Similar debate surrounds the singleton $\{A\}$ as an entity distinct from A; see, for example, Russell (1903), 68. Zermelo, on the other hand, does not classify the singleton as fictitious. Gödel treats singletons in the same terms as the empty set in the excerpted passage from his (1944), 131.

shall call this element the [empty set] and our sets are, from now on, the elements which have members as well as the [empty] set' (Fraenkel, Bar-Hillel, and Levy (1973), 24).

The extrinsic nature of their argument is clear from the summary:

> Let us, however, stress at this point that whereas the existence of at least one individual is required for serious philosophical reasons [that is, to get the construction going], referring to one of the individuals as the [empty set] is done only for reasons of convenience and simplicity, and can be regarded as a mere notational convention. (Ibid.)

The contrast drawn here is not between intrinsic and extrinsic justifications, but between an extrinsic justification that is essential—the recovery of set theory cannot be carried out without some individual to start from—and one that is merely convenient—we could do without the empty set, as long as we have an individual of some kind, but it would be more cumbersome to do so.

Another style of argument for the Empty Set Axiom begins from a conception of set that underlies Zermelo's cumulative hierarchy, now called the *iterative conception*.[6] The idea is that sets are formed in a series of stages, beginning from the things that are not sets; at every stage, all possible collections of things at previous stages are formed. The contrast is with the Fregean picture of a set as the extension of a concept: on the Fregean conception, all the things in the universe (including the sets) are divided into two piles, depending on whether they do or don't have the property in question;[7] on the *iterative conception*, we begin with non-sets and generate the sets in stages. These are sometimes called the 'logical' and the 'mathematical' notion of collection, respectively; the mathematical notion is sometimes called 'combinatorial', because at each stage, a set is formed for every combination of things available at that stage, regardless of whether or not there is some law or property or whatever to single out precisely the things in that combination.[8]

Various things follow from the *iterative conception*. For example, a set can have as members only things occurring at stages earlier than the first

---

[6] For discussion, see Boolos (1971), Shoenfield (1967), ch. 9, Shoenfield (1977), Parsons (1977), Scott (1974), Wang (1974a), Hallett (1984), 214–23.

[7] I use 'having a property' as shorthand for a range of related ideas, including falling under a concept (Frege), satisfying a propositional function (Russell), yielding a true sentence when a name is substituting in an open sentence, etc.

[8] For discussion of this contrast, often identified with the class/set distinction, see Parsons (1974), Gödel (1964), 258–9, Martin (SVC), and Maddy (1983). The combinatorial idea appears in Bernays (1934); see II. 4. ii for more.

stage at which it appears, so a set cannot be self-membered. Furthermore, at any stage, the set of all previously-formed sets is formed. At the first stage, the set of all previously-formed sets is the empty set. So the Empty Set Axiom follows from the *iterative conception*.

If we adopt the *iterative conception* of set, that is, if we assume that it characterizes sets, gives the meaning of the word 'set', explicates the concept of 'set', or whatever—there are many idioms in which to couch this claim—then this justification for the Empty Set Axiom counts as intrinsic. It doesn't depend on what follows from the axiom, or what sort of theory the axiom makes possible or facilitates. Instead, it rests on an analysis of what sets are, on the nature of sets themselves. The *iterative conception* lies behind the cumulative hierarchy of Zermelo (1930), where it provides a rationale for his axioms beyond the purely extrinsic justifications of Zermelo (1908b).[9]

(iii) *Pairing and Union.* The Pairing and Union Axioms are the most elementary and uncontroversial ways of generating new sets from old; the former says that for any A and B, there is a set with exactly these two as members (i.e. $\{A,B\}$), and the latter says that for any set A, there is a set consisting of precisely the members of the members of A. This last may look unfamiliar, but the ordinary union of two sets C and D (in symbols, $C \cup D = \{x \mid x \in C \text{ or } x \in D\}$) can be obtained using the two axioms in succession: by Pairing, the set $\{C,D\}$ exists; by Union, the set whose members are precisely the members of the members of $\{C,D\}$ exists, and this last is just $C \cup D$. Pairing also yields the singleton of A, for any A, as $\{A\} = \{A,A\}$ (by Extensionality).

The Pairing Axiom was included in Zermelo's Axiom of Elementary Sets in (1908b); it appeared as a single axiom in his (1930). The Union Axiom appears on both lists. Both axioms are so straightforward as to elicit scant comment from commentators, but such discussion as does occur centres around two modes of argument. One is based on the *iterative conception*, the other on a doctrine called *limitation of size*. Let's take the second first.

In his illuminating historical and philosophical study of *limitation of size*, Hallett traces its first appearance to the writings of Cantor himself, to Cantor's notion of the Absolute Infinite (Hallett (1984), 165–76). Recall that Cantor distinguished between the ordinary transfinites, which are open to rational, mathematical treatment, and the Absolute Infinite,

---

[9] Mirimanoff (1917) was a partial precursor.

which can never be known or comprehended. Having shown how to deal with the infinity of the natural numbers, and with its successors, he concludes: 'I have no doubt at all that in this way we extend ever further, never reaching an insuperable barrier, but also never reaching any even approximate comprehension of the Absolute' (Cantor (1883), translated in Hallett (1984), 42). Thus the sequence of (finite and transfinite) ordinal numbers itself is identified with the Absolute: 'The absolutely infin - ite sequence of numbers therefore seems to me in a certain sense a suitable symbol of the Absolute' (ibid.). In an 1899 letter to Dedekind, this becomes the notion of 'absolutely infinite collections': 'a multiplicity can be such that the assumption that *all* of its element "are together" leads to a contradiction, so that it is impossible to conceive of the multiplicity as a unity, as "one finished thing"' (Cantor (1899), 114). The collection of all ordinal numbers is such a collection: if it were 'one finished thing', it would be well-ordered, and hence, it would itself have an ordinal number that would have to be strictly greater than every ordinal number, including itself.[10]

Cantor goes on to argue that the collection of all cardinal numbers is also absolutely infinite, because it is equinumerous with the collection of all ordinal numbers. Collections that are not absolutely infinite are called 'sets', and the mathematical theory of sets is concerned only with them. Sets can be numbered, can be increased, can be understood mathematically; absolutely infinite collections cannot be numbered, cannot be increased, cannot be understood at all. Here, then, is the principle of *limitation of size*: sets are those collections that are not too large, that is, collections that are not as large as the collection of all ordinal numbers.

A few years later, when the paradoxes had taken centre stage, Russell suggested this diagnosis: 'This difficulty does not concern the infinite as such, but only certain very large infinite classes' (Russell (1903), 362). This idea reappears in Russell (1906).[11] Russell, like Zermelo, sees the problem as how to limit Unlimited Comprehension: if not every property has an extension, how are we to circumscribe those that do? The sug-

---

[10] This is the reasoning of the Burali-Forti paradox. See Burali-Forti (1897).

[11] At this point in his development, Russell had proposed and rejected type theory (see Russell (1903), App. B), and he now reviews three possible approaches to the paradoxes. Two of these are addressed directly to the problem of how to limit Unlimited Comprehension. The first, the zig-zag theory, would admit extensions only for properties of a certain simple form. (Quine's set theories in (1937) and (1940) are descendants of this idea.) The second is the theory of limitation of size. (The third suggestion is the no-class theory, which eventually took its place, alongside ramified type theory, in the overall doctrine of *Principia Mathematica*. See III. 2 for more.)

gestion behind his 'theory of limitation of size' is that a property has an extension only if that extension would not be too big. The trick, of course, is in specifying what counts as 'too big'.

Before confronting this problem, it is worth noting that Russell claims *limitation of size* 'can be recommended as plausible by the help of certain *a priori* logical considerations' (Russell (1906), 145). This suggests that Russell might have classified *limitation of size* arguments as intrinsic. It seems that Cantor so understood them, given that they arise directly out of his considered description of the nature of collections, large and small, transcendent and immanent. In contrast, Russell's analysis goes like this: 'there are a number of processes, of which the generation of ordinals is one, which seem essentially incapable of terminating, although each process is such that the class of all terms generated by it . . . ought to be the last term generated by that process' (Russell (1906), 152). For example, at any point in the generation of the ordinals, the class of ordinals generated so far can be seen as the end of the sequence. Obviously, such a process of generation cannot end.

Thus it is natural to suppose that the terms generated by such a process do not form a class. And, if so, it seems also natural to suppose that any aggregate embracing all the terms generated by one of these processes cannot form a class. Consequently there will be (so to speak) a certain limit of size which no class can reach; and any supposed class which reaches or surpasses this limit is an improper class, i.e. is a non-entity. (Ibid.)

Here Russell is hoping to found set theory on a Limited Comprehension Axiom along the following lines: any property that doesn't apply to every member of some 'self-reproductive process' (ibid.) has an extension. Once the inherently problematic nature of self-reproductive processes is understood, this version of Limited Comprehension would appear as a minor, necessary adjustment to Unlimited Comprehension, and would thus inherit its intuitive force.

The problem, then, is to specify what counts as 'too big' or what processes are 'self-reproductive'. Here Russell remarks that for properties that generate contradictions, 'It is probable . . . that . . . we can actually construct a series, ordinally similar to the series of all ordinals, composed entirely of terms having the property' (ibid. 144). This suggests that a property is not 'self-reproductive', that its extension is not 'too big', exactly when it cannot be put in one-to-one correspondence with the ordinals. This suggestion appears in Jourdain (1904), which is cited by Russell; in his correspondence with Jourdain, Cantor notes the similarity of this idea to his own view that the series of ordinals is Absolutely Infinite.[12]

So an attractive concrete version of *limitation of size* is the claim that any property has an extension if and only if it is not possible to establish a one-to-one correspondence between the ordinal numbers and things with that property. The trouble with this proposal, as a fundamental axiom, is that it presupposes the ordinal numbers; without a prior theory of the ordinals, the proposed axiom is useless. Russell illustrates the problem: 'A great difficulty of this theory is that it does not tell us how far up the series of ordinals it is legitimate to go. It might happen that ω is already illegitimate: in that case, all [legitimate] classes would be finite' (ibid. 153). To see Russell's point about ω, suppose 0, 1, 2, and 3 have been generated. The set of these is in fact the next ordinal, 4. Does this mean that the set of natural numbers is self-reproducing, and hence illegitimate? If so, any infinite set will be illegitimate, because any such set contains a subset equinumerous with ω. Unless we have some independent way of showing that ω is not 'too big', this theory of *limitation of size* doesn't get off the ground.

Russell puts the point this way: 'We need further axioms before we can tell where the series [of ordinals] begins to be illegitimate' (ibid.); 'it is not easy to see where this series begins to be non-existent, if such a bull[13] may be permitted' (ibid. 144). More generally, and in more precise language, Hallett writes:

Since nobody has been able to specify any means of recognizing whether a collection is intrinsically small (safe) or not, the only alternative is to specify an external measure of size via a measure collection as Jourdain did. Thus the existence of some collection of objects (sets) must be guaranteed independently of considerations of size. This does not preclude the use of limitation of size principles, but it means that they cannot be the sole arbiters of set existence. (Hallett (1984), 185)

In other words, *limitation of size* cannot, by itself, serve as a replacement for Unlimited Comprehension, but it might help to justify other axioms.[14]

---

[12] For a valuable survey of Cantor, Jourdain, and Russell on *limitation of size*, see Hallett (1984), ch. 4.

[13] Webster's defines 'bull', from Middle English, as 'a ludicrously illogical or incongruous mistake in statement (Ex: I'm glad I hate onions because if I liked onions, I'd eat them, and I can't stand onions).' (*Webster's New World Dictionary of the American Language*, 2nd college edn. (Cleveland, Ohio: William Collins, 1979)).

[14] In von Neumann's system, a principle of *limitation of size* is adopted explicitly as an

One way this idea has functioned in the post-Russellian development of axiomatic set theory can be seen in this passage from Fraenkel, Bar-Hillel, and Levy:

The axiom of [unlimited] comprehension turned out to be inconsistent and therefore cannot be used as an axiom of set theory. However, since this axiom is so close to our intuitive concept of set we shall try to retain a considerable number of instances of this axiom scheme. . . . Our guiding principle, for the system ZF,[15] will be to admit only those instances of the axiom schema of comprehension which assert the existence of sets which are not too 'big' compared to sets which we already have. We shall call this principle *the limitation of size doctrine*. (Fraenkel, Bar-Hillel, and Levy (1973), 32)

The suggestion that Zermelo's approach can be motivated in this way is widespread; for example, referring to Russell's zig-zag theory and his theory of *limitation of size*, Gödel writes: 'The most characteristic feature of the second (as opposed to the first) would consist in the non-existence of the [set of all sets]. . . . Axiomatic set theory as later developed by Zermelo and others can be considered as an elaboration of this idea' (Gödel (1944), 124–5).

To produce a justification along these lines, we begin with a Russellian diagnosis of the paradoxes: 'Zermelo's protection against the paradoxes consists essentially in eschewing too big classes' (Quine (1969c), 278). An axiom can then be defended on the grounds that it doesn't produce collections that are too big. Or better—given that we have no independent way of identifying sets as too big—an axiom that generates new sets from old can be defended on the grounds that the collections generated aren't substantially bigger than those from which they are generated; in other words, the axiom doesn't make matters any worse.

Again, a true Cantorian might base this first step—the rejection of 'too-bigness'—on the 'insuperable barrier' to 'any even approximate comprehension of the Absolute', and this might well count as intrinsic, that is, as based on an analysis of the nature of collections. But even without the connection to theology, I suspect this style of argument will strike most today as a mite too mystical. One could, instead, base the first step on a case-by-case analysis of the known paradoxes. This way, the result-

axiom: a collection is 'too big' iff it can be brought into one-to-one correspondence with the collection of all sets (see von Neumann (1925)). In the company of other axioms, this axiom is equivalent to three of the standard ZFC axioms (separation, replacement, and choice). For simplicity, I stick to ZFC.

[15] ZF is just ZFC without the Axiom of Choice.

ing defence would be fully extrinsic: things like this lead to contradictions; this axiom is good because it doesn't lead to things like this. This is still vague, of course, but the position that our axioms do not generate sets that are too big receives some support from the facts that known paradoxes cannot be derived from them, and no new paradoxes have been shown to follow from them in decades of use.

In any case, however it is understood, *limitation of size* applies easily to the case of Pairing: $\{A,B\}$ has only two members, so it can hardly be 'too big', in any relevant sense. Fraenkel, Bar-Hillel, and Levy, for example, characterize the pair set as a set of 'very modest size' ((1973), 32). Union is slightly trickier. Again, Fraenkel, Bar-Hillel, and Levy put the case this way: 'According to our program of not introducing 'too large' sets, the sets whose union is to be formed will not be taken arbitrarily—they must be members of a single given set' (ibid. 34). If we see ourselves as generating 'small' sets from other 'small' sets, then it is important that the collection of sets whose union we are taking be 'small', as Fraenkel, Bar-Hillel, and Levy note, but it is also important that each of the individual sets be 'small'. Thus von Neumann remarks: 'If a is a set, not too big, of sets that are themselves not too big, then the set b of the elements of the elements of a is not too big either' (von Neumann (1925), 401). The basic claim is that the union of a small collection of small collections must be small.

This position has been criticized, for example, by Hallett, who writes that 'The union set axiom is rather harder to justify along these lines, for it is certainly expansive, the union of a frequently having more members than a' (Hallett (1984), 205). Of course, adherents of the argument insist that the union is 'not much bigger' (Levy (1979), 18). Hallett imagines that this sort of claim might be fleshed out by cardinality considerations: 'For if one knows the cardinality of a collection X and the cardinality of each of its members, one can quite easily assign a cardinal bound to the union of X' (Hallett, loc. cit.). So even Hallett sees some force to the *limitation of size* argument for the Union Axiom.

Though he doesn't mention *limitation of size*, Zermelo may have been influenced by these considerations in his (1908b) list.[16] By (1930), however, his central motivating concept is the *iterative conception*. Notice that the *iterative conception* can be seen as implying a version of *limitation of*

---

[16] Hallett ((1984), 241) argues that he was, citing Zermelo's reference to Hessenberg (Zermelo (1908b), 202), who entertained a notion of 'ultrafinite' collections (that is, collections that are too big). See I. 3. iv below.

size: if sets are generated in stages, each set must occur for the first time at some stage, and all its members must occur at earlier stages. But a new ordinal is formed at every stage, so there is no stage at which the set of all ordinals is formed. The same goes for any collection that never stops acquiring new members; it cannot be a set, because there is no stage at which all its members are available to be collected. These are the collections that are too big, like the collection of all ordinals, of all cardinals, and the collection of all sets.

In any case, arguments for the Pairing and Union Axioms based on the *iterative conception* are straightforward and easy: each of A and B first occurs at some stage; let α be the later of the two. Then A and B are available for collection at stage $\alpha + 1$, so $\{A,B\}$ is formed there. This establishes Pairing. Similarly, if A is a collection of sets, then A first occurs at some stage α, and every member of A first occurs at a stage before α. This means that the members of the members of A are all available for collection by stage α at the latest; so $\cup A$ is formed by stage α. This establishes Union. Arguments in these styles can be found, for example, in Boolos ((1971), 496) and Shoenfield ((1977), 325).

(iv) *Separation.* The Axiom of Separation (or the Axiom of Subsets, as it is sometimes called) is the key to Zermelo's system, his substitute for Unlimited Comprehension. Here he places two constraints on the notion that for every property P, there is a set containing exactly the things with P: 'In the first place, sets may never be *independently defined* by means of this axiom but must always be *separated* as subsets from sets already given' (Zermelo (1908b), 202). To use a property to form a set, we must already have some set from which to separate out the elements of the new set. In other words, though we cannot simply form the set of all things with the property P, we can form the set of all things *in some given set* that have P. Zermelo continues: 'thus contradictory notions such as "the set of all sets" or "the set of all ordinal numbers" . . . are excluded' (ibid.). To see this, suppose there is a set V of all sets. Then by Separation, there would be a set R of elements x of V with the property of being non-self-membered. But such an R is self-membered if and only if it is not; this is Russell's paradox. So there is no such set V.

The second constraint concerns the property P itself. Ramsey had yet to provide his division of the paradoxes into two varieties—those involving purely logical or mathematical notions and those involving linguistic or semantic terms—but Zermelo's constraint on P is aimed at eliminating the second variety from his system. He requires 'the defining cri-

terion [for the set, that is, the property *P*] must always be definite . . .
with the result that . . . all criteria such as "definable by means of a finite
number of words" . . . vanish' (ibid.). In this way, we avoid the Berry
paradox and other such problems.

In fact, Zermelo had no clear account of the crucial notion of 'definiteness'. The axiom was criticized on this ground by Russell, Jourdain,
Poincaré, and others (see Moore (1982), § 3. 3). By (1922), Skolem had
devised a solution, anticipated by Weyl, and equivalent to a simultaneous
proposal of Fraenkel: a definite property is one expressible in a language
for first-order logic with '∈' (for membership) as its only non-logical
symbol. In his (1930), Zermelo argued for a second-order account, but
Skolem's position has carried the day.

So the contemporary Axiom of Separation says that for every set *A*
and every property *P* expressible in first-order logic with '∈' as the sole
non-logical symbol, there is a set *B* containing exactly those elements of
A that have *P* (in symbols, $B = \{x \in A \mid x \text{ has } P\}$). This statement cannot itself be expressed in first-order form—where the variables range
over sets, not formulas—so it is actually what's called an 'axiom schema':
for every first-order formula $\phi(x)$, the statement 'for every set *A*, there is
a set *B* containing exactly those members *a* of *A* such that $\phi(a)$' is an
axiom. The Axiom of Separation in fact consists of infinitely many individual axioms of this form.

Implicit in these remarks of Zermelo is an extrinsic argument for
Separation on the grounds that it blocks the derivation of known paradoxes. Of course, it also sacrifices much of the set-forming power of
Unlimited Comprehension, given that it cannot produce a set without
beginning from a previously-given set. Thus Separation requires the co-operation of Zermelo's other axioms to reproduce the bulk of Cantorian
set theory. A more complete version of this extrinsic justification would
support Separation in the company of the rest of ZFC.

In addition, Separation is clearly well-suited for a *limitation of size* defence: if the original set *A* is not too big, then the separated set *B*, a subset of *A*, cannot be too big. In other words, as a way of generating new
sets from old, Separation cannot make matters worse as far as size is concerned. Arguing that Zermelo himself was influenced by this line of
thought, Hallett notes his remark that with the Axiom of Separation, 'the
"ultrafinite paradoxes", to use Hessenberg's expression . . . are excluded'
(Zermelo (1908b), 202). Hallett continues:

Zermelo's reference to Hessenberg's term 'ultrafinite paradoxes' is a fairly clear indication that he did accept the limitation of size hypothesis. For Hessenberg remarks: 'It can be shown of the paradoxical sets which we investigate here that they are of greater power than any aleph.' And such sets are just what he calls 'ultrafinite' meaning that they fall outside (are too big for) transfinite set theory. Although this characterization of 'too big' is really a cardinal characterization, something which Zermelo himself did not explicitly rely on, by using the term 'ultrafinite' Zermelo is clearly saying that the separation axiom cannot approach the *very big sets* which cause the paradoxes. In this sense, separation acts as a limitation of size principle. (Hallett (1984), 241)

So the doctrine of *limitation of size* provides a second line of defence, either intrinsic or extrinsic, depending on what support one gives for the doctrine itself.

Finally, consider Separation from the point of view of the *iterative conception*: our set A is first formed at some stage α; all the members of A must have been formed before stage α, so every member of A that satisfies the formula $\phi(x)$ must have been formed before stage α; thus, the set B is formed by stage α at the latest. Versions of this straightforward *iterative conception* defence of the Axiom of Separation can be found in Boolos ((1971), 497–8) and Shoenfield ((1977), 325).

(v) *Infinity.* The assumption that there are infinite sets, completed infinite collections, was the revolutionary move that marked the beginning of Cantor's set theory. From the time of the ancients, paradoxes like Zeno's had brought the notion under suspicion. Aristotle's solution was to insist that mathematicians could and should get by with the potential infinite (for every number, there is a next; for any length, there is a shorter) and renounce the completed infinite (the collection of all numbers; the line as a collection of points). Though it necessitated a sharp separation between arithmetic and algebra, on the one hand, and geometry on the other, this point of view was arguably tenable until the rise of the calculus. The line of development that finally led to a coherent foundation for the calculus (see I. 2) also led to the explicit introduction of completed infinities: each real number is identified with an infinite collection of rationals.[17]

Hallett identifies a Cantorian notion he calls *Cantorian finitism*:

it expresses a certain 'finitistic' attitude to sets . . . Namely, sets are treated as

---

[17] On Dedekind's account (see Dedekind (1872) or Enderton (1977), ch. 5). Other accounts make use of other infinite sets (e.g. in Cantor's case, infinite Cauchy sequences of rationals).

simple objects, regardless of whether they are finite or infinite . . . We saw that the Cantor and Dedekind definitions of real number force us to admit certain infinite collections as single objects, as individuals. Thus, while in construction (i.e. in terms of their definition) these real numbers are highly complex, the theory says that once we have defined them we can treat them as simple objects—forget the complexity. What Cantor does is to extend this doctrine to *all* collections that one wishes to subject to mathematical examination. They can all be treated as single objects. (Hallett (1984), 32)

This Cantorian idea lies behind the Axiom of Infinity: to claim that there are infinite sets is to claim that completed infinite collections can be treated mathematically. In its standard contemporary form, the axiom asserts the existence of the set of all finite ordinals.[18]

A *limitation of size* theorist might say that the set of all finite ordinals is not too big, an *iterative conception* theorist might say there is a stage after all the finite stages, but these claims can hardly be defended on the basis of either of these doctrines. The standard justification is purely extrinsic:

Dealing with natural numbers without having the set of all natural numbers does not cause more inconvenience than, say, dealing with sets without having the set of all sets. Also, the arithmetic of the rational numbers can be developed in this framework. However, if one is already interested in analysis [the calculus] then infinite sets are indispensable since even the notion of a real number cannot be developed by means of finite sets only. Hence we have to add an existence axiom that guarantees the existence of an infinite set. (Fraenkel, Bar-Hillel, and Levy (1973), 45)

Cantor may have envisioned a theological justification (see Hallett (1984), § 1. 3), but for anyone alive to the value of modern mathematics, this extrinsic argument will be eminently persuasive.

(vi) *Power Set.* The Power Set Axiom is another way of generating new sets from old; it asserts that for any set A, there is a set $\wp(A)$ containing exactly the subsets of A. Recall that Cantor proved the power set of A has greater cardinality than A. This is easy to see for finite sets—a set with 5 elements has 2^5 subsets; Cantor showed that this is also true for infinite sets. So, in particular, given that ω (the set of finite ordinals) has $\aleph_0$ elements, the power set of ω (the set of all sets of finite ordinals) has

---

[18] Contemporary texts usually state the axiom along these lines: there is a set that contains the empty set, and which contains, for each of its elements a, the set $a \cup \{a\}$.

$2^{\aleph_0}$ elements. A set of finite ordinals A determines a function from ω to $\{0,1\}$ (e.g. the function that sends n to 0 if $n \notin A$ and 1 if $n \in A$); thinking of such functions as representations of real numbers in binary notation, it isn't hard to show that the reals are equinumerous with $\wp(\omega)$. So there are $2^{\aleph_0}$ reals, as well.[19]

Hallett sees *Cantorian finitism* as including the idea that infinite sets should be treated like finite ones (see Hallett (1984), 32). Assuming that all finite sets are unproblematic, we can assert the existence of the power set of any finite set, and so, by applications of *Cantorian finitism*, we should do the same for infinite sets (see Hallett (1984), 212). Others, including Fraenkel, argue that the power set of a 'not too large' set must also be 'not too large', thus defending Power Set by means of *limitation of size*, but Hallett exposes such arguments to considerable criticism (see Hallett (1984), § 5.1). Perhaps the *iterative conception* provides the most satisfying account: if A is first formed at stage α, then all the members of A are available at or before stage α, so any subset of A is formed at stage α at the latest; thus, the power set of A is formed at stage $\alpha + 1$. (See Boolos (1971), 496–7; Shoenfield (1977), 326.)

There is also an extrinsic argument for Power Set that runs along the same lines as the argument just given for the Axiom of Infinity. The set theoretic account of the real numbers depends on the existence of infinite sets, yes, but it cannot be carried out without also taking the power set of an infinite set. Perhaps this is not surprising, given the close connection noted above between the reals and $\wp(\omega)$. This argument is implicit in Fraenkel, Bar-Hillel, and Levy ((1973), 34–5), and explicit in Hallett:

Is there any evidence that [the Power Set Axiom] is legitimate . . .? In a certain sense, there is. The reason here is quite simple, namely, the crucial involvement of the . . . power-set axiom in the set theoretic construction of the continuum. . . . the argument is: the power-set principle . . . was revealed in our attempts to make our intuitive picture of the continuum analytically clearer; in so far as these attempts are successful, then the power-set principle gains some confirmatory support. At least the development of the set-theoretic continuum shows that one application of the power-set principle to an infinite set has productive and intelligible, although strong, consequences. (Hallett (1984), 212–13)

Again, this style of argument will be persuasive for anyone alive to the

---

[19] See Enderton (1977), 149.

value of the set theoretic reduction of the continuum, and the wide range of mathematics that it underlies.

(vii) *Choice*. As noted in I. 1, the Axiom of Choice was the critical ingredient in Zermelo's (1904) proof of the Well-Ordering Theorem. Its effects are aptly illustrated in a famous example from Russell: it's easy to prove the existence of a choice set for an infinite collection of pairs of shoes; for example, take the set of all the left shoes. But what about an infinite collection of pairs of socks? As Fraenkel, Bar-Hillel, and Levy remark,

as long as manufacturers adhere to the regrettable custom of producing equal stockings for both feet there is no condition which simultaneously distinguishes one stocking in each of the infinitely many pairs. Hence a set containing just one stocking from each pair exists only by virtue of the axiom of choice. (Fraenkel, Bar-Hillel, and Levy (1973), 63)

Choice was by far the most controversial of Zermelo's axioms; passionate debate reverberated through all corners of the mathematical community. Moore (1982) provides a readable and compelling account of its development and eventual resolution.

Zermelo himself presents two basic varieties of arguments for his Axiom, which map neatly onto our categories of intrinsic and extrinsic justification. Both are present at the outset of his reply to his critic Peano:

how does Peano arrive at his own fundamental principles . . .? Evidently by analyzing the modes of inference that in the course of history have come to be recognized as valid and by pointing out that the principles are intuitively evident and necessary for science—considerations that can all be urged equally well in favor of the disputed principle. (Zermelo (1908a), 187)

To support a hypothesis on the grounds that it is 'intuitively evident' clearly qualifies as intrinsic. Zermelo develops the case this way:[20]

That this axiom, even though it was never formulated in textbook style, has frequently been used, and successfully at that, in the most diverse fields of mathematics, especially in set theory, by Dedekind, Cantor, F. Bernstein, Schoenflies, J. König, and others is an indisputable fact . . . Such extensive use of a principle can be explained only by its *self-evidence*. (Ibid.)

---

[20] Fraenkel, Bar-Hillel, and Levy ((1973), 85) second Zermelo's reading of history here. Hallett ((1984), 159) disagrees, drawing a sharper distinction than the others do between using the axiom and using a mode of inference that can be analysed as an equivalent of the axiom.

Indeed, versions of the axiom were often used unconsciously, even in the early work of the French analysts Baire, Borel, and Lebesgue, who later joined the ranks of its leading critics. This is counted as evidence for the naturalness or intuitiveness of the assumption.

More elaborate intrinsic defences (and critiques) of the axiom rest on philosophical analyses of the nature of sets or of mathematical objects more generally. As in the famous exchange between Hadamard, a defender of Choice, and Lebesgue, Borel, and Baire, opponents of Choice (see Baire *et al.* (1905)), the debate often takes the form of a face-off between those who hold mathematical things to exist objectively (Realism), and those who take them to be constructed or defined by us (Constructivism or Definabilism).[21]

A more narrowly-focused argument with a similar flavour sees the conflict between pro-Choice forces and anti-Choice forces as resting on a confusion about the notion of collection:

> much of the traditional concern about the axiom of choice is probably based on a confusion between sets and definable properties. In many cases it appears unlikely that one can *define* a choice function for a particular collection of sets. But this is entirely unrelated to the question of whether a choice function *exists*. Once this kind of confusion is avoided, the axiom of choice appears as one of the least problematic of the set theoretic axioms. (Martin (SVC), 1–2)

One strand of this argument advocates realism much in the spirit of Hadamard against those who hold that sets depend for their existence on our definitions. A second strand contrasts the logical notion of collection—the extension of a predicate—with the mathematical notion of collection—generated combinatorially in stages.

This second strand emerges most distinctly in arguments for Choice from the *iterative conception*: if the family $\mathfrak{S}$ of disjoint, non-empty sets is first formed at stage α, then every member A of $\mathfrak{S}$ is first formed before α, and the members of A before that; so the members of the members of $\mathfrak{S}$ are all available at stage α; every combination of available elements is then formed at stage α, including a choice set. *Iterative conception* theorists disagree over the viability of this argument (e.g. Shoenfield ((1977), 335–6) is in favour, but Boolos ((1971), 501–2) against).

Zermelo concludes his intrinsic defense of Choice by admitting that

---

[21] I return to this version of the controversy in II. 4. ii and III. 4. ii.

'this self-evidence is to a certain degree subjective' (Zermelo (1908a), 187). He then switches to his extrinsic defence:

But the question that can be objectively decided, whether the principle is *necessary for science*, I should now like to submit to judgment by presenting a number of elementary and fundamental theorems and problems that, in my opinion, could not be dealt with at all without the principle of choice. (ibid. 187–8)

This remark is followed by a list of seven theorems from set theory and analysis that Zermelo takes to rest on the axiom. To illustrate the fundamental nature of the consequences of the axiom, we should recall Cantor's Well-Ordering Theorem, the Aleph Theorem (every cardinal number appears in the list $\aleph_0$, $\aleph_1$, $\aleph_2$, . . .), and Cardinal Comparability (for any two distinct cardinal numbers, κ and λ, either $\kappa < \lambda$ or $\lambda < \kappa$). It takes little imagination to see that the deep and intricate theory of infinite cardinal numbers would be undermined without these results. Since Zermelo's day, it has become clear that consequences or equivalents of the axiom play similarly fundamental roles in fields as diverse as analysis, topology, abstract algebra, and mathematical logic.[22]

An uncompromising opponent of Choice might insist on rejecting all the mathematics that rests on it, but history shows that such an opponent would be swimming against the tide. To take just one example, Moore tells the story of van der Waerden's famous *Modern Algebra*. The first edition, published in 1930, included numerous recent applications of the axiom, which had taken on great importance in algebra in the 1920s. Despite the wide influence of the first edition, some opponents of the axiom among van der Waerden's Dutch colleagues persuaded him to delete the axiom from the second, 1937 edition. The resulting restricted picture of the subject so incensed his fellow algebraists that the axiom and its consequences were reinstated in the third edition of 1950. Moore concludes, 'Algebraists insisted that the Axiom . . . had become indispensable to their discipline' (Moore (1982), 235). Thus the algebraists, along with mathematicians in many other fields, agreed with Zermelo's analysis:

no one has the right to prevent the representatives of productive science from continuing to use this 'hypothesis'—as one may call it for all I care—and developing its consequences to the greatest extent . . . We need merely separate the theorems that necessarily require the axiom from those that can be proved with-

---

[22] Moore provides tables of consequences and equivalents in various fields in App. 2 to his (1982). For a short introduction, see Jech (1977).

out it in order to delimit the whole of Peano's mathematics as a special branch, as an artificially mutilated science, so to speak. . . . principles must be judged from the point of view of science, and not science from the point of view of principles fixed once and for all. (Zermelo (1908a), 189)

Note the final sentence: Zermelo's ringing endorsement of extrinsic justifications.

The contemporary system ZFC includes two further axioms not prefigured in Zermelo's (1908b). They are:

(viii) *Replacement.* Around 1922, both Skolem and Fraenkel noticed a deficiency in Zermelo's system: 'It is easy to show that Zermelo's axiom system is not sufficient to provide a complete foundation for the usual theory of sets' (Skolem (1922), 296). (See also Fraenkel (1922).) To see the problem, consider ω, $\wp(\omega)$, $\wp(\wp(\omega))$, and so on. It is surely in the spirit of Cantorian set theory to allow $\{\omega,\ \wp(\omega),\ \wp(\wp(\omega)),\ \dots\}$, but Skolem demonstrates that the existence of this set cannot be proved from Zermelo's axioms. He does this by showing that all the axioms are true in $V_{\omega+\omega}$, but the set in question does not exist.[23] Fraenkel made a similar observation.

Skolem suggests that 'in order to remove this deficiency' ((1922), 297), we add a new axiom: if F is a function and A is a set, then there is a set B containing exactly the $F(a)$ for $a \in A$ (i.e. $B = \{F(a) \mid a \in A\}$). The function F replaces each member a of the set A with $F(a)$ to produce the new set B, hence, Axiom of Replacement. Now ω is a set (by the Axiom of Infinity) and F that maps 0 to ω, 1 to $\wp(\omega)$, 2 to $\wp(\wp(\omega))$, and so on, is a function, so by Replacement, $\{F(n) \mid n \in \omega\} = \{\omega,\ \wp(\omega),\ \wp(\wp(\omega)) \dots\}$ exists. Notice that the function F is subject to the same difficulties as the property P in the Separation Axiom. Skolem used the same solution; he took Replacement as a schema, one Replacement axiom for every first-order formula $\phi(x,y)$: if A is a set, and if $\phi(a,b)$ and $\phi(a,b')$ imply that $b = b'$ for every $a \in A$, then $\{b \mid \text{for some } a \in A,\ b = F(a)\}$ exists.

The axiom was anticipated by Cantor (1899) and Mirimanoff (1917), and put to good use by von Neumann in (1925). While Skolem and

---

[23] If σ is provable from Zermelo's axioms, then it is true in every model of those axioms, that is, in every structure in which all Zermelo's axioms are true. This is the Soundness Theorem. Completeness (Gödel (1930)) is the converse: if σ is true in every model of a theory T, then σ is provable from T. See Enderton (1972) for a textbook treatment.

Fraenkel used the axiom to obtain sets that seemed unobjectionable from the point of view of the pre-axiomatic set theorists, von Neumann did much more: he showed that Replacement was needed for fundamental set theoretic results. For example, though Zermelo had proved Cantor's Well-Ordering Theorem in the form 'every set can be well-ordered', his system was too weak to prove it in Cantor's original form: 'every set can be put in one-to-one correspondence with some ordinal'. (This can be seen along the lines of Skolem's argument: all Zermelo's axioms are true in $V_{\omega+\omega}$, but $V_{\omega+\omega}$ contains no uncountable ordinals, and so no ordinal for e.g. $\wp(\omega)$.) Von Neumann proved the stronger Well-Ordering Theorem and the fundamental principle of Transfinite Recursion. Zermelo added the axiom to his list in (1930) (though, as in the case of Separation, he argued for a second-order formulation).

Like Separation, Replacement is a good fit for *limitation of size* theorists:

our guiding principle . . . is to admit only axioms which assert the existence of sets which are not too 'big' compared to sets already ascertained. If we are given a set *a* and a collection of sets which has no more members than *a* it seems to be within the scope of our guiding principle to admit that collection as a new set. (Fraenkel, Bar-Hillel, and Levy (1973), 50)

The function F maps each member of A to at most one new set, so $\{F(a) \mid a \in A\}$ has no more members than A itself. Admittedly, when Replacement is combined with other axioms, like Union and Power Set, it generates some larger sets than are possible in Zermelo's system; for example, it produces sets of size $\aleph_\omega$.[24]

Iterative conception theorists disagree on whether or not Replacement follows from their understanding of sets. After deriving Zermelo's axioms (except Choice and Extensionality) from his theory of stages, Boolos writes:

There is an extension of the stage theory from which the axioms of replacement could have been derived. We could have taken as axioms all instances . . . of a principle which may be put, 'If each set is correlated with at least one stage (no matter how), then for any set z there is a stage s such that for each member w of z, s is later than some stage with which w is correlated.' (Boolos (1971), 500)

But he adds: 'This *bounding* or *cofinality* principle is an attractive further

---

[24] Map 0 to $\aleph_0$, 1 to $\aleph_1$, 2 to $\aleph_2$, and so on, and apply Replacement to get $\{\aleph_0, \aleph_1, \aleph_2, \ldots\}$. The union of this set has size $\aleph_\omega$.

thought about the interrelation of sets and stages, but it does seem to us to be a *further* thought, and not one that can be said to have been meant in the rough description of the iterative conception' (ibid.). So, for Boolos, the Replacement Axioms go beyond the iterative conception.

Shoenfield, in contrast, builds a maximality idea into his description of stage theory. He begins:

Stages are important to us because they enable us to form sets. Thus suppose that x is a collection of sets and that S is a collection of stages such that each member of x is formed at a stage which is a member of S. If there is a stage after all the members of S, then we can form x at this stage. Thus the fundamental question for us is: given a collection S of stages, is there a stage after all the members of S? (Shoenfield (1977), 323)

By way of answer, he writes:

We would like the answer to this question to be yes whenever possible. We know by the paradoxes that not every collection of sets is a set; but we have avoided the paradoxes by restricting ourselves to sets which are formed at some stage. We do not wish to further restrict the notion of set by not having sufficiently many stages. (Ibid.)

In particular, if x is a set, and with each y in x, there is correlated a stage S_y, then there should be a stage after all the stages S_y. For this conclusion, Shoenfield provides the following argument: 'Suppose that as each stage S is completed, we take each y in x which is formed at S and complete the stage S_y. When we reach the stage at which x is formed, we will have formed each y in x and hence completed each stage S_y' (ibid. 324). Thus on Shoenfield's version of the iterative conception, there is a stage after all the S_ys, and from this the Axiom of Replacement follows.

But beyond all these considerations lie the purely extrinsic arguments, beginning with von Neumann's fundamental results. Until recently, the important known consequences of Replacement had all been squarely within set theory itself, like Transfinite Recursion, but in the mid-1970s, Martin used the axiom to establish a welcome regularity property of certain definable sets of reals (see Martin (1975)). A few years earlier, Harvey Friedman had shown that this conclusion could not be proved from Zermelo's theory alone (see H. Friedman (1971)). Thus Martin's theorem demonstrates that Replacement plays a central role in the theory of sets of reals, a theory of central interest to the early analysts.[25]

---

[25] I return to these topics in I. 4.

It is worth noting, in connection with the *iterative conception*, that Replacement also allows us to define the V_αs within our formal theory. As Boolos remarks, 'Then we can prove as theorems . . . the axioms of stage theory' (Boolos (1971), 500). Whether or not we think Replacement follows from the *iterative conception* alone, this may well strike us as a welcome result. In sum, then, we have Boolos's analysis of the case for Replacement: 'the reason for adopting the axioms of replacement is quite simple: they have many desirable consequences and (apparently) no undesirable ones' (ibid.). The extrinsic argument, unadorned.

(ix) *Foundation*. The Axiom of Foundation (or the Axiom of Regularity, as it is sometimes called) rules out self-membership entirely. It also rules out membership loops like $A \in B$ and $B \in A$, and infinite descending $\in$-chains like $A_0 \ni A_1 \ni A_2 \ldots$. In the presence of the other axioms, it is equivalent to the claim that every set is a member of some V_α. This presents a clear and useful picture of the universe of sets, but in fact, the bulk of ordinary set theoretic results can be proved without appeal to Foundation.

In the earliest known version of his axiomatization, a notebook from 1905, Zermelo used a weak form of Foundation—the assumption that no set is self-membered—to block Russell's paradox. No version of the axiom appears in his (1908b), perhaps because Zermelo now felt Separation was enough to block the paradoxes. Mirimanoff, in (1917), focused his attention on well-founded sets (i.e. those without infinite descending $\in$-chains); though he didn't assume there were no other sets, he did argue that restricting attention to these—essentially, assuming Foundation—was a practical and fruitful approach. Von Neumann adopted Foundation in his (1925), as did Zermelo in (1930).

Von Neumann's goal was to specify the universe of sets as uniquely as possible, so he used Foundation to rule out structures with self-membership. In (1930), Zermelo applied the axiom to generate the picture of the set theoretic universe as composed of the V_αs; he felt this picture provided an attractive rationale for his axiomatization that went beyond the purely extrinsic justifications of his (1908b). Recent *iterative conception* theorists often take Foundation to be built into their notion of collection (see Shoenfield (1977), 326–7). Boolos derives it from the axioms of his stage theory (Boolos (1971), 498), as does Scott (Scott (1974), 211; Shoenfield (1977), 327).

Still, most theorists leave open the question of the truth of Foundation, that is, the question of whether or not all sets are well-founded. Most take a position rather like Mirimanoff's: well-founded sets are flexible, well-behaved, and suitable for fruitful study. Fraenkel, Bar-Hillel, and Levy put the point this way:

Let us now remark that even if one does not agree that only well-founded sets can be rightfully called sets, one can advance no argument for retaining sets which are not well-founded other than the desire for greater generality. This greater generality is not of much use since no field of set theory or mathematics is in any need of sets which are not well-founded. Opposing the desire for more generality there is always a desire for more restricted and definite notions, if by restricting the discussion no interesting mathematical results are lost. . . . Thus one can accept [Foundation] not as an article of faith but as a convention for giving a more restricted meaning to the word 'set', to be discarded once it turns out that it impedes significant mathematical research. (Fraenkel, Bar-Hillel, and Levy (1973), 88–9)

Foundation is seen as a way of weeding out 'pathologies' or 'oddities' (see Boolos (1971), 491), a way of obtaining a clear picture of the set theoretic universe, without giving up anything in return.

Recently, in response to problems in computer modelling, Aczel (1988) devised a set theory with non–well-founded sets called AFA (for 'Anti-Foundation Axiom'), and Barwise and others have also applied the theory to problems in the semantics for natural languages. Supporters of AFA argue that it accomplishes these modelling jobs more naturally than ZFC would do. To the extent that these cases would support an accusation of 'impeding mathematical research' against Foundation, this would count as extrinsic evidence against the insistence on Foundation.[26] On the other hand, in contrast to ZFC with the *iterative conception*, the cumulative hierarchy and the formal V_αs, 'We have not been able to produce any such plausible, intuitive model . . . which contains ill founded sets from any hypotheses that do not beg the question' (Moschovakis (1994), 182). To date, models of AFA are constructed inside models of ZFC.[27] Without an underlying picture comparable to the *iterative conception*, AFA is less appealing as a fundamental notion of collection.

So, these are some of the considerations most commonly offered for (and

---

[26] Notice that adopting Foundation in our fundamental theory of sets does not preclude our studying AFA, especially given that it is relatively consistent with ZFC (see Moschovakis (1994), 259–62). But the following point—that there is no intuitive model of AFA—may count against using it as the fundamental theory.

[27] I return to this case in III. 6. i.

against) the standard axioms of ZFC. All the objects and theorems of classical mathematics, and much more, can be derived in this system. The next order of business is to see why these very powerful axioms are not powerful enough.

4

Independent Questions

The first and most famous of the independent questions is Cantor's Continuum Hypothesis (often abbreviated CH), which was first formulated in a weak form in Cantor (1878).[1] In that paper, Cantor proves that many infinite sets are countable—the integers, the rationals, any union of countably many countable sets,[2] the algebraic numbers—and that many others have the cardinality of the reals—in particular, the set of all ordered pairs of reals, and even the set of all ordered n-tuples of reals, the set theoretic counterpart to an n-dimensional space. He then remarks:

And now that we have proved for a very rich and extensive field of [sets], the property of being capable of correspondence with the [reals] . . . the question arises . . .: Into how many and what different classes (if we say that [sets] of the same or different [cardinality] are grouped in the same or different *classes* respectively) do [infinite sets of reals] fall? (Cantor (1878), as translated in Jourdain (1952), 45)

In other words, how many different infinite cardinalities are represented by sets of real numbers? Cantor replies: 'By a process of induction, into the further description of which we will not enter here, we are led to the theorem that the number of classes is two' (ibid.). The first of these classes contains the countably infinite sets of reals, and the second contains the sets of reals that can be brought into one-to-one correspondence with the set of all reals. Cantor's hypothesis is that there are no other infinite sets of reals.

Notice that here Cantor refers to his hypothesis as a 'theorem'; he remarks that he will 'defer to a later occasion the exact investigation of this question' (Cantor (1878), as translated in Moore (1989), 82). Cantor did return to this problem, many times, but his efforts to prove CH were, as we now know, doomed to failure.

---

[1] The following discussion of the early history of the continuum problem (1877–1908) relies heavily on the very helpful Moore (1989).

[2] The proof of this theorem—the countable union theorem—requires (a weak form of) the Axiom of Choice, but Cantor didn't notice this. See Moore (1982).

By 1882, Cantor had developed his ordinal numbers and considered the set of all countable ordinals, ω_1. He showed that ω_1 has a cardinality larger than $\aleph_0$, and that every infinite subset of ω_1 smaller than ω_1 has cardinality $\aleph_0$; in other words, the cardinality of ω_1 is the very next infinite cardinality after $\aleph_0$. He then states his conjecture in a new form:

I believe that I can rigorously prove that the set of all real numbers . . . can be put into one–one correspondence with the collection [ω_1]. If this theorem is combined with [the fact that the cardinality of ω_1 comes immediately after $\aleph_0$], one obtains without further ado the *long* sought proof for the theorem mentioned in the conclusion to the memoir [1878]: Every *infinite* [set of reals] . . . is either [countable] . . . or can be put in one–one correspondence with the collection of all real numbers. (Letter of 1882 from Cantor to Mittag-Leffler, as translated in Moore (1989), 85)

This statement is actually stronger than the earlier one, as it requires that the continuum be well-ordered. It is equivalent to the familiar contemporary version of CH—$2^{\aleph_0} = \aleph_1$—which appears in a letter of Cantor's in 1895 (see Moore (1989), 99).

Several times during the 1880s and 1890s, Cantor thought he had proved CH, only to be disappointed. Others, including Bendixson, Tannery, and Pierce, also joined in the effort, to be followed in the early decades of the twentieth century by Bernstein, Hausdorff, and Hilbert. At the International Congress of Mathematicians in Paris in 1900, Hilbert included the Continuum Problem—is CH true?—as the first on his famous list of the twenty-three most important open problems of mathematics. At the International Congress of Mathematicians in Heidelberg in 1904, König announced that CH is false, because the continuum cannot be well-ordered. The error in König's proof was discovered the next day, by Zermelo, which led directly to his proof of the Well-Ordering Theorem and his isolation of the Axiom of Choice.

The truth about the deep intractability of CH only began to be understood with Gödel's work in the late 1930s.[3] Gödel showed, in brief, that if ZFC is consistent, then it cannot disprove CH, or, to put the matter another way, if ZFC is consistent, then so is ZFC + CH.[4] Intuitively, this result is proved by constructing an alternative, called L, to Zermelo's

---

[3] See Gödel (1939), and Solovay (1990).
[4] He also showed, by the same general method, that if ZF is consistent, then so is ZFC. In other words, adding the Axiom of Choice to ZF cannot turn a consistent theory into an inconsistent theory—considerable comfort to the supporters of the axiom! For textbook treatments, see Drake (1974), ch. 5, Kunen (1980), ch. VI, Devlin (1984), ch. II.

cumulative hierarchy, V, an alternative in which all the axioms of ZFC are true, and CH is also true. If CH were disprovable from ZFC, that is, if not-CH were a theorem of ZFC, then not-CH would also be true in L, which it is not.

This model, L, of ZFC is obtained by a modification of the stage-wise definition of V. There, at stage $\alpha + 1$, we add all combinatorially-determined subsets of V_α. For L, in contrast, Gödel takes inspiration from Russell's theory of orders.[5] Russell's collections are determined by propositional functions, and (in the theory without the Axiom of Reducibility, which Gödel rejects as contrary to the VCP), these propositional functions must be predicative. To capture these notions, at stage $\alpha + 1$ in the construction of L, we add only those subsets of L_α that are definable by a first-order formula whose quantifiers range over, and whose parameters are drawn from, L_α. L is the union of these L_αs, just as V is the union of the V_αs. But Gödel departs boldly from Russell's scruples when he allows α to range over all ordinals, predicative and impredicative, just it does in the construction of V.

It must be admitted that this talk of L and V is rather loose, because neither of these collections is a set: there is no stage at which all their members are available for collecting. For this reason, none of what's been said about them can be proved in ZFC, which is fortunate, because if ZFC were able to prove the existence of a model of ZFC, it would be inconsistent.[6] In official terms, Gödel's argument works like this: there is a first-order formula $\exists\alpha(x \in L_\alpha)$, usually written $\mathcal{L}(x)$ or $x \in L$,[7] and a sentence $\forall x \exists \alpha(x \in L\alpha)$, usually written $V = L$,[8] such that for every axiom σ of ZFC $+$ $V = L$, $\sigma^{x \in L}$ is provable in ZFC, where $\sigma^{x \in L}$ is the result of relativizing all quantifiers of σ to L;[9] CH is provable in ZFC $+$ $V = L$, so $CH^{x \in L}$ is provable in ZFC; therefore, if ZFC were to prove not-CH (and hence, not-$CH^{x \in L}$), then ZFC would be inconsistent. So, if ZFC is consistent, ZFC does not prove not-CH. This official argument makes no use of the objectionable L or V, or any models of ZFC.

Gödel's results leave open the possibility that ZFC can prove CH; this

---

[5] See Gödel (1938), 26, Gödel (1944), 136, and Solovay (1990), 8. But cf. Solovay (1995a), 119–20.

[6] This is Gödel's incompleteness theorem, plus his completeness theorem: if a first-order theory (like ZFC) has a model, it is consistent.

[7] Terminology: this is read 'x is constructible'.

[8] Terminology: this is called the 'Axiom of Constructibility'.

[9] That is, '$\forall x(\ldots x \ldots)$' is replaced by '$\forall x(x \in L \supset \ldots x \ldots)$', and '$\exists x(\ldots x \ldots)$' is replaced by '$\exists x(x \in L \wedge \ldots x \ldots)$'.

was, after all, what Cantor and many of his contemporaries and successors had hoped for. But whatever Gödel may have thought in the late 1930s, by the mid-1940s, he believed CH to be unprovable from ZFC.[10] His efforts to establish its unprovability were unsuccessful, however, and that breakthrough came only in the 1960s, from another source. In his (1963/4), Cohen presents the method of forcing, which produces a new model of ZFC from an old model by appending a carefully chosen 'generic' set. In particular, Cohen shows how to append a sequence of, say, $\aleph_2$ distinct subsets of ω, so that $2^{\aleph_0} \geq \aleph_2$, thus falsifying CH.[11] The same method can be used to obtain models in which $2^{\aleph_0}$ takes a wide range of different values.[12]

So CH can't be proved or disproved from the axioms of ZFC (assuming they are consistent); it is independent of ZFC. Though this is the original independent question, it is not the only one, nor is it the simplest one. Let me explain.

We saw earlier how Cantor's interest in sets of reals grew out of his work in ordinary analysis, his study of functions given by trigonometric series expansions. This work can be seen against a backdrop of a long-term development of the notion of function itself, a development stretching from before the Greeks up to the time of Cantor and the rise of set theory. Along the way, various forces from applied as well as pure mathematics consistently pushed toward an ever broader, more inclusive account of functionality. I look a bit more closely at this story later (in II. 4. ii), but for now, the salient point is that the most general notion of function—that of a completely arbitrary correspondence—arose along with the concepts of set theory during the late nineteenth century. Investigations into the foundations of analysis had produced a series of so-called 'pathological' functions, odd creatures that served as counterexamples to previously accepted assumptions. The pure combinatorial collections of set theory and the completely arbitrary functions invoked in the foundations of analysis were two sides to the same coin.[13]

---

[10] See Gödel (1947), 184–5.

[11] That is, the expanded model thinks these are $\aleph_2$ distinct subsets of ω, and thus, that $2^{\aleph_0} \geq \aleph_2$

[12] See Kunen (1980) for a modern textbook treatment. As in Gödel's method, some care has to be taken because ZFC (if it is consistent) cannot prove the existence of any model of ZFC. See ibid. 232–5 for a range of 'official' versions of forcing arguments.

[13] Notice that sets and functions are interdefinable: to any set $A \subseteq X$, there corresponds the characteristic function fA from X to $\{0,1\}$ that sends $a \in X$ to 1 iff $a \in A$; to any function f from B to C, there corresponds the set $\{\langle b,c \rangle \mid f(b) = c\}$.

By 1900, the pathological functions were subjects of considerable controversy. At that time, the French analysts Baire, Borel, and Lebesgue set out to classify functions from reals to reals according to complexity, and it soon became clear that this problem could be reduced to the problem of classifying sets of reals according to their complexity. For these purposes, the simplest sets of reals are the closed sets, and their complements, the open sets: if $A \subseteq \mathbb{R}$ and $r \in \mathbb{R}$, then r is a *limit point* of A iff there are elements of A (other than r) arbitrarily close to r;[14] A is *closed* iff it contains all its limit points; $B \subseteq \mathbb{R}$ is open iff the complement of B, $\mathbb{R} - B$ ($= \{r \in \mathbb{R} \mid r \notin B\}$) is closed.[15] The connection with properties of functions goes like this: a function f from $\mathbb{R}$ to $\mathbb{R}$ is continuous iff for every open $A \subseteq \mathbb{R}$, the inverse image of A ($= \{r \in \mathbb{R} \mid f(r) \in A\}$) is also open. Borel went on to define a hierarchy of sets of reals, beginning with these: $\Sigma^0_1 =$ the open sets; $\Pi^0_1 =$ the closed sets; $\Sigma^0_{\alpha+1} = \{A \subseteq \mathbb{R} \mid A$ is the union of countably many sets in $\Pi^0_\alpha\}$; $\Pi^0_{\alpha+1} = \{A \subseteq \mathbb{R} \mid \mathbb{R} - A$ is in $\Sigma^0_{\alpha+1}\}$; and $\Delta^0_\alpha = \Sigma^0_\alpha \cap \Pi^0_\alpha$. A set of reals is Borel iff it occurs in some Σ^0_α.[16]

Despite their complexity, the Borel sets turned out to be fairly well-behaved. For example, they have reasonable 'length'. As mentioned in I. 2, Lebesgue had devised a general notion of measure for point sets; he did this in order to generalize the central notion of integration. The Axiom of Choice guarantees that there are non-measurable sets of reals; by 1902 Lebesgue was able to show that these oddities will not occur among the Borel sets.

The isolation of Borel sets also allowed the generalization of some of Cantor's work on CH. In (1884b), Cantor had proved that any infinite closed set of reals is either countable or has the cardinality of the continuum, in other words, that CH holds for closed sets of reals. This result follows from the Cantor–Bendixson theorem—every infinite closed set of reals can be partitioned into a countable set and perfect set—and Cantor's theorem that every non-empty perfect set has the cardinality of

---

[14] Formally, for any $\varepsilon > 0$, there is an $a \in A$ such that the distance between a and r is less than ε.

[15] So, 0 and 1 are limit points of the set of all reals between 0 and 1; the set of reals between 0 and 1, including 0 and 1, is closed; the set of reals between 0 and 1, excluding 0 and 1, is open. (An equivalent definition is: $A \subseteq \mathbb{R}$ is *open* iff for every $a \in A$, there is an $\varepsilon > 0$ such that every real less than ε from a is in A.)

[16] For limit ordinals λ, Σ_λ is the union of the Σ^0_αs for $\alpha < \lambda$. (I apologize for muddling these definitions in the hardback edition of Maddy (1990), 111–12; corrected versions appear in the paperback.)

the continuum. (A closed set of reals is perfect iff every point in it is a limit point.) Cantor was optimistic that the full CH could be proved by a generalization of this theorem. Such generalizations were eventually proved for some Π_2^0 sets (by Young, in 1902), for all Π_2^0 sets (by Hausdorff, in 1914), and eventually for all Borel sets (by Hausdorff, again, in 1916). Unfortunately, this method cannot be used to prove CH, because, as Bernstein had shown back in 1908, there are uncountable sets without perfect subsets. But again, these oddities do not occur among the Borel sets: every uncountable Borel set does contain a perfect subset.[17]

   This process of building more and more complex sets of reals was carried further in the teens and twenties by the Russian school of Luzin and Suslin using the notion of projection: closed subsets of the plane—that is, of $\mathbb{R}^2$, the set of all ordered pairs of reals—can be defined analogously to closed subsets of the line; then the *projection* of a closed $A \subseteq \mathbb{R}^2$ is, figuratively, the shadow A casts on the x-axis, or, formally, $\{r \in \mathbb{R} \mid$ for some $s \in R, (r,s) \in A\}$. Luzin and Suslin then define the *projective sets*: $\Sigma_0^1 =$ the open sets; $\Pi_0^1 =$ the closed sets; $\Sigma^1{}_{\alpha+1} =$ projections of Π_α^1 sets; $\Pi^1{}_{\alpha+1}$ complements of $\Sigma^1{}_{\alpha+1}$ sets; and $\Delta_\alpha^1 = \Sigma_\alpha^1 \cap \Pi_\alpha^1$. Suslin proved that the Borel sets are precisely the sets that are both Σ_1^1 and Π_1^1, that is, the Δ_1^1 sets.

   Luzin and Suslin quickly showed that the Σ_1^1 and Π_1^1 sets are Lebesgue measurable and that uncountable Σ_1^1 sets have perfect subsets. Here, however, progress sudden ceased: the measurability of Σ_2^1 sets remained stubbornly unresolved, and the existence of 'thin' Π_1^1 sets (uncountable Π_1^1 sets without perfect subsets) remained a possibility.

   The forces behind this impasse were clarified along similar lines to those affecting CH. In his (1938), Gödel announced that L contains a non-measurable Σ_2^1 (indeed, Δ_2^1) set and a thin Π_1^1 set, but he provided no detailed proof there or elsewhere. Addison later (in his (1959)) showed how these results can be understood as following from the overall well-ordering of L: to show that the Axiom of Choice holds in L, Gödel noted that the entire class could be well-ordered in a particularly straightforward way; Addison showed that the resulting well-ordering of the reals is especially simple, that it is a 'good' Δ_2^1 well-ordering, and from this he derived the non-Lebesgue measurable and thin sets. From all this, it follows, as for CH, that ZFC cannot rule out such oddities low down in the

---

[17] Terminology: every Borel set has the perfect subset property, that is, if it is uncountable, then it contains a perfect subset. For more detail and references on the history of these results, see Hallett (1984), 103–10.

projective hierarchy. And, again, the converse results were proved by forcing: soon after Cohen's discovery, Solovay constructed forcing models in which all projective sets are Lebesgue measurable and every uncountable projective set has a perfect subset.[18] So, ZFC also can't prove the existence of non-measurable Σ^1_2 sets or thin Π^1_1 sets.

This study of simple sets of reals—initiated by the analysts Borel, Baire, and Lebesgue—is now called 'descriptive set theory'.[19] Though some of its fundamental questions have been shown to be independent of ZFC, like CH, it is worth noting that the questions themselves (especially the question of Lebesgue measurability) are significantly more down-to-earth. The notions involved—Borel set, Lebesgue measure, projective set—arose in the ordinary pursuit of natural questions in analysis; by comparison, Cantor's CH involves one of his greatest conceptual innovations, the notion of infinite cardinality. Furthermore, the sets of reals involved are simply definable; by contrast, CH essentially involves the notion of all arbitrary, combinatorially-determined subsets of an infinite set. So it is striking that simpler questions like these also turn out to be independent of ZFC.

And these aren't the only examples. As the use of set theoretic concepts and methods gradually spread beyond set theory and analysis, into areas like algebra, topology, and mathematical logic, new independent questions arose. Let me sketch just one example, this one from algebra. Without getting into the details, one central notion of modern algebra is the group,[20] and one central notion of group theory is that of a *free* group.[21] It can be shown that every free group has a unique extension by the integers, or, to use the terminology, that every free group is a Whitehead group. Whitehead asked if the converse is also true, that is, if the free groups are precisely the Whitehead groups. In 1951, Stein found a partial answer—every countable Whitehead group is free—but the problem for uncountable Whitehead groups remained open. Finally,

---

[18] See Solovay (1965) and (1970). To get these results, Solovay assumes the consistency of a theory slightly stronger than ZFC, namely ZFC plus the existence of an inaccessible cardinal (see I. 5). Shelah (1984) has shown that the inaccessible is necessary.

[19] For a comprehensive survey of the field, see Moschovakis (1980).

[20] A group is a set A with a binary function $+$ that is associative (for all $a,b,c \in A$, $a + (b + c) = (a + b) + c$), and has an identity i (for all $a \in A$, $a + i = i + a = a$) and additive inverses (for every $a \in A$, there is a $b \in A$ such that $a + b = i$). For example, the integers (positive and negative whole numbers) with ordinary addition. A group is commutative iff for all $a,b \in A$, $a + b = b + a$. In what follows, I use 'group' to mean 'commutative group'.

[21] A group is free iff every element is uniquely representable in terms of a set of basic elements.

his (1974), showed that the answer in L is yes—every Whitehead group in L is free—but that a forcing model can be generated with an unfree Whitehead group of size $\aleph_1$. Thus, Whitehead's problem is independent of ZFC.[22]

So, we've seen that there is a wide range and variety of independent questions, and we are left wondering what we are to make of this phenomenon. One early reaction was to project a fragmentation of set theory: 'Probably we shall have in the future essentially different intuitive notions of sets just as we have different notions of space, and will base our discussions of sets on axioms which correspond to the kind of sets we want to study' (Mostowski (1972), 94, from a talk given in 1965). An especially simple version of this view, no doubt simpler than what Mostowski had in mind, holds that every consistent extension of ZFC is as good as any other, that set theory is just a matter of determining which conclusions do and don't follow from which assumptions. I call this 'Glib Formalism'. From the Glib Formalist's point of view, all there is to say about CH and the rest is contained in results of the sort we've been citing: it follows from some set theories, doesn't follow from others.

But Gödel, as early as (1947), was taking a very different line. As noted above, even before Cohen's discoveries, Gödel felt confident that CH is independent:

> there are (assuming the consistency of the axioms) a priori three possibilities for Cantor's conjecture: It may be either demonstrable or disprovable or undecidable. The third alternative . . . is the most likely, and to seek a proof for it is at present one of the most promising ways of attacking the problem. (Gödel (1947), 181)

He argues for this position from the fact that both L and V provide models of ZFC:

> there are two quite differently defined classes of objects which both satisfy all axioms of set theory written down so far. One class consists of the sets definable in a certain manner by properties of their elements [L], the other of the sets in the sense of arbitrary multitudes irrespective of if, or how, they can be defined [V]. Now, before it is settled what objects are to be numbered, and on the basis of what one-to-one correspondences, one could hardly expect to be able to determine their number. (ibid. 183)

---

[22] Devlin (1977), § IV. 3, discusses the first part of this claim. Eklof (1976) provides an exposition of both parts.

Here Gödel suggests that L and V are different, but his argument does not depend on this assumption. He continues:

If, however, someone believes that it is meaningless to speak of sets except in the sense of extensions of definable properties, or, at least, that no other sets exist, then, too, he can hardly expect more than a small fraction of the problems of set theory to be solvable without making use of this, in his opinion essential, characteristic of sets, namely, that they are all derived from (or in a sense even identical with) definable properties. (Ibid.)

In particular, if you believe that $V = L$, you expect many theorems of set theory to depend on this fact, and thus, to be independent of ZFC alone.

In general, Gödel takes the moral of the as-yet-unproved independence results to be that 'the axiomatic system of set theory as known today is incomplete' (ibid. 182). He goes on to note that additional axioms have been proposed, and he argues that there are grounds for decisions on the adoption or rejection of such axiom candidates. First, he cites axiom candidates which 'show clearly . . . that [ZFC] can be supplemented without arbitrariness by new axioms which are only the natural continuation of the series of those set up so far' (ibid.). Beyond these, he envisions 'other (hitherto unknown) axioms of set theory which a more profound understanding of the concepts underlying logic and mathematics would enable us to recognize as implied by these concepts' (ibid.). These justifications would be intrinsic, but Gödel explicitly recognizes the possibility of extrinsic justifications as well:

Furthermore, however, even disregarding the intrinsic necessity of some new axiom, and even in case it had no intrinsic necessity at all, a decision about its truth is possible also in another way, namely, inductively by studying its 'success', that is, its fruitfulness in consequences and in particular, in 'verifiable' consequences, i.e., consequences demonstrable without the new axiom, whose proofs by means of the new axiom, however, are considerably simpler and easier to discover, and make it possible to condense into one proof many different proofs. . . . There might exist axioms so abundant in their verifiable consequences, shedding so much light upon a whole discipline, and furnishing such powerful methods for solving given problems . . . that quite irrespective of their intrinsic necessity they would have to be assumed at least in the same sense as any well-established physical theory. (Ibid. 182–3)

Obviously, Gödel does not take any consistent extension of ZFC to be as good as any other; he doesn't even seem to think there are equally good intuitive notions of set. Rather, he imagines the 'non-arbitrary' extension of ZFC in defensible directions, and holds that in this way 'a decision of the question [CH], even if it is undecidable from the axioms in their present form, might nevertheless be obtained' (ibid. 181). From this point of view, there is much more to be said about CH (and the other independent questions); we can even hope to answer them.

Given the styles of argument adduced for the axioms of ZFC, it doesn't seem unreasonable to suppose that persuasive intrinsic or extrinsic justifications might be devised for additional axioms, and that some (if not all) of the independent questions might one day be settled in this way. This approach has, in fact, been adopted by a substantial school of contemporary set theorists. So, for example, Martin writes: 'Although the ZFC axioms are insufficient to settle CH, there is nothing sacred about these axioms, and one might hope to find further axioms which seem clearly true of our notion of set (in the same way the ZFC axioms appear clearly true) and which do settle CH' (Martin (1976), 84). Here Martin appeals only to intrinsic evidence, but in connection with a particular new axiom candidate, he writes: 'The author regards [the candidate in question] as an hypothesis with a status similar to that of a theoretical hypothesis in physics. Three kinds of quasi-empirical evidence . . . have been produced' (Martin (1977), 814). And he goes on to describe these: the failure to refute the hypothesis, the verification (in Gödel's sense) of some of its consequences, and the plausibility and coherence of its consequences. In his (199?), Martin argues directly for the propriety of extrinsic evidence.

This school of thought on the independent questions and on the investigation and evaluation of new axiom candidates is the central focus of this book. My goal is to understand the structure and underpinnings of this portion of contemporary set theoretic practice, to explicate and analyse its distinctive modes of justification. Given the range, depth, and complexity of the work of this school, I can't undertake to deal with all of it here, so I hope to cast some light by concentrating on one particular new axiom candidate. But first, we need a sense of the general styles of these hypotheses and of their interrelations.

5

New Axiom Candidates

One obvious candidate for a new axiom has already been introduced, that is, $V = L$, the Axiom of Constructibility, which claims that every set is constructible in Gödel's sense. The relative consistency of ZFC + $V = L$—if ZFC is consistent, then so is ZFC + $V = L$—shows the Axiom to be a safe way of extending ZFC: if ZFC + $V = L$ implies a contradiction, then so does ZFC all by itself.[1] We've also see that $V = L$ is a powerful potential addition to ZFC: it settles the CH (CH is true in L), the open questions of descriptive set theory (there are non-measurable Σ_2^1 sets and thin Π_1^1 sets in L), the Whitehead problem (every Whitehead group in L is free), and much more.

So $V = L$ is a safe and powerful hypothesis, but is it actually independent? Gödel's relative consistency result also shows that $V = L$ cannot be disproved from ZFC, but perhaps it can be proved. To show that it cannot be proved, we rely on a fundamental feature of L, namely, the absoluteness[2] of the notion of constructibility: for any transitive[3] model M of ZFC and any ordinal α, whatever M thinks is L_α really is L_α. From this, we can see that L is a minimal model for ZFC in a quite precise sense: if M is a transitive model of ZFC containing all ordinals, then the constructible sets of M are the real constructible sets, and thus, $L \subseteq M$. The same goes for models that don't contain all the ordinals: if N is such a model, and α is the first ordinal not in N, then the constructible sets of N are precisely the sets in L_α, and thus $L_\alpha \subseteq N$. It follows that any forcing extension of a model of ZFC + $V = L$ will contain sets different from all the relevant constructible sets, thus be a model of ZFC + $V \neq L$; so ZFC (if it is consistent) cannot prove $V = L$. All this makes $V = L$ a genuine contender: safe, powerful, and in some sense, minimal.

A second style of new axiom candidate—the large cardinal axiom—

---

[1] Of course, I needn't speak of ZFC here; ZF alone would do, as V = L implies the Axiom of Choice.

[2] $\phi(x)$ is *absolute* for M iff (for all $a \in M$, $\phi(a)$ is true in M iff $\phi(a)$ is true in V).

[3] A model M is *transitive* iff for all x and y, if $x \in y \in M$, then $x \in M$.

includes a wide variety of particular axioms, all of which can be understood, in one way or another, as asserting that there are more and more stages in the cumulative hierarchy. The Axiom of Infinity can be seen as the first of these—implying the existence of an ω-th stage—and the Axiom of Replacement pushes further in this direction—implying the existence of an $\omega + \omega$-th stage, an ω_1-st stage, an ω_ω-stage, and so on.[4] Typically, large cardinal axioms, as their name suggests, assert the existence of a large cardinal number which serves as an index to a late stage in the hierarchy.

The first new large cardinal axiom, the Axiom of Inaccessible Cardinals, implies the existence of a stage after all those whose existence is implied by ZFC. An *inaccessible* cardinal κ is such that (i) the union of any collection of fewer than κ sets of size less than κ has size less than κ,[5] and (ii) if λ is a cardinal less than κ, then 2^λ is also less than κ.[6] In other words, κ cannot be reached by taking unions of small collections of smaller sets or by taking power sets, the operations that underlie the force of Replacement and Power Set. This is much true of $\aleph_0$; the Axiom of Inaccessible Cardinals asserts the existence of such a cardinal greater than $\aleph_0$. If κ is such an inaccessible, it can be shown that V_κ is a model of ZFC, and thus, that ZFC is consistent. So it is not possible to prove the relative consistency of the axiom: if we could prove relative consistency—if ZFC is consistent, then so is ZFC + I (where I is the Axiom of Inaccessible Cardinals)—then we could prove this in ZFC, and hence in ZFC + I; then ZFC + I would prove both the relative consistency of ZFC + I and the consistency of ZFC, and by modus ponens, its own consistency; but if it is consistent, Gödel's second incompleteness theorem implies that it cannot do this. The same argument applies to all large cardinal axioms, so this style of axiom candidate is not as safe as $V = L$.

Inaccessibles were introduced by Hausdorff, in the same issue of the same journal as Zermelo (1908b), though the axiom wasn't explicitly formulated until Tarski did so in the late 1930s.[7] In the early teens, Mahlo considered a cardinal κ so large that there are κ inaccessible cardinals smaller than κ, and a cardinal λ so large that there are λ cardinals

---

[4] ω_ω is the first ordinal after ω_1, ω_2, ω_3, and so on. Its cardinality is $\aleph_\omega$.

[5] Terminology: κ is regular. For example, $\aleph_0$ is regular, but $\aleph_\omega$ is not (because a set of size $\aleph_\omega$ can be formed by taking a union of $\aleph_0$ sets of sizes $\aleph_0$, $\aleph_1$, $\aleph_2$, and so on).

[6] Terminology: κ is strong limit. Again, $\aleph_0$ is strong limit, but $\aleph_1$ is not (because $\aleph_0 < \aleph_1$, but $2^{\aleph_0} \geq \aleph_1$).

[7] See Kanamori (1994), § 1. 1 for history and references.

like κ smaller than λ, and so on; these are sometimes called 'hyperinaccessibles'. Mahlo also found a way to generalize this 'build from below' strategy to even larger large cardinals, which now bear his name. In Zermelo (1930), thinking about inaccessibles is tied in with the picture of the cumulative hierarchy: he describes the set theoretic universe as consisting of a series of larger and larger models of ZFC, one for each inaccessible stage:

> The unlimited series of Cantor's ordinal numbers is matched by just as infinite a double series of essentially different set-theoretic models, the whole classical theory [ZFC] being manifested in each of them. . . . This series in its boundless progression does not have a true conclusion, only relative stopping points, namely those 'limit numbers' [inaccessibles] which separate the higher from the lower model types. (Zermelo (1930), 47, as translated in Kanamori (1994), 20)

In other words, we are to think of V has the union of $V_{\kappa'}$, $V_{\kappa''}$, . . ., $V_{\kappa'''}$, . . . where the κs are the successive inaccessibles and each entry is a model of ZFC.

Large as they may seem, all these—inaccessibles, hyperinaccessibles, Mahlos—are now thought of as small large cardinals; we'll see why in a moment. The most widely studied of the larger large cardinals—measurable cardinals—arose from a line of development quite different from the systematic closure operations described so far.[8] In fact, the roots of the concept go back to Lebesgue and his work on the notion of measure: while the notion of the length of a interval on the real line is unproblematic, the study of complex sets of reals raised the problem of how their 'length' could be assessed. Lebesgue set the problem of assigning a number to every set of reals in such a way that (i) not all sets are assigned 0, (ii) two sets of reals are assigned the same number if one is the result of shifting the other some fixed distance to the right or left, (iii) the number assigned to the union of a countable collection of disjoint sets of reals is the sum of the numbers assigned to the individual members of that collection. In 1905, Vitali used the Axiom of Choice to show that there is no such assignment; Lebesgue's own theory of measure satisfies these conditions, but does not make assignments to every set of reals. During the teens and twenties, the question was gradually simplified and generalized (by Banach and others) to this form: is there a set S and an assignment of either 0 or 1 to each subset of S such that (i) S itself is assigned 1, (ii) for $s \in S$, $\{s\}$ is assigned 0, (iii) the number assigned to the union of a

---

[8] See ibid. §§ 2, 4, for history and references.

collection of fewer than the cardinality of S disjoint subsets of S is the sum of the numbers assigned to the individual members of that collection? For $S = \omega$, the answer is yes; in his (1930), Ulam defined a measurable cardinal to be a cardinal number greater than $\aleph_0$ that admits such an assignment of 0s and 1s to its subsets (the assignment itself is the measure on it), and showed what is not immediately obvious: measurable cardinals are inaccessible.

It wasn't until the early 1960s that the true size of measurable cardinals was understood: Tarski, Hanf, and Keisler at last succeeded in showing that there are many small large cardinals below the first measurable. Around the same time, Scott hit on the breakthrough result in the theory of large cardinals; he showed that if there is a measurable cardinal, then the measure on that cardinal is not constructible, that thus $V \neq L$. Soon Rowbottom, using different methods, improved the result to this form: if there is a measurable cardinal, then there are only countably many constructible subsets of ω, so there are non-constructible subsets of ω, and thus $V \neq L$. Eventually, Silver provided the last word in this direction. He showed that if there is a measurable cardinal, then there is a particular non-constructible subset of ω, called $0^{\#}$, that codes up information on exactly how L differs from V: for example, because L is so short on one-to-one correspondences, it can't tell one uncountable cardinal from another, and what it takes for the first uncountable cardinal, for $\aleph_\omega$, for the first inaccessible (if there is one) are all in reality mere countable ordinals. Solovay and Silver both showed that the non-constructible set $0^{\#}$ is quite simple; it is Δ_3^1.[9]

In the course of his original proof, Scott also pointed the way toward another characterization of measurable cardinals. Call M an *inner model* of ZFC iff there is a formula ϕ such that (i) M is the collection of all sets that satisfy ϕ, (ii) ZFC proves that every ordinal number satisfies ϕ, and (iii) for every axiom σ of ZFC, ZFC proves $\sigma^{\phi(x)}$. (So L is the canonical example of an inner model, with $\mathcal{L}(x)$ as the relevant ϕ.) Scott showed that if there is a measurable cardinal κ, then there is a mapping from V into an inner model M that preserves first-order formulas—$a_1, a_2, \ldots, a_n$ satisfy ψ iff their images satisfy ψ in M—and κ is the first ordinal that isn't sent to itself[10] (we say that κ is the 'critical point' of an 'elementary

---

[9] $0^{\#}$ is a set of natural numbers, so we can think of it as coding a real number in binary notation and ask after the complexity of its singleton. See Kanamori (1994), §§ 5, 8, 9, and 14, for history and references.

[10] For a sense of how Scott's argument goes, suppose κ is the smallest measurable cardinal. Then M thinks the image of κ, which is different from, indeed, greater than κ, is the

embedding' of V into M). Keisler soon proved the converse. Nowadays, it is considered more informative to view a measurable cardinal as the critical point of an elementary embedding of V into an inner model M, and this is sometimes regarded as defining the term.

This form of definition has the added advantage of being easily generalized. The inner model M generated by a measurable cardinal κ contains any sequence of its members that is κ terms long, but not all sequences of its members that are κ^+ terms long, where κ^+ is the next cardinal number after κ; in other words, M is closed under κ sequences, not under κ^+ sequences. Stronger large cardinal axioms can be generated by positing critical points for elementary embeddings into inner models with stronger closure conditions: e.g. a cardinal κ is λ-*supercompact* (for $\lambda \geq \kappa$) iff it is the critical point of an elementary embedding of V into an inner model M such that (i) the image of κ under the embedding is greater than λ, and (ii) M is closed under λ sequences; a cardinal κ is *supercompact* iff it is λ-supercompact for all λ. The strongest potential axiom along these lines requires than $M = V$—that is, that there be a non-trivial elementary embedding of the universe of sets into itself—but by 1970, Kunen had showed this to be impossible. Some extremely large, large cardinal axioms have been formulated by examining Kunen's proof and positing cardinals that seem as large as possible without allowing the argument to go through.[11]

Another important line of development in the theory of large cardinals has been the study of minimal inner models in which the cardinal retains its characteristics. To see what this means, notice that if there is a measurable cardinal, that cardinal is also present in L, but its measure is missing from L, so the cardinal is not measurable there. On the other hand, it can be shown that if there are inaccessibles, hyperinaccessibles, Mahlo cardinals, etc., these cardinals retain these properties in L; so, L itself is the minimal inner model for the small large cardinals. (These cardinals are considered small because they, unlike measurables, are consistent with $V = L$.) During the 1960s and early 1970s, Solovay, Kunen, and Silver developed the theory of minimal inner models with measurable cardinals. These inner models share many structural features with L: e.g. CH is true, there is a simple well-ordering of the reals (though Δ_3^1 is the

---

first measurable cardinal. So M can't think κ is measurable, and thus, the measure on κ is not in M. But by the minimality of L, $L \subseteq M$, so the measure on κ is not constructible.

[11] See my (1988), § VI, for some discussion. See Kanamori (1994), §§ 22, 23, 24, for more.

best possible this time, rather than Δ^1_2), and there is a simple thin set of reals (though again, it is Π^1_2, rather than Π^1_1). Since then, the project of providing 'canonical' inner models for large cardinals has become one of the liveliest and most productive areas of contemporary set theory.[12] Early on, Gödel had high hopes for large cardinal axioms. In a 1946 lecture, he notes the incompleteness of any (sufficiently strong) formal system and considers ways of generating stronger systems, and he continues:

In set theory, e.g., the successive extensions can most conveniently be represented by stronger and stronger axioms of infinity . . . It is not impossible that for such a concept of demonstrability some completeness theorem would hold which would say that every proposition expressible in set theory is decidable from the present axioms plus some true assertion about the largeness of the universe of all sets. (Gödel (1946), 151)

Gödel's prediction has proved correct to the extent that the larger large cardinals have turned out to imply important results about sets of reals. We've already seen that the existence of a measurable cardinal implies the existence of non-constructible reals, but along more conventional lines, Solovay (1969) used the existence of a measurable cardinal to extend Lebesgue measurability and the perfect subset property from Σ^1_1 sets to the Σ^1_2 sets. (Here we see quite directly the clash with L, where there is a non-Lebesgue measurable Σ^1_2 set and a thin Π^1_1 set.) Assuming the existence of a supercompact cardinal, Woodin (1988) extended these same properties to all projective sets,[13] but this result came quite late, in the course of another line of development (as we'll see in a moment). In any case, soon after the invention of forcing, the hopes that large cardinal axioms would settle the full CH were dashed by Levy and Solovay in their (1967).

The third popular variety of new axiom candidate has a very different flavour from the first two: it is a direct assertion about sets of real numbers, rather than a general assertion about the universe of sets that happens, indirectly, to yield information about sets of reals. The idea grew out of the mathematical study of infinite games—games with an infinite number of moves—which were first studied in Poland in the 1930s. If we

---

[12] The introduction to Martin and Steel (1994) provides a survey. I return to this topic in III. 6.

[13] Actually, all that's needed for this result is $\aleph_0$ Woodin cardinals, which are smaller than supercompacts. For a definition of Woodin cardinal, see Kanamori (1994), 360. I return to this topic in III. 6.

think of a real number as an infinite sequence of 0s and 1s, we can imagine that a pair of players who take turns playing 0 or 1 will generate a real if they play infinitely long. If A is a set of reals, there is an associated game of this sort, called $G(A)$: the first player wins if the real generated by the play of the game is in A; otherwise, the second player wins. The game $G(A)$, and derivatively, the set of reals A, is said to be *determined* iff one of the two players of $G(A)$ has a winning strategy. The study of determinacy began in the 1950s, when Gale and Stewart showed that open games (the games associated with open sets of reals) are determined and that the Axiom of Choice implies the existence of an undetermined set.[14]

Determinacy is a particularly welcome property because it implies the various regularity properties: during the mid-1960s, Mycielski, Swierczkowski, and Davis showed that if a set is determined, then it is Lebesgue measurable, has the perfect subset property, etc. In the course of the 1960s and 1970s, it was gradually shown that all Borel sets (that is, the Δ_1^1 sets) are determined; Martin's (1975) proof of the all-inclusive result is especially noteworthy as a clear case in which the Axiom of Replacement is essential.[15] Martin's theorem is the best possible in this direction using only ZFC, because $V = L$ is relatively consistent, and ZFC $+ V = L$ implies that not all Δ_2^1 sets are Lebesgue measurable. Continuing the earlier pattern, the addition of a measurable cardinal extends determinacy to Σ_1^1 sets (Martin (1970)). In fact, determinacy alone is enough to contradict $V = L$; if the Σ_1^1 sets are determined, then $0^\#$ exists.[16]

Determinacy hypotheses, then, go beyond ZFC as soon as they go beyond the determinacy of Borel sets. The Axiom of Determinacy, first discussed by Mycielski and Steinhaus in (1962), is the assumption that all sets of reals are determined, but Gale and Stewart's early result had already established that the axiom is inconsistent with the Axiom of Choice. Given the widespread acceptance of Choice, the hypotheses actually considered in a serious way are restricted determinacy assumptions like the Axiom of Projective Determinacy (PD), which asserts that

---

[14] For some discussion and references, see my (1988), § V, Kanamori (1994), ch. 6. Moschovakis (1980) provides the complete picture.

[15] This example was mentioned in connection with Replacement in I. 3.

[16] For every real number x, there is a counterpart to $0^\#$ called $x^\#$. (See Drake (1974), 257, Kanamori (1994), 110.) The determinacy of the Σ_1^1 sets is actually equivalent to the existence of $x^\#$ for every real, including 0. Martin (1970) proves determinacy implies the sharps, and Harrington (1978) establishes the converse.

all projective sets are determined.[17] By 1980, an elegant and nearly-complete theory of the properties and behaviour of projective sets of reals had been derived from ZFC + PD, as documented in Moschovakis's compendium, (1980).

Thus ZFC + PD provides a powerful alternative to ZFC + $V = L$, generating a very different picture of the projective sets.[18] The trouble is that PD, in itself, seems too specialized, too opaque, to serve as a basic axiom for set theory. In the words of Martin and Steel: 'Because of the richness and coherence of its consequences, one would like to derive PD itself from more fundamental principles concerning sets in general, principles whose justification is more direct' (Martin and Steel (1989), 72). This hope led to a new take on the possible use of large cardinal axioms: 'The success of determinacy axioms led to a revised program for doing descriptive set theory based on large cardinal axioms: Show that large cardinal axioms imply determinacy axioms' (Martin and Steel (1988), 6582). Martin's (1970) derivation of the determinacy of Σ_1^1 sets from the existence of a measurable cardinal could be viewed as the first step along this path.

The next step was also taken by Martin; in (1978), he derived the determinacy of Σ_2^1 sets from a very large, large cardinal axiom, namely the then-largest of those generated by going as far as seemed possible without falling prey to Kunen's inconsistency theorem. Welcome as this result was, it was also worrisome: first, the danger that the axiom used might be inconsistent was very real, given its genesis; second, if so much power was needed to yield determinacy at the Σ_2^1 level, the full PD might well outstrip the resources of large cardinal theory. In 1984, Woodin erased the second of these worries by wedging yet another large cardinal axiom between the one Martin had used and Kunen's inconsistency, and he used this new large cardinal to prove PD.[19] While the first worry remained, a surprising result came from another quarter.

Building on work of Foreman, Magidor and Shelah, Woodin (1988) showed that if there is a supercompact cardinal, then every projective set

---

[17] There is actually a more natural hypothesis that subsumes this one, namely the assumption that all sets of reals in $L(\mathbb{R})$ are determined, written $AD^{L(\mathbb{R})}$. (To construct $L(\mathbb{R})$, begin with the set of reals and proceed as in the construction of L, that is, at any stage, take all predicatively definable subsets of what's available at the previous stage. $L(\mathbb{R})$ is the smallest model of ZF containing all ordinals and reals.)

[18] See my (1988), § V. 1, for more on the contrast between these two theories of projective sets.

[19] Indeed, he proved $AD^{L(\mathbb{R})}$.

is Lebesgue measurable and has the perfect subset property.[20] Could it be that proving PD truly requires a large cardinal hypothesis ever so much stronger than the one needed for the regularity properties? This seemed unlikely, and with other indicators pointing in the same direction, Martin and Steel were led to the culminating theorem: if there is a supercompact cardinal, then all projective sets are determined.[21] All the welcome results of PD can be obtained in the theory ZFC + SC (where SC says 'there is a supercompact cardinal').[22] Notice this also implies that PD—for all its power—can be no help in settling CH (because SC cannot).

So these are the three main styles of new hypothesis: the Axiom of Constructibility ($V = L$), large cardinal axioms, and determinacy axioms. They are interconnected in fundamental ways: sufficiently large large cardinal axioms (measurable and above) imply the falsity of $V = L$; the most salient form of $V \neq L$, the existence of the sharps, including $0^{\#}$, is equivalent to the first determinacy hypothesis that goes beyond ZFC, the determinacy of Σ_1^1 sets; and a sufficiently strong large cardinal axiom, for example, the Axiom of Supercompact Cardinals, implies the determinacy, and hence the regularity, of all projective sets. Material for extending ZFC is available; the question is, on what grounds are we to proceed from here?

---

[20] Again, this result actually only requires $\aleph_0$ Woodin cardinals.

[21] Indeed, using another result of Woodin's, Martin and Steel showed that every set of reals in $L(\mathbb{R})$ is determined. Again, the actual hypothesis for PD is $\aleph_0$ Woodin cardinals. For $AD^{L(\mathbb{R})}$, one needs $\aleph_0$ Woodins and a measurable cardinal above them.

[22] For more on this development, see the introductions to Martin and Steel (1988; 1989), my (1988), § VI. 4, Kanamori (1994), §§ 31 and 32.

$V = L$

The question of how axioms should be evaluated is obviously a very large one; for purposes of discussion here, it seems best to focus on a single example. The standard axioms are now so well-entrenched that assessment of their justification is inevitably coloured by custom; on the other hand, some of the independent questions are too new, too ill-understood, or too controversial for dependable analysis. Against this backdrop, one candidate stands out: the first far-reaching choice point after the axioms of ZFC, and one on which there is a settled consensus among practitioners. I'm referring, of course, to the Axiom of Constructibility.

When Gödel introduced the axiom in his (1938), under the rather colourless name 'Proposition A', he wrote: 'The proposition A added as a new axiom seems to give a natural completion of the axioms of set theory, in so far as it determines the vague notion of an arbitrary infinite set in a definite way' (Gödel (1938), 27). It isn't clear whether or not Gödel means to endorse the Axiom, whether or not he means 'natural completion' here in the sense of his (1947). There, referring to the small large cardinal axioms available at the time, he writes that they show 'not only that the axiomatic system of set theory as known today is incomplete, but also that it can be supplemented without arbitrariness by new axioms which are only the natural continuation of the series of those set up so far' (Gödel (1947), 182). It may be that the (1938) remark about the 'naturalness' of $V = L$ is meant in a weaker sense, indicated by the 'in so far as' clause, and not in the sense that large cardinal axioms are 'natural'.

But however we read the earlier remark, from (1947) on, Gödel's view of the axiom as a potential new axiom for set theory is unambiguously negative, for two distinct reasons. The first is simple: $V = L$ implies CH, and Gödel believes that CH is false.[1] For example, he writes: 'certain facts (not known or not existing at Cantor's time) . . . seem to indicate

---

[1] Many set theorists have opinions about CH, but there is no consensus. For a survey, see my (1988), § II.

that Cantor's conjecture will turn out to be wrong . . . There exists a considerable number of facts of this kind which, of course, at the same time make it likely that not all sets are [constructible]' (Gödel (1947), 184–5). The facts Gödel has in mind are various 'paradoxical' (ibid. 185) consequences of CH, consequences of the general form: there is a set of reals of size $2^{\aleph_0}$ with such-and-such smallness property.

Now Gödel admits that there are 'highly unexpected and implausible' (ibid. 186) results about sets of reals that do not depend on CH— e.g. Peano's space-filling curves—but he claims that these have a different source. As it happens, Gödel's opinions on this matter are not widely shared; for example, Martin writes:

Gödel cites some facts which he believes are evidence against CH. He lists a number of known consequences of CH which he thinks are intuitively implausible. These consequences assert that very thin subsets of the real line exist of cardinality the continuum. Gödel says that such assertions are counterintuitive in a sense different from that in which the existence of Peano curves is counterintuitive. While Gödel's intuitions should never be taken lightly, it is very hard to see that the situation *is* different from that of Peano curves, and it is even hard for some of us to see why the examples Gödel cites are implausible at all. (Martin (1976), 87)[2]

In addition, Gödel's attempts to axiomatize his picture of the continuum were not notably successful.[3]

In contrast, Gödel's second reason for rejecting the Axiom of Constructibility is now common coin. It is only a glimmer in (1947), where he notes that $V = L$ implies CH, then remarks in a footnote: 'On the other hand, from an axiom in some sense directly opposite to this one the negation of Cantor's conjecture could perhaps be derived' (Gödel (1947), 184). By Gödel (1964), the second edition of this paper, this theme has become more explicit. The corresponding footnote begins with the above-quoted sentence, then continues: 'I am thinking of an axiom which . . . would state some maximum property of the system of all sets, whereas [$V = L$] states a minimum property' (Gödel (1964), 262–3).

In case we doubt which sort of axiom Gödel himself supports, the footnote concludes: 'Note that only a maximum property would seem to harmonize with the concept of set' (ibid.). The relevant concept of set

[2] See also Martin and Solovay (1970), 177.
[3] See Moore (1990), § 7, and Solovay (1995b).

comes earlier in the article: 'a set is something obtainable from the integers (or some other well-defined objects) by iterated application of the operation "set of"' (ibid. 259; cf. Gödel (1947), 180). In footnotes, he explains that 'iterated application' 'is meant to include transfinite iteration, i.e., the totality of sets obtained by finite iteration is considered to be itself a set and a basis for further applications of the operation "set of"' (Gödel (1964), 259; cf. Gödel (1947, 180), and that

The operation 'set of x's' (where the variable 'x' ranges over some given kind of objects) cannot be defined satisfactorily (at least not in the present state of knowledge), but can only be paraphrased by other expressions involving again the concept of set, such as: 'multitude of x's', 'combination of any number of x's', 'part of the totality of x's', where 'multitude' ('combination', 'part') is conceived of as something which exists in itself no matter whether we can define it in a finite number of words (so that random sets are not excluded). (Gödel (1964), 259; cf. Gödel (1947, 180)

This is essentially the combinatorially-determined, iterative conception, so Gödel's claim is that $V = L$ in a minimizing principle and that only a maximizing principle would be consistent with the iterative conception of set.

On this point, Gödel has lots of company. For a sampling:

The key argument against accepting $V = L$ . . . is that the axiom of constructibility appears to restrict unduly the notion of *arbitrary* set. (Moschovakis (1980), 610)

Most set theorists regard $[V = L]$ as a restriction which may prevent one from taking every subset at each stage, and so reject it (this includes Gödel, who named it). (Drake (1974), 131)

The axiom of constructibility should have better been called the constructibility hypothesis, but its present name is already in general use. When added as an axiom to ZF it yields a set theory which is usually understood to describe not the full universe of sets but a limited universe which consists of the constructible sets only. (Levy (1979), 291)

Beautiful as they are, [Gödel's] so-called constructible sets are very special being almost *minimal* in satisfying formal axioms in a first-order language. They just do not capture the notion of set in general (and they were not meant to). (Scott (1977), xii)

We hear again and again that $V = L$ is restrictive, limiting, minimal, and that these things are antithetical to the general notion of set.

There are also more clearly extrinsic arguments against $V = L$—e.g.

that there should not be a well-ordering of the reals so simple as Δ^1_2, that there should not be a non–Lebesgue measurable set so simple as Δ^1_2, that there should not be a thin set of reals so simple as Π^1_1, etc.—but I leave these aside here.[4] And, as suggested above, there are also arguments in favor of $V = L$: it is safe and powerful.[5] But its numerous detractors clearly hold that its merits are far outweighed by its demerits.

My focus, then, is the Axiom of Constructibility. Given that it is independent of ZFC, does it remain a legitimate mathematical question? If it does, how is this question to be resolved, and on what grounds? To tip my hand early, I take the answers to be: yes, it remains a legitimate mathematical question; it should be resolved in the negative ($V = L$ should be rejected); it should be so resolved on the grounds that $V = L$ is restrictive, in some sense or other. But it's a long way from here to a rational defence of these answers, even the partial one I hope to present in this book. I begin (in Part II) with a tempting mode of approach and explain why I think it cannot be made to work. Part III sketches another, for which I have higher hopes, and applies it to the case of $V = L$.

---

[4] For discussion and references, see my (1988), §§ II. 2, II. 3. 1, and V. 1.

[5] For examples of such sentiment, see Fraenkel, Bar-Hillel, and Levy (1973), 108–9, ('As an additional axiom for set theory the axiom of constructibility is somewhat attractive'), and much more strongly, Devlin (1977), iv ('one can provide persuasive arguments which justify the adoption of the axiom').

II

REALISM

Perhaps the most straightforward way of underwriting the legitimacy of the independent questions is to embrace some form of realism: there is a world of sets which ZFC only partly describes; the sets therein have the properties they do and stand in the relations they do objectively, that is, independently of our ability or inability to discover them; in this world, CH (and the independent questions of descriptive set theory) have determinate truth values; we can attempt to learn these truth values by searching for new axioms. From this point of view, good evidence for (or against) an axiom candidate is good evidence that it is true (or false) in the real world of sets.[1]

Apart from providing a distinctive take on the independent questions, realism has the merit of squaring with a well-known aspect of the experience of doing mathematics, of what might be called the 'phenomenology' of mathematical experience. I have in mind the oft-noted impression amongst mathematicians that they are not free to proceed as they please, that their work is constrained by the properties of something external. Moschovakis, speaking for many, puts the point this way:

> The main point in favor of the realistic approach to mathematics is the instinctive certainty of most everybody who has ever tried to solve a problem that he is thinking about 'real objects', whether they are sets, numbers, or whatever; and that these objects have intrinsic properties above and beyond the specific axioms about them on which he is basing his thinking for the moment. (Moschovakis (1980), 605)

Realism gives literal backing to these sentiments.

My purpose in this part is to explore the strengths and weaknesses of

---

[1] I use 'realism' for the view that there is one objectively-determinate set theoretic universe, so that CH (and the rest) must be either true or false there. Other forms of realism are possible—e.g. positing many universes of sets, or positing objective but incompletely-determinate objects—and some of these come up later (e.g. in III. 4), but unless explicitly qualified, I use 'realism' in this simple sense.

the realistic approach. In II. 1 and II. 2, I survey Gödelian and Quinean forms of mathematical realism, and in II. 3, I sketch a version of my own, set theoretic realism, which is developed at much greater length in my (1990a). An argument against $V = L$ from this point of view is constructed in II. 4. II. 5–7 start from shortcomings in the case against $V = L$ and proceed into deeper flaws in set theoretic realism itself. The tenor of these defects motivates the turn toward naturalism in Part III.

1

Gödelian Realism

In his (1947) and (1964), Gödel undertakes a direct defence of the legitimacy of CH, and a prominent theme in that defence is a staunch realism:

It is to be noted, however, that on the basis of the point of view here adopted, a proof of the undecidability of Cantor's conjecture from the accepted axioms of set theory . . . would by no means solve the problem. For if the meanings of the primitive terms of set theory as explained on page 262 and footnote 14 [these present the iterative conception, as quoted in I. 6 above] are accepted as sound, it follows that the set-theoretical concepts and theorems describe some well-determined reality, in which Cantor's conjecture must be either true or false. Hence its undecidability from the axioms being assumed today can only mean that these axioms do not contain a complete description of that reality. (Gödel (1964), 260)

Elsewhere, he argues for the view that 'the objects and theorems of mathematics are as objective and independent of our free choice and our creative acts as is the physical world' (Gödel (1951), 312, n. 17). Here we find a hint of the experiential theme—that mathematical progress is constrained by something external—plus a new element central to Gödel's thinking: a strong analogy between mathematics and physical science.[1]

Gödel traces this analogy to the early Russell. For example, in his (1920), Russell disapproves of Meinong's argument that 'we can speak about "the golden mountain", "the round square", and so on; we can make true propositions of which these are the subjects; hence they must have some kind of logical being, since otherwise the propositions in which they occur would be meaningless' (Russell (1920), 169). Russell would deal with these true propositions by means of his theory of descriptions, but he thinks more is going wrong here than the lack of a logical device. He continues:

In such theories, it seems to me, there is a failure of that feeling for reality which

---

[1] For useful recent discussions of Gödel's realism, see Parsons (1990) and (1995), Boolos (1995), and Goldfarb (1995). (See also Gödel (1933), 50, and Feferman (1995), 39–40, for discussion of a period of his life when Gödel seems not to have been a realist.) What I give in this section is only a crude sketch of one theme in Gödelian thought.

ought to be preserved even in the most abstract studies. Logic, I should maintain, must no more admit a unicorn than zoology can; for logic is concerned with the real world just as truly as zoology, though with its more abstract and general features. (Ibid.)

Gödel cites this final clause with approval (Gödel (1944), 120), and elaborates the analogy in some detail.

We've seen (in I. 4) how he compares extrinsic justifications for axioms to theoretical justifications in physical science:

There might exist axioms so abundant in their verifiable consequences, shedding so much light upon a whole field, and yielding such powerful methods for solving problems . . . that, no matter whether or not they are intrinsically necessary, they would have to be accepted at least in the same sense as any well-established physical theory. (Gödel (1964), 261; cf. Gödel (1947), 182–3)

This passage recalls Gödel's earlier report on Russell:

The analogy between mathematics and a natural science is enlarged upon by Russell also in another respect . . . He compares the axioms of logic and mathematics with the laws of nature and logical evidence with sense perception, so that the axioms need not necessarily be evident in themselves, but rather their justification lies (exactly as in physics) in the fact that they make it possible for these 'sense perceptions' to be deduced. (Gödel (1944), 121)

Again, the more theoretical parts of mathematics, on the one hand, and physical science, on the other, are justified by their consequences.

If extrinsic justifications are to work on the model of this science/mathematics analogy, there must be another, more basic form of mathematical insight that plays a role parallel to that of sense perception, and indeed, Gödel believes there is such a thing. At first, he speaks simply of our perception of mathematical things or facts: 'The truth, I believe, is that [mathematical] concepts form an objective reality of their own, which we cannot create or change, but only perceive and describe' (Gödel (1951), 320). A bit later, he introduces the notion of mathematical intuition, with explicit reference to the analogy:

The similarity between mathematical intuition and a physical sense is very striking. It is arbitrary to consider 'This is red' as immediate datum, but not so to consider the proposition expressing modus ponens or complete induction (or perhaps some simpler propositions from which the latter follows). For the difference, as far as it is relevant here, consists solely in the fact that in the first case a relationship between a concept and a particular object is perceived, while in the second case it is a relationship between concepts. (Gödel (1953/9), 359)

The most elaborate presentation occurs in Gödel (1964), where he writes:

despite their remoteness from sense experience, we do have something like a perception also of the objects of set theory, as is seen from the fact that the axioms force themselves upon us as being true. I don't see any reason why we should have less confidence in this kind of perception, i.e., in mathematical intuition, than in sense perception, which induces us to build up physical theories and to expect that future sense perceptions will agree with them, and moreover, to believe that a question not decidable now has meaning and may be decided in the future. (Gödel (1964), 268)

Notice that the science/mathematics analogy seems to have slipped a bit here: set theoretic axioms are now intuited, while the laws of natural science are not perceived. In fact, it seems that for Gödel, both intuitive and extrinsic evidence is relevant to the assessment of set theoretic axioms.[2]

It is natural to wonder how this mathematical intuition is supposed to work; Gödel's answer consists of a single paragraph, a paragraph Parsons calls 'possibly the most difficult and obscure passage in Gödel's finished philosophical writing' ((1995), 67). It begins:

It should be noted that mathematical intuition need not be conceived of as a faculty giving an *immediate* knowledge of the objects concerned. Rather it seems that, as in the case of physical experience, we *form* our ideas also of those objects on the basis of something else which *is* immediately given. Only this something else here is *not*, or not primarily, the sensations. That something besides the sensations actually is immediately given follows (independently of mathematics) from that fact that even our ideas referring to physical objects contain constituents qualitatively different from sensations or mere combinations of sensations, e.g., the idea of object itself, whereas, on the other hand, by our thinking we cannot create any qualitatively new elements, but only reproduce and combine those that are given. Evidently the 'given' underlying mathematics is closely related to the abstract elements contained in our empirical ideas. (Gödel (1964), 268)

This passage echoes Kant, and also Husserl (whom Gödel took to have understood and carried out Kant's central ideas),[3] though the exact

---

[2] Cf. Parsons (1995), 68–9.

[3] Noting that 'there is hardly any later direction that is not somehow related to Kant's ideas', Gödel remarks that 'none of [these] really did justice to the core of Kant's thought' and asks, alluding to Husserl's phenomenology: 'But now, if the misunderstood Kant has already led to so much that is interesting in philosophy, and also indirectly in science, how much more can we expect it from Kant correctly understood?' (Gödel (1961/?), 387)

structure of these echoes is still under investigation by commentators.[4] At a crude first approximation, Gödel seems to hold that our experience of physical objects is built up from sensory input and some abstract or conceptual elements, and that these latter are of the same sort as the 'givens' of mathematical intuition.

It is important to note that Gödel explicitly rejects any idealistic reading of this view:

> It by no means follows, however, that the data of this second kind, because they cannot be associated with actions of certain things upon our sense organs, are something purely subjective, as Kant asserted. Rather they, too, may represent an aspect of objective reality, but, as opposed to the sensations, their presence in us may be due to another kind of relationship between ourselves and reality. (Gödel (1964), 268)

Føllesdal (1995) points to a strong connection between this position and Husserl's (presumably, as opposed to Kant's). In any case, however mystified we might be about the nature of the 'other kind of relationship', Gödel's realism is unambiguous.

In sum, then, this line of Gödelian thought is based on a strong analogy between mathematics and natural science:

> It seems to me that the assumption of [sets and mathematical concepts] is quite as legitimate as the assumption of physical bodies and there is quite as much reason to believe in their existence. They are in the same sense necessary to obtain a satisfactory system of mathematics as physical bodies are necessary for a satisfactory theory of our sense perceptions. (Gödel (1944), 128)

Here, as Parsons admits ((1990), 107–8), it is hard to avoid the interpretation that mathematical objects are posited to explain our mathematical experiences, much as physical objects explain our sensory experiences. In any case, it is clear that, according to Gödel, the set theorist studies sets much as astronomers study stars, botanists study flowers and trees, and physicists study the small parts of matter.

A Gödelian realism along these lines has been subject to considerable philosophical criticism, most prominent being the simple objection that we have not been given a convincing account of this mathematical intu-

---

[4] Much of the relevant material is only newly available with the publication of previously unpublished material in vol. iii of Gödel's collected works (Gödel (1995)). For more on Gödel's understanding of Kant, see Parsons (1995), Gödel (1946/9), and Stein (1995); for the connections with Husserl, see Gödel (1961/?) and Føllesdal (1995).

ition.[5] While natural science itself provides the beginnings of an account of how the stimulation of our senses by our surroundings generates reliable, though not infallible, beliefs about those surroundings, there is no chapter of any science, no branch of mathematics, no part of philosophy, that gives a parallel account of how we come to reliable, if not infallible, beliefs about mathematical things on the basis of mathematical experiences. The problem is exacerbated if one adds, as Gödel does, that 'the objects of transfinite set theory . . . clearly do not belong to the physical world' (Gödel (1964), 267). If mathematical things are non-spatiotemporal, and thus presumably acausal, the problem of explaining how they generate our mathematical experiences, how our cognitive apparatus can respond to them, begins to appear insurmountable. In this form, it is the issue raised by Benacerraf in his (1973), a paper with an immense influence on philosophy of mathematics in recent decades.[6]

Without an account of the workings of mathematical intuition, it is hard to see how our mathematical experiences can provide a basis from which to infer the objective existence of mathematical things. Some people report religious experiences, but without a compelling story of how these experiences are generated by theological entities, there is always the attractive alternative of explaining those experiences as caused by something other than supernatural beings. Similarly, though people report mathematical experiences, there is the attractive alternative of explaining them without reference to mathematical things. For example, we might try emphasizing the creative aspects of mathematical activity, drawing a parallel with a sort of collective creative fiction-writing, rather than with natural science.[7] Where the Gödelian explains the strong tendency toward agreement among mathematicians as a result of their describing one and the same mathematical reality, we might appeal to their similar training and innate equipment; where the Gödelian explains the phenomenon of axioms 'forcing themselves upon us as being true' as a result of our perception-like contact with that reality, we might appeal to the impression, commonly reported by novelists, that characters, once created, tend to develop minds of their own. My point is not to endorse

---

[5] See Chihara (1973), ch. 2, and Chihara (1982), or Dummett (1967), 204. For discussion of Chihara (1973), see Steiner (1975b).

[6] For recent discussions, see Field (1989), 25–30, Burgess (1990), or my (1990a), 36–48. My (1996a) sketches the influence and legacy of this paper.

[7] Chihara's 'mythological platonism' ((1973), 61–75) is a version of Fictionalism. (Chihara himself does not endorse this view.)

this Fictionalism, but to note that nothing Gödel shows us seems to rule it out. In other words, we're given no reason to regard the claims of mathematics as literally true.

Fortunately, another recent version of mathematical realism is structured to provide just this: an argument for the truth of (as least some) mathematical claims. It originates with Quine.

2

Quinean Realism

Though his defence of realism is one of the most influential of recent years, Quine certainly did not start out as a realist. In their (1947), he and Goodman write:

We do not believe in abstract entities. No one supposes that abstract entities— classes, relations, properties, etc.—exist in space-time; but we mean more than this. We renounce them altogether . . . Why do we refuse to admit the abstract objects that mathematics needs? Fundamentally this refusal is based on a philosophical intuition that cannot be justified by appeal to anything more ultimate. (Goodman and Quine (1947), 105)

Notice that this rejection of mathematical things is motivated by a philosophical intuition, rather than anything mathematical or scientific. In the bibliography to a later collection of his papers, Quine writes:

Lest the reader be led to misconstrue passages in the present book by trying to reconcile them with the appealingly forthright opening sentence of the cited paper [that is, of Goodman and Quine (1947), quoted above], let me say that I should now prefer to treat that sentence as a hypothetical statement of the conditions for the construction in hand. (Quine (1980), 173–4)

Quine's change of heart on mathematical realism springs from his interactions with Carnap, so let me begin there.

Carnap's attitude toward mathematical existence claims stands in sharp contrast to that of Goodman and Quine: he emphatically denies that questions like these—'are there abstract objects?', 'do numbers (or sets) exist?'—are deep philosophical questions. Rather, according to Carnap, a statement like 'five is a number' is part of what constitutes the linguistic framework of number theory, and 'there are numbers' follows as a trivial consequence; if we have adopted the linguistic framework of number theory, we will reply that there are numbers. Now, obviously, philosophers intend to ask some other, non-trivial question about the ontological status of numbers—not 'is the existence of numbers implied by the linguistic framework of number theory?', but 'are there numbers, independently of any linguistic framework?'—a question they insist must be answered before we decide whether or not to adopt the relevant linguistic framework. But for Carnap, a legitimate question must be posed as an 'internal question'—that is, it must be asked inside a linguistic framework that provides the evidential rules that determine what counts as an answer—and the question philosophers attempt to ask is 'external': 'our judgement must be that they have not succeeded in giving to the external question and to the possible answers any cognitive content. Unless and until they supply a clear cognitive interpretation, we are justified in our suspicion that their question is a pseudo-question' (Carnap (1950), 245). The philosopher's prior question, which is supposed to guide our choice of linguistic frameworks, is actually a pseudo-question.

There remains, of course, the question of whether or not to adopt a given linguistic framework: the thing language (which speaks of medium-sized physical objects), the number language, the set language, etc. This question has no cognitive content, it is not a 'theoretical question', in need of a theoretical answer, because it does not take place inside a linguistic framework:

If someone decides to accept the thing language, there is no objection against saying that he has accepted the world of things. But this must not be interpreted as if it meant his acceptance of a *belief* in the reality of the thing world; there is no such belief or assertion or assumption, because it is not a theoretical question. To accept the thing world means nothing more than to accept a certain form of language, in other words, to accept rules for forming statements and for testing, accepting or rejecting them. The acceptance of the thing language leads, on the basis of observations made, also to the acceptance, belief and assertion of certain statements. But the thesis of the reality of the thing world cannot be among these statements, because it cannot be formulated in the thing language, or, it seems, in any other theoretical language. (Ibid. 243–4)

The same goes for the number language, or the set language: if we adopt the language, with its evidential rules, we are led to assert the existence of numbers or sets, of many particular numbers or sets, and likewise, to deny the existence of other numbers or sets. But the external questions—are there numbers? Are there sets?—cannot be posed; only their trivial, internal counterparts.

So we cannot decide whether or not to adopt a given linguistic framework on the basis of the answer to a prior (deep, philosophical) external question: there is no such question. According to Carnap,

To be sure, we have to face at this point an important question; but it is a practical, not a theoretical question; it is the question of whether or not to accept the new linguistic forms. The acceptance cannot be judged as being either true or false because it is not an assertion. It can only be judged as being more or less expedient, fruitful, conducive to the aim for which the language is intended. (Ibid. 250)

Thus, the decision on adopting a linguistic framework is pragmatic, not theoretical. For example, 'The efficiency, fruitfulness and simplicity of the use of the thing language may be among the decisive factors . . . The thing language in the customary form works indeed with a high degree of efficiency for most purposes of everyday life' (ibid. 244). And more generally, 'the acceptance or rejection of any . . . linguistic forms in any branch of science, will finally be decided by their efficiency as instruments, the ratio of the results achieved to the amount and complexity of the efforts required' (ibid. 256–7). The key, for Carnap, is realizing that 'it would be wrong to describe this situation by saying: "The fact of the efficiency of the thing language is confirming evidence for the reality of the thing world"; we should rather say instead: "This fact makes it advisable to accept the thing language"' (ibid. 244). So, for example, the immense usefulness of mathematical language in the pursuit of natural science provides good reason for us to adopt the set language over and above (some scientific elaboration of) the thing language, but it does not provide evidence for the existence of sets.

In time, Quine came to agree that much of mathematical language should be adopted on pragmatic grounds, contrary to his earlier view, but he could not follow his respected mentor in the distinction between internal and external questions. He agrees that the decision on adopting a linguistic framework is properly made in terms of power, effectiveness, and fruitfulness for the purposes at hand, but he suggests that all scientific hypotheses are adopted on similar grounds; in other words, he thinks there is no clear distinction between the internal evidential standards of science and the pragmatic standards by which Carnap would have us judge linguistic frameworks.

For example, imagine we've adopted the language of scientific enquiry before the introduction of atomic theory, and we're wondering about the addition of atoms.[1] Carnap would say that we're wondering whether or not to switch to a new, more inclusive, linguistic framework—that is, a new framework which contains, as a proper part, a syntactically identical copy of our current linguistic framework—and he urges that we base our

---

[1] I come back to this case in II. 6.

decision on the power, fruitfulness, and efficiency of the new framework, as compared with the old. Quine could put his point like this: our current framework includes familiar canons of scientific method, and among these is the admonition to judge new hypotheses on the basis of their power, fruitfulness, and efficiency. So Carnap is drawing a distinction without a difference when he calls some questions internal and some external; they are being judged on the same principles, that is, pragmatically:

Ontological questions . . . are on a par with questions of natural science . . . Now Carnap has maintained that this is a question not of matters of fact but of choosing a convenient language form, a convenient conceptual scheme or framework for science. With this I agree, but only on the proviso that the same be conceded for scientific hypotheses generally. (Quine (1951), 45)

Both agree that decisions should be approached with 'tolerance and an experimental spirit' (Quine (1948), 19, quoted approvingly by Carnap (1950), 250), but as Carnap puts Quine's point, this does not support a sharp boundary 'between the acceptance of a language structure and the acceptance of an assertion formulated in the language' (Carnap (1950), 250). Carnap takes Quine's position to 'deviate considerably from customary ways of thinking' (ibid.).

Aside from their disagreement over whether it is better to say 'The pragmatic virtues of the linguistic framework of xs confirms the existence of xs' or 'The pragmatic virtues of the linguistic framework of xs make it advisable to adopt the x language', Quine and Carnap are not so very far apart at this point: they see the adoption of an overall scientific language/theory as justified by similar considerations. But there is a further disagreement between them. To see this, recall that to accept the thing language is 'to accept rules for forming statements and for testing, accepting or rejecting them. The acceptance of the thing language leads, on the basis of observations made, also to the acceptance, belief and assertion of certain statements' (Carnap (1950), 243–4). To take a crude example, the thing language might include a rule to the effect that experiences of such-and-such a sort provide good evidence for the statement that there is a tree outside my window. If I adopt the thing language, and I have those experiences, then I have good evidence for the existence of a tree outside my window. Sceptical rejoinders—for example, that an evil demon may be falsely manipulating my senses, so that my experiences are not, in fact, good evidence—take place outside the linguistic framework, in the realm of the pseudo-question, and are thus irrelevant.

Compare the number language. Here, once again, we are to accept rules for forming statements—now including numerals like 'five', statements like 'five is a number', and so on—plus the relevant evidential rules—the axioms and deductive rules. Carnap writes: 'Here again there are internal questions, e.g., "Is there a prime number greater than a hundred?" Here, however, the answers are found, not by empirical investigation based on observations, but by logical analysis based on the rules for the new expressions' (ibid. 244). Such a logical analysis, using the relevant evidential rules, might lead us to assert that '2 + 2 = 4'. But notice that this time, the conclusion is based exclusively on the evidential rules of the linguistic framework. Carnap concludes, 'Therefore the answers are here analytic' (ibid.), as opposed to the thing language, where the answers are often (as in the example above) synthetic.

Finally, consider the full language of scientific enquiry, as we know it, a linguistic framework that includes both mathematical and physical terms, predicates, variables, evidential rules, etc. Carnap would like to distinguish the mathematical portion of this framework from the physical portion, to classify the mathematical claims as analytic and the physical claims as synthetic. Following the lead of our discussion of the thing and number languages, it might seem possible to do this by separating those hypotheses asserted on the basis of 'empirical investigation based on observations' from the rest; the former would be physical and the latter mathematical.

Carnap made a series of efforts to spell out this distinction, all of which were undermined by Quine's criticisms.[2] Carnap eventually held that the mathematical part of the language of science is true by virtue of the meanings of the words involved (words like 'not' and 'plus'), while the physical part is true by virtue of the way the world is. In his famous (1951), Quine criticizes various attempts to separate what is 'true by virtue of meaning' from what is 'true by virtue of the way the world is', and finally concludes that

It is obvious that truth in general depends on both language and extralinguistic fact. The statement 'Brutus killed Caesar' would be false if the world had been different in certain ways, but it would also be false if the word 'killed' happened rather to have the sense of 'begat'. Thus one is tempted to suppose in general

---

[2] See Quine (1951) and (1954). For discussion, see Friedman (1988).

that the truth of a statement is somehow analyzable into a linguistic component and a factual component. Given this supposition, it next seems reasonable that in some statements the factual component should be null; and these are the analytic statements. But, for all its a priori reasonableness, a boundary between analytic and synthetic statements simply has not been drawn. That there is such a distinction to be drawn at all is an unempirical dogma of empiricists, a metaphysical article of faith. (Quine (1951), 36–7)

So Quine's disagreement with Carnap is twofold: he denies that ontological questions are external, in Carnap's sense, and he denies that the linguistic parts of our overall scientific theory can be separated in principled way from its factual parts.[3]

But Quine does not disagree with Carnap on his fundamental commitment to empiricism; both hold that 'whatever evidence there *is* for science *is* sensory evidence' (Quine (1969d), 75). The trouble for the scientifically-minded empiricist, like Carnap or Quine, is that mathematics does not seem to be based on sensory evidence—it seems a priori[4]—and it seems to be certain, not fallible, as beliefs based on such evidence must be.[5] The most direct solution is to follow Mill's lead, to treat mathematical claims as ordinary empirical generalizations, and to explain the illusion that they are certain as due to their being so very highly confirmed (Mill (1843)).

In a work influenced by Carnap's point of view, Ayer rejects Mill's approach on the grounds that mathematical statements are not, in fact, subject to empirical refutation:

It might easily happen, for example, that when I came to count what I had taken to be five pairs of objects, I found that they amounted only to nine . . . But . . . one would not say that the mathematical proposition '$2 \times 5 = 10$' had been confuted. One would say that I was wrong in supposing that there were five pairs of objects to start with, or that one of the objects had been taken away while I was counting, or that two of them had coalesced, or that I had counted wrongly. One would adopt as an explanation whatever empirical hypothesis fitted in best with the accredited facts. The one explanation which would in no circumstances be adopted is that ten is not always the product of two and five. (Ayer (1946), 318)

Of course, the fact that we would prefer to change various empirical hypothesis before repudiating '$2 \times 5 = 10$' is also explicable on Mill's ac-

---

[3] Of course, both are aspects of the same general disagreement over the separability of language and fact.

[4] An a priori belief is one that is not based on sensory experience, as opposed to a posteriori.

[5] See Ayer (1946) for a classic statement of the problem.

count: the mathematical proposition is more highly confirmed than the others, so they are first to be rejected. As Ayer admits, 'In rejecting Mill's theory, we are obliged to be somewhat dogmatic' (ibid.).

But assuming the empiricist has rejected Mill's theory, Carnap presents an alterative. How do I know that $2 \times 5 = 10$?—Because it is part of the linguistic framework I have adopted.—Why won't I allow it to be denied?—Because to do so is inconsistent with the very language I speak; in Ayer's words, 'we cannot abandon [the principles of mathematics] without contradicting ourselves, without sinning against the rules which govern the use of language, and so making our utterances self-stultifying' (ibid. 319). On this view, mathematical propositions are a priori—known independently of sense experience—and certain—undeniable. But if Quine is right, and the distinction between linguistic and factual truths cannot be maintained, the empiricist is once again face-to-face with the original difficulty. So Quine cannot leave the matter here.

And he doesn't. Against Carnap, he has argued that the mathematical parts of our overall scientific theory cannot be separated from the physical parts on the basis of a distinction between analytic and synthetic, and on the alterative picture he presents, the two cannot be separated in any epistemically significant way. The crude idea behind Carnap's distinction is that some statements answer to experience and some do not—as we may say, that some statements are a posteriori and some a priori. But this picture requires that we isolate the evidence pertinent to the justification of a single statement, something Quine insists that we cannot do: to test a scientific theory against experience, we draw testable consequences using premises from many sectors of that theory, including mathematical premises. In his words, 'a self-contained theory which we can check with experience includes, in point of fact, not only its various theoretical hypotheses of so-called natural science but also such portions of logic and mathematics as it makes use of' (Quine (1954), 367).[6] This insight Quine traces to Duhem, who puts it this way:

the physicist can never subject an isolated hypothesis to experimental test, but only a whole group of hypotheses; when the experiment is in disagreement with his predictions, what he learns is that at least one of the hypotheses constituting

---

[6] Compare: 'The fact is that only laws of nature *together* with mathematics (or logic) have consequences verifiable by sense experience. It is, therefore, arbitrary to place all content in the laws of nature' (Gödel (1953/9), 348–9). This argument is quite similar to Quine's, but Gödel concludes only that mathematics and science are analogous, not that mathematics and science are inseparable parts of the same over-all theory. See Goldfarb (1995) for discussion.

this group is unacceptable and ought to be modified; but the experiment does not designate which one should be changed. (Duhem (1906), 187)

Quine insists that even the mathematics might be changed:

> our statements about the external world face the tribunal of sense experience not individually but only as a corporate body . . . The totality of our so-called knowledge or beliefs, from the most casual matters of geography and history to the profoundest laws of atomic physics or even of pure mathematics and logic, is a man-made fabric which impinges on experience only along the edges . . . Any statement can be held true come what may, if we make drastic enough adjustments elsewhere in the system . . . Conversely, by the same token, no statement is immune to revision. (Quine (1951), 41, 42, 43)

On this view, called 'holism', mathematics is of a piece with the science in which it functions: empirical confirmation of the theory as a whole confirms the mathematics involved in that theory; disconfirmation puts the mathematics, like the rest, up for revision.

For Quine, as for Mill, mathematics is fallible and responsive to empirical evidence, though for Quine, that evidence is more indirect than Mill's simple inductive generalizations. Thus Quine rejects yet another dichotomy: 'Now the very distinction between a priori and empirical begins to waver and dissolve' (Quine (1954), 367). But recall Ayer's objection to Mill: if Quine is to reject the a priority and certainty of mathematical statements, he must explain our tendency to preserve them come what may. This tendency, Quine argues, is nothing but the exercise of reasonable scientific principles; faced with a falsified prediction

> the choice of which of the beliefs to reject is indifferent only so far as the failed observation . . . is concerned, and not on other counts. It is well . . . not to rock the boat more than need be. Simplicity of the resulting theory is another guiding consideration, however, and if the scientist sees his way to a big gain in simplicity he is even prepared to rock the boat very considerably for the sake of it. (Quine (1990), 15)

A change in the mathematical items of the disconfirmed theory would inevitably cause large scale changes throughout: 'mathematics infiltrates all branches of our system of the world, and its disruption would reverberate intolerably' (ibid.) Or tolerably only if the payoff is very large, as with the replacement of Euclidean by Riemannian geometry in relativity theory.

If asked why he spares mathematics, the scientist will perhaps say that its laws are necessarily true [or a priori or infallible]; but I think we have here an explanation, rather, of mathematical necessity itself. It resides in our unstated policy of shielding mathematics by exercising our freedom to reject other beliefs instead. (Ibid.)

We revise the mathematical portions of our theory only as a last resort—a policy which makes good pragmatic sense—and this is why we take mathematics to be a priori, infallible, etc.

We are now quite close to Quine's mathematical realism. We know that ontological questions are to be settled by scientific means:

Our acceptance of an ontology is, I think, similar in principle to our acceptance of a scientific theory, say a system of physics: we adopt, at least insofar as we are reasonable, the simplest conceptual scheme into which the disordered fragments of raw experience can be fitted and arranged. Our ontology is determined once we have fixed upon the over-all conceptual scheme which is to accommodate science in the broadest sense; and the considerations which determine a reasonable construction of any part of that conceptual scheme, for example, the biological or the physical part, are not different in kind from the considerations which determine a reasonable construction of the whole. (Quine (1948), 16–17)

When we form this overall theory, it involves a considerable amount of mathematics. And finally, we judge the ontology of a theory, not by looking at its names or predicates, but by noting what it says 'there is'; this is Quine's 'criterion of ontological commitment'.[7] By this standard, in adopting our best scientific theory of the world, we commit ourselves to an ontology including mathematical things; we become mathematical realists.[8]

This line of argument for realism has been further developed by Putnam,[9] who emphasizes not only that mathematics is extremely useful in science, but that many hypotheses of physical science cannot even be stated without the use of mathematics:

one wants to say that the Law of Universal Gravitation makes an objective statement about bodies—not just about sense data or meter readings. What is that

[7] Introduced in Quine (1948).

[8] Though Duhem is also a holist, he is not a mathematical realist, or at least, he would not accept Quine's argument for mathematical realism. See my (199?a) for a discussion of their agreements and disagreements.

[9] I am glossing over implicit differences between Quine's and Putnam's versions. A crude characterization would be that Carnap imagines a distinction between the pragmatically justified and the factual; Quine and Putnam agree that there is no such distinction; Quine sees all as pragmatic, while Putnam sees all as factual. In what follows, I lean toward the Putnamian version.

statement? It is just that bodies behave in such a way that the quotient of two numbers *associated* with the bodies is equal to a third number *associated* with the bodies. But how can such a statement have any objective content at all if numbers and 'associations' (i.e. functions) are alike mere fictions? It is like trying to maintain that God does not exist and angels do not exist while maintaining at the very same time that it is an objective fact that God has put an angel in charge of each star and the angels in charge of each of a pair of binary stars were always created at the same time! If talk of numbers and 'associations' between masses, etc. and numbers is 'theology' (in the pejorative sense), then the Law of Universal Gravitation is likewise theology. (Putnam (1975), 74–5)

In other words, 'mathematics and physics are integrated in such a way that it is not possible to be a realist with respect to physical theory and a[n anti-realist] with respect to mathematical theory' (ibid. 74). He concludes:

I have been developing an argument for realism along roughly the following lines: quantification over mathematical entities is indispensable for science . . . therefore we should accept such quantification; but this commits us to accepting the existence of the mathematical entities in question. This type of argument stems, of course, from Quine, who has for years stressed both the indispensability of quantification over mathematical entities and the intellectual dishonesty of denying the existence of what one daily presupposes. (Putnam (1971), 347)

This is called the 'indispensability argument' for mathematical realism.[10] Over the past few decades, the indispensability argument has been as influential a factor in support of realism as Benacerraf's problem has been against it.[11]

We should note a few of the peculiarities of the version of mathematical realism this argument delivers. Some will be troubled by its underlying empiricism; anyone moved, for example, by Ayer's insistence that mathematical claims cannot be denied without something like self-

[10] Compare: 'it is applicability alone which elevates arithmetic from a game to the rank of a science' (Frege (1903), 187). Field (1980) argues that mathematics is, despite appearances, dispensable in science, but commentators remain unconvinced. For a mere sampling, Malament (1982) doubts that Field's methods can be extended to quantum mechanics; Resnik (1985a; 1985b) questions the claim that Field's formulations are actually mathematics-free; my (1990b) and (1990c) dispute the advantages of Field's view over realism; and Shapiro (1983) raises some important technical considerations. Field (1989) contains some replies. See also Burgess and Rosen (1997).

[11] e.g. Steiner ((1975a), 122–3) and Maddy ((1990a), 28–35) appeal to indispensability considerations in defense of versions of realism; Field ((1980), 2; (1989), 14–20) and Chihara ((1973), chs. III and V) are motivated by their anti-realism to argue that (some or all) mathematics is dispensable after all.

contradiction will not be satisfied with Quine's attempt to explain those feelings away. Pure mathematicians will most likely be even more displeased to realize that the defence only extends to applied mathematics. Putnam draws this conclusion quite explicitly; speaking of 'the set theoretic "needs" of physics', he writes:

Insofar, then, as the indispensability of quantification over sets is any argument for their existence . . . we may say that it is a strong argument for the existence of at least predicative sets, and a pretty strong, but not *as* strong, argument for the existence of impredicative sets. When we come to the higher reaches of set theory, however—sets of sets of sets of sets—we come to conceptions which are today not needed outside of pure mathematics itself. The case for 'realism' being developed in the present section is thus a qualified one: at least sets of things, real numbers, and functions from various kinds of things to real numbers should be accepted as part of the presently indispensable (or nearly indispensable) framework of . . . physical science . . . and as part of that whose existence we are presently committed to. But sets of very high type or very high cardinality (higher than the continuum, for example), should today be investigated in an 'if-then' spirit. One day they may be as indispensable to the very *statement* of physical laws as, say, rational numbers are today; then doubt of their 'existence' will be as futile as extreme [anti-realism] now is. But for the present we should regard them as what they are—speculative and daring extensions of the basic mathematical apparatus of science. (Putnam (1971), 346–7)

At some points, Quine has sounded even more severe, denying that the claims of pure mathematics are even meaningful:

So much of mathematics as is wanted for use in empirical science is for me on a par with the rest of science. Transfinite ramifications are on the same footing insofar as they come of a simplificatory rounding out, but anything further is on a par rather with uninterpreted systems. (Quine (1984), 788)

Recent writings have been a bit more generous, if grudgingly so; speaking of the 'higher reaches of set theory', he allows that 'We see them as meaningful because they are couched in the same grammar and vocabulary that generate the applied parts of mathematics. We are just sparing ourselves the unnatural gerrymandering of grammar that would be needed to exclude them' (Quine (1990), 94). Concerning the independent questions, he reasons:

Further sentences such as the continuum hypothesis and the axiom of choice, which are independent of those axioms, can still be submitted to the considerations of simplicity, economy, and naturalness that contribute to the molding of scientific theories generally. Such considerations support Gödel's axiom of constructibility, $V = L$. It inactivates the more gratuitous flights of higher set theory, and incidentally it implies the axiom of choice and the continuum hypothesis. (Ibid. 95)

Note the oddity of this conclusion: Quine's application of indispensability considerations has led him to a stand (on $V = L$) precisely opposite to that of the set theoretic community (see I. 6).[12]

The general pattern here is clear. If a mathematician is asked to defend a mathematical claim, she will most likely appeal first to a proof, then to intuitions, plausibility arguments, and intra-mathematical pragmatic considerations in support of the assumptions that underlie it. From the point of view of the indispensability theorist, what actually does the justifying is the role of the claim, or of the assumptions that underlie its proof, in well-confirmed physical theory. In other words, the justifications given in mathematical practice differ from those offered in the course of the indispensability defence of realism. This, by itself, would be an unsettling peculiarity of Quinean realism, even if the two modes of justification invariably led to the same conclusions, but as the examples from pure mathematics to $V = L$ show, this isn't the case: the conclusions of indispensability theory conflict with the actual practice.

To these, let me add one last peculiarity. On the indispensability picture, mathematics enters at a fairly high level of theorizing, when we are moved to mathematize our scientific theorizing. But, as a purely phenomenological matter, various mathematical claims, elementary truths of arithmetic or set theory, seem obvious; as Gödel says, they 'force themselves upon us as being true' ((1964), 268). Parsons puts the problem this way:

The empiricist view, even in the subtle and complex form it takes in the work of Professor Quine, seems subject to the objection that it leaves unaccounted for precisely the *obviousness* of elementary mathematics . . . It seeks to meet the difficulties of early empiricist views of mathematics by assimilating mathematics to the theoretical part of science. But there are great differences . . . [e.g.] the existence of very general principles that are universally regarded as obvious, where on

---

[12] Between these two quotations comes: 'I recognize indenumerable infinites only because they are forced on me by the simplest known systematizations of more welcome matters. Magnitudes in excess of such demands, e.g. $\beth_\omega$ or inaccessible numbers, I look upon only as mathematical recreation and without ontological rights. Sets that are compatible with '$V = L$' . . . afford a convenient cut-off' (Quine (1986), 400). Again the clash with practice is clear; aside from the sentiment against $V = L$, already noted, the accepted axioms of ZFC imply the existence of $\beth_\omega$, and arguments are offered in favour of inaccessibles.

an empiricist view one would expect them to be bold hypotheses, about which a prudent scientist would maintain reserve, keeping in mind that experience might not bear them out. (Parsons (1980), 151–2)

Once again, indispensability theory comes in conflict with the actual experience of doing mathematics.

In sum, then, Quinean realism avoids the difficulties of the Gödelian version—it has an argument for the truth of (some) mathematical claims, and it has no counterpart to the controversial mathematical intuition—but doing so brings it into conflict with the actual practice of mathematics.

3

Set Theoretic Realism

The hope behind set theoretic realism is to produce a version of realism with the strengths of both the Gödelian and the Quinean varieties and the weaknesses of neither. As the delineation and defence of this view is the central burden of my (1990a), I will be brief here. For our purposes, I need just enough to set up the difficulties to be explored later. The trouble with Gödelian realism is that it gives us no reason to believe that mathematical claims are true. Quine provides this, in the form of the indispensability argument. The drawback of the indispensability defence is that it conflicts with the actual practice of mathematics. And sensitivity to practice, again, is one of the strengths of Gödel's analysis.

The compromise goes like this. Take the indispensability arguments to provide good reasons to suppose that some mathematical things (e.g. the continuum) exist. Admit, however, that the history of the subject shows the best methods for pursuing the truth about these things are mathematical ones, not those of physical science. (Note that these methods condone the pursuit of pure mathematics and seem to counsel against $V = L$.) To give an account of these methods and their justificatory force, begin with the level of the obvious, by explicating mathematical intuition. (I do this by replacing Gödel's rather mystical faculty with a down-to-earth neurophysiological model that describes both physical and mathematical perception and uses these as the basis of both physical and mathematical intuition.) Proceed from there to demonstrate the rationality of extrinsic methods of justification. (This is posed as the leading open problem at the end of my (1990a).)

From the point of view of the set theoretic realist, we have good reason to suppose that the continuum exists, and thus, to suppose that the independent questions have determinate answers. Here realism is used to support the legitimacy of CH and the rest, just as it was in Gödel (1947) and (1964). In the subsequent search for new axioms, we have mathematical intuition and extrinsic methods with which to evaluate new axiom candidates (assuming the open problem from my (1990a) can be solved). In short, we seem to have a position with the desired payoffs and none of the detriments. The next step would be to apply the methods at hand to the actual evaluation of axiom candidates.

I don't pretend that set theoretic realism actually lives up to this description; for a sampling of objections, see Lavine (1992), Balaguer (1994), Riskin (1994), Carson (1996). But, in fact, I do think that the most serious and far-reaching objection is the one I raise in II. 5–7 below. Before turning to its difficulties, though, let me first make an effort to apply set theoretic realism to the evaluation of an axiom candidate, as it was intended.

4

A Realist's Case against $V = L$

Given the interrelations between the various new axiom candidates, one way to argue against $V = L$ would be to argue for the existence of measurable cardinals (MC), then derive $V \neq L$. One drawback to this approach is that we can't then use Scott's 1961 theorem (MC $\rightarrow V \neq L$) as an extrinsic argument for MC! In fact, as Gödel (1947) shows, there was considerable sentiment against $V = L$ even before this result; my goal in this section is to sketch an argument that would have worked even then.

The literature contains hints at more than one such line of reasoning, but I concentrate here on what I take to be the most widely shared and the most promising. It appears, for example, in the continuation of a passage from Moschovakis (1980) quoted above (in I. 6). He begins: 'The key argument against accepting $V = L$ . . . is that the axiom of constructibility appears to restrict unduly the notion of *arbitrary* set of integers' (Moschovakis (1980), 610). He then elaborates: 'there is no a priori reason why every subset of ω should be definable from ordinal parameters, much less by an elementary definition over some countable L_ξ' (ibid.). The suggestion is that the trouble with $V = L$ is that it requires every set to be definable in a certain uniform way, and that this requirement is implausible, undesirable, to be avoided. This is the line of thought I try to fill in.

The role of realism in all this is twofold. First, realism is to underwrite the assumption that there is a real question to be decided here, that it isn't enough to say that ZFC + $V = L$ and ZFC + $V \neq L$ are equally acceptable because they are both equiconsistent with ZFC. For the realist, as we've seen, there is a fact of the matter about which of $V = L$ and $V \neq L$ is true in the world of sets, and only the true member of the pair is acceptable as a new axiom. The second contribution of realism is a feature that set theoretic realism inherits from the Gödelian variety, namely, the strong science/mathematics analogy. This implies that in mathematics, as in science, there are legitimate forms of evidence beyond the sensory and the intuitive, that is, evidence based on the consequences of a given hypothesis, or more generally, on the virtues of the type of theory it produces. This is what we've been calling 'extrinsic evidence', as contrasted with the intrinsic (now understood as perceptual or intuitive).

Notice that a strong analogy between mathematics and science does not require that the canons of extrinsic evidence in mathematics be precisely the same as those in natural science. We are free to admit the obvious: that mathematics has methods of its own that are not identical with those of science. (This is how Gödelian and set theoretic realism avoid the conflicts with practice that mar Quinean realism.) But there are high-level structural similarities that I hope to exploit.

Let me begin (in (i)) with a sketch of the strategy behind the realist's argument against $V = L$. I turn then (in (ii)) to an analysis of the mathematical facts that might stand behind Moschovakis's complaint, and I conclude (in (iii)) by applying the methodological morals to the case of $V = L$.

(i) *Strategy.* The realist's case against $V = L$ depends on the status of a general methodological maxim. The line of argument draws on a parallel between the role of such maxims in mathematics and in natural science. So, to set the stage, we need a familiar scientific example for comparison. Consider, then, the principle of Mechanism.[1]

In their illuminating history (1938), Einstein and Infeld describe the sources of the Mechanism:

Science connecting theory and experiment really began with the work of Galileo . . . Throughout two hundred years of scientific research force and matter were the underlying concepts in all endeavors to understand nature . . . The easiest forces to imagine are those of attraction and repulsion. In both cases the force vectors lie on a line connecting the material points. The demand for simplicity leads to the picture of particles attracting or repelling each other; any other assumption about the direction of the acting forces would give a much more complicated picture.

Can we make an equally simple assumption about the length of the force vectors? Even if we want to avoid too special assumptions we can still say one thing: The force between any two given particles depends only on the distance between them . . .

With matter and force as our fundamental concepts we can hardly imagine simpler assumptions than that forces act along the line connecting the particles and depend only on the distance. But is it possible to describe all physical phenomena by forces of this kind alone? (Einstein and Infeld (1938), 52–3)

---

[1] As will become clear, I draw heavily here on the history and analysis of Einstein and Infeld (1938).

Mechanism, as a methodological maxim, counsels that we attempt such descriptions in every case, and a wonderfully effective maxim it was:

The great achievements of mechanics in all its branches, its striking success in the development of astronomy, the application of its ideas to problems apparently different and non-mechanical in character, all these things contributed to the belief that it *is* possible to describe all natural phenomena in terms of simple forces between unalterable objects. (Ibid. 53–4)

Mechanism was explicitly formulated and endorsed by Helmholtz in the mid-nineteenth century; in the late nineteenth century, it led to the development of the kinetic theory, 'one of the greatest achievements directly influenced by the mechanical view' (ibid. 55).[2] Thus, Mechanism arose as a generalization from successful practice, and after its formulation, its guidance produced one of the deepest and most far-reaching theories of our time. The isolation and application of such methodological maxims would seem an uncontroversial component of sound scientific procedure.

But there were problems. First, the use of purely mechanical ideas in the treatment of electrostatics and magnetism (beginning in the mid-eighteenth century) was awkward; Einstein and Infeld conclude their discussion like this:

Although we can consistently carry out the mechanical view in the domain of electric and magnetic phenomena introduced here, there is no reason to be particularly proud or pleased about it. Some features of the theory are certainly unsatisfactory if not discouraging. New kinds of substances had to be invented; two electric fluids and the elementary magnetic dipoles. The wealth of substances begins to be overwhelming! . . . The forces are simple. They are expressible in a similar way for gravitational, electric and magnetic forces. But the price paid for this simplicity is high: the introduction of new weightless substances. These are rather artificial concepts, and quite unrelated to the fundamental substance, mass. (Ibid. 84)

Bad as this sounds, the next trouble was worse: an outright contradiction to the existing Mechanistic doctrine. Rowland (in 1876), improving on experiments of Oersted (in 1820), showed that a moving electric charge will deflect a magnetic needle, neither by attracting nor repelling, but along a line *perpendicular* to the plane of motion, and that the force of that deflection increases as the velocity of the charge increases:

Not only does the force fail to lie on the line connecting charge and magnet, but

---

[2] I return to the kinetic theory in II. 6. i.

the intensity of the force depends on the velocity of the charge. The whole mechanical point of view was based on the belief that all phenomena can be explained in terms of forces depending only on the distance and not the velocity. The result of Rowland's experiment certainly shakes this belief. (Ibid. 89)

Thus Mechanism is shaken, though a conservative approach might 'seek a solution within the frame of old ideas', perhaps by broadening 'the previous point of view and introduc[ing] more general forces between the elementary particles' (ibid. 90). As long as the recalcitrant phenomenon are small and localized, we may chose to retain 'the apparently well-founded and successful mechanical theories' (ibid.).[3]

The third difficulty was eventually decisive, though indirectly. It involves the propagation of light waves in the ether, a central assumption of the nineteenth century. Physicists at first hoped that light was a longitudinal wave—like a sound wave in air, where the points in the medium oscillate back-and-forth in the same direction as the propagation of the wave—rather than a transverse wave—like the wave in a length of string, where the movement of points of the medium is up-and-down in a direction perpendicular to that of the propagation of the wave. The difference was important:

Obviously, we should be fortunate if light waves were longitudinal. The difficulties in designing a mechanical ether would be much simpler in this case. Our picture of ether might very probably be something like the mechanical picture of a gas that explains the propagation of sound waves. It would be much more difficult to form a picture of ether carrying transverse waves. (Ibid. 117)

The trouble with modelling light as a transverse wave in the ether is that our best picture of the medium in which such waves propagate requires an elastic solid (like jelly, or even steel), while the planets must move through the ether without impediment.

Einstein and Infeld ask: 'Was nature, in this case, merciful to the physicists attempting to understand all events from a mechanical point of view?' (ibid.). The answer, of course, is no: polarization phenomena, for example, can be explained only by a transverse wave.[4] Einstein and Infeld summarize the resulting the situation like this:

---

[3] Note the echo of Quinean holism: unexpected phenomena can be reconciled with a theory by many different sorts of revisions, with conservative ones as the first choice.

[4] e.g. suppose we observe a light source through two thin crystals, and turning the second crystal along the axis of the light ray causes the light to vanish. For a longitudinal wave, nothing along the axis itself changes, so the phenomenon is inexplicable. In 1817, Fresnel gave an explanation of polarization in terms of transverse waves; the phenomenon itself was discovered by Malus in 1808.

The discussion of all the various attempts to understand the mechanical nature of the ether as a medium for transmitting light, would make a long story . . . In order to construct the ether as a jelly-like mechanical substance [so that it could transmit transverse waves] physicists had to make some highly artificial and unnatural assumptions. (Ibid. 119)

At this point, Mechanism could be maintained only at a considerable cost.

Overlapping these developments in mechanistic theory was a contrary motion: 'During the second half of the nineteenth century new and revolutionary ideas were introduced into physics; they opened the way to a new philosophical[5] view, differing from the mechanical one' (ibid. 125). The revolutionary idea in question is that of a field, particularly the electromagnetic field, which reached its full mathematical form in Maxwell's equations of 1855. 'The formulation of these equations is the most important event in physics since Newton's time,[6] not only because of their wealth of content, but also because they form a pattern for a new type of law' (ibid. 143). Unlike mechanical laws, the field laws do not concern the forces between bodies separated in space. Rather, 'Maxwell's equations describe the structure of the electromagnetic field. All space is the scene of these laws and not, as for mechanical laws, only points in which matter or charges are present . . . In Maxwell's theory, there are no material actors' (ibid. 146). Eventually, field theory led to the identification of light waves as a species of electromagnetic waves, that is, to the unification of optics with electricity and magnetism:

This great result is due to the field theory. Two apparently unrelated branches of science are covered by the same theory . . . If it is our aim to describe everything that ever happened or may happen with the help of one theory, then the union of optics and electricity is, undoubtedly, a very great step forward. (Ibid. 150)

Thus, the field concept evolved from a helpful way of expressing familiar facts about electric fluids to a powerful tool for generating new theories.

So, as Mechanism experienced mounting difficulties, the Field Conception—the admonition to seek field theoretic descriptions—racked up huge successes:

---

[5] I explore the notion of 'philosophical' being used here in III. 4. ii.

[6] Cf.: 'From a long view of the history of mankind—seen from, say, ten thousand years from now—there can be little doubt that the most significant event of the 19th century will be judged as Maxwell's discovery of the laws of electrodynamics. The American Civil War will pale into provincial insignificance in comparison with this important scientific event of the same decade' (Feynman, Leighton, and Sands (1964), 1–11).

In the beginning, the field concept was no more than a means of facilitating the understanding of phenomena from the mechanical point of view. In the new field language it is the description of the field between the two charges, and not the charges themselves, which is essential for an understanding of their action. The recognition of the new concepts grew steadily, until substance was overshadowed by the field. It was realized that something of great importance had happened in physics . . . Slowly and by a struggle the field concept established for itself a leading place in physics and has remained one of the basic physical concepts. (Ibid. 151)

At the same time, the underlying relationship between Mechanism and the Field Concept emerged only gradually:

The field was at first considered as something which might later be interpreted mechanically with the help of the ether. By the time it was realized that this program could not be carried out, the achievements of the field theory had already become too striking and important for it to be exchanged for a mechanical dogma. On the other hand, the problem of devising the mechanical model of ether seemed to become less and less interesting and the result, in view of the forced and artificial character of the assumptions, more and more discouraging. (Ibid. 152–3)

Physicists were faced with a troubled maxim—Mechanism—and a powerful and effective rival—the Field Conception—and they naturally opted to switch.

The story of Mechanism might be described this way: (1) a strong and effective methodological maxim is formulated by generalization from successful scientific practice; application of that maxim leads to further breakthroughs. (2) Gradually, various annoying anomalies crop up; each of these can be dealt with by accepting otherwise unattractive treatments of the phenomena involved (e.g. electric fluids), by various modifications of the maxim (e.g. to deal with Oersted and Rowland's results), or by adopting long-term research projects (e.g. to mechanize the ether). (3) An alternative maxim arises, again by generalization; application of that maxim sheds helpful light on the ground already covered by application of the old maxim; application of the new maxim gradually outstrips the old in fruitfulness, explanatory power, etc.; the new maxim cannot be made consistent with the old; the old maxim is overthrown in favour of the new. On this picture, no particular anomaly leads to the rejection of the maxim—any particular anomaly can be dealt with in one way or another, as conservativeness recommends—but the accumulated effects of a number of anomalies, combined with an attractive alternative maxim, do the job together.

I take it as given that this line of scientific development is rational, that physicists were right to formulate and apply Mechanism in the first place, just as they were also right to replace it by the Field Conception in the end. My realistic case against $V = L$ works by analogy: I describe a mathematical maxim with a history similar to that of Mechanism (in (ii)), and I suggest that $V = L$ is suspicious in light of its connections with that maxim (in (iii)).[7] Assuming the science/mathematics analogy, if it is rational to proceed as the natural scientists did, it should be rational for set theorists to hold this attitude towards $V = L$.

(ii) *The Rise and Fall of Definabilism.* The mathematical maxim I have in mind is Definabilism, the requirement that all mathematical things be definable in a certain uniform way. I leave open the exact specification of this 'uniform way' to allow for different versions of the same general maxim.

Definabilism arose during the development of one of the most central mathematical concepts of all, the concept of a function. The first representations of what we would now call functions were tables of squares, square roots, etc., from as early as 2000 BC.[8] The Greeks went further, to verbal descriptions of such dependencies as the positions of the planets on time. Arabic thinkers added tables of sines and cosines. Medieval mathematicians gave graphic representations of such variations as heat intensity with time. But in none of this did a general notion of function emerge.

The turning-point came in the early seventeenth century. By that time, algebraic symbolism had been introduced, more sophisticated measuring devices allowed earlier verbal descriptions to be replaced by quantitative ones, and natural science had shifted focus from astronomy to mechanics, especially dynamics. But for all that, functions were still represented by tables, graphs, or verbal descriptions. Then, in 1637, both Descartes and Fermat hit on the idea of applying algebra to geometry. Fermat wrote down the equation for a line. Given an equation in x and y, Descartes showed how to calculate a value of y for every value of x. That he also showed how to do the reverse—calculate a value of x for every value of y—suggests his notion was closer to our idea of a binary relation than to our idea of a dependent variable as a function of an independent

---

[7] This argument is essentially that of my (1993a).

[8] The following discussion of the history of the function concept rests heavily on Youschkevitch (1976).

variable.[9] But for our purposes, it is most important to note that Descartes distinguished between 'geometric curves'—those determined by an equation—and 'mechanical curves'—those for which no equation can be given. When he excluded the mechanical curves from his geometry, Descartes introduced the first hint of Definabilism: attention should be restricted to curves definable by algebraic equations.

In the first half of the eighteenth century, Bernoulli wrote to Leibniz of 'a quantity somehow formed from indeterminate and constant' quantities, and later of 'diverse quantities given somehow by an indeterminate [quantity] x and by constants . . . either algebraically'[10] or using logarithms or trigonometric notions. Here the independent and dependent variables emerge, and some variety of expressibility requirement is imposed. Leibniz agreed to this understanding of the notion of function,[11] and in 1871, Bernoulli published the following definition: 'I call a function of a variable magnitude a quantity composed in any manner whatsoever from this variable magnitude and from constants.'[12] Just how the variable quantity is to be 'composed' is not explicitly specified, but the context assured that Bernoulli has in mind the use of symbolic means.

Finally, in 1748, Euler is explicit: a variable quantity ranges over

all numbers, both positive and negative, both integer and factional, both rational and irrational and transcendental.[13] Even zero and imaginary numbers are not excluded from the meaning of a variable quantity . . . A function of a variable quantity is an analytic expression composed in any way from this variable quantity and numbers or constant quantities.[14]

Euler's analytic expressions are more generous than Descartes's equations; in addition to algebraic operations, they allow trigonometric and logarithmic notions, power series expansions, and 'innumerable others which the integral calculus supplies in abundance'.[15] For Euler, a

---

[9] During this period, dependent variables were typically associated with the study of curves: x- and y-values vary along a curve, as do the tangent, the arc length, and so on. Leibniz used the word 'function' already in 1673, but he had in mind relations between purely geometric quantities. This usage continued into the eighteenth century. See Bos (1974/5).

[10] As quoted and translated in Youschkevitch (1976), 57. This is Johann, one of the many scientific Bernoullis.

[11] See n. 9 above.

[12] As quoted and translated in another valuable resource, Bottazzini (1986), 9.

[13] This includes the use of non-algebraic notions, such as sines, cosines, and logarithms.

[14] As quoted and translated in Youschkevitch (1976), 61.

[15] As quoted and translated in Bottazzini (1986), p. 9.

function is identified with such an expression, the purest form of Definabilism. Descartes ruled 'mechanical functions' out of his geometry, but Euler's definition leaves no room even for the existence of functions without analytic representations.

In sum, then, over this long period, mathematicians gradually developed the notion of a function as a dependence of one variable on the values of another. The means of this dependence, the way the y value depends on the x value, was identified with a symbolic expression, and the resources available for such expressions expanded with mathematics itself. Definabilism, as a powerful maxim for the treatment of functions, arose out of this historic development, much as Mechanism did in the history of physics.

The analogy with Mechanism continues as Definabilism is faced with a series of anomalies. The first of these appeared in the famous debate between d'Alembert and Euler over the mathematical treatment of a vibrating string.[16] This is an extremely important episode in the history of mathematics, as d'Alembert initiated the study of partial differential equations with his wave equation. For our purposes, the salient feature is the resulting disagreement between d'Alembert and Euler over what counts as a function.

The controversy centred on two initial conditions: the initial shape of the string and the initial velocity of its points. D'Alembert's solution to the wave equation is stated in terms of these two; a good Definabilist, he requires (among other things) that they both be given by analytic expressions. If the initial conditions fail to meet these conditions, d'Alembert judges the problem to be unsolvable.

The trouble with this position is obvious when we consider that a common way to set a string vibrating is to pluck it, and that this initial shape does not meet d'Alembert's conditions: it can be given by two separate analytic expressions, but not by a single one. D'Alembert rules out such initial conditions, despite admitting that they are 'the most ordinary, and perhaps the only ones that have ever existed for vibrating strings'.[17] Stunning as this may seem to us now, d'Alembert considers such functions 'not at all proper for analysis',[18] that is, for mathematical treatment.

---

[16] My treatment of this episode is guided by Bottazzini (1986), § 1. 3, and especially the detailed Truesdell (1960), Pt. III.

[17] As quoted and translated in Truesdell (1960), 288.

[18] As quoted and translated ibid. 274.

In a conflict between the requirements of existing mathematics and the needs of physical mechanics, Euler took the other side: he denies that initial positions must be given by a single analytic expression and allows that they 'are equally satisfactory, whether they are expressed by some equation or whether they are traced in any fashion, in such a way as not to be subject to any equation'.[19] In defence of this view, he insists that 'the first vibration depends on our pleasure, since we can, before letting the string go, give it any shape whatsoever'.[20] Thus Euler, under pressure from the needs of mathematical physics, gives up his Definabilism, while d'Alembert, under the same pressure, maintains the integrity of his mathematics.

It should be emphasized that d'Alembert was doing just that; he was quite right to insist that solutions to his wave equation must be twice differentiable, and that Euler's solutions (generated by his 'inadmissible' initial conditions) are not. Euler agrees, but defends his approach nevertheless: 'I do not deny that in applying the calculus to such a case, one commits some error, but I claim that the totality of this error becomes infinitely small and entirely zero.'[21] (Amusing to imagine Berkeley having a go at this remark!) Cavalier as this sounds, Euler in fact made considerable efforts to explain how and why these problems can be safely ignored, and these efforts touched on ideas so far ahead of his time that it took as much as a century for mathematics to develop the tools to treat them adequately.[22]

In any case, it is clear that Euler was led to reject his earlier notion of function. Commentators disagree over whether or not he had the modern, completely general notion of an arbitrary correspondence,[23] but it is clear from the passages quoted here that he no longer identified functions with symbolic expressions. D'Alembert, on the other hand, elevates Definabilism to a binding methodological maxim with potentially limitative force: certain initial conditions are inadmissible, even if this constrains the application of mathematics to physics; certain studies fall

---

[19] As quoted and translated ibid. 246.

[20] As quoted and translated in Bottazzini (1986), 26.

[21] As quoted and translated in Truesdell (1960), 285.

[22] See ibid. 286, 289–91, 296–7, Bottazzini (1986), 27, Youschkevitch (1976), 72. Truesdell writes: 'it is Euler's signal merit to have been led by the most secure intuition to results which the subsequent course of mathematics and rational mechanics has justified in all detail, though he himself lacked the experience and the apparatus to present an adequate argument for them' ((1960), 297).

[23] e.g. see Youschkevitch (1976), §§ 10 and 13, who thinks Euler's conception was the modern one, or Truesdell (1960), 247, who thinks it wasn't.

outside legitimate mathematics. D'Alembert's position, though defensible, was undeniably uncomfortable. Thus mechanics produced the first anomaly for Definabilism.

Given the analogy with Mechanism, we should not be surprised to find that Definabilism retained its attractions in the aftermath of the first anomaly partly by relaxing its requirements, that is, by allowing more generous means of definition. The first hint came from another Bernoulli,[24] during the d'Alembert–Euler debates: he claims, without proof, that every function is representable by the expansion of an infinite trigonometric series. Euler was painfully undecided on this question for the rest of his life,[25] and little clarity was to be found anywhere until the beginning of the nineteenthth century, when Fourier launched his study of heat.

In the course of solving his heat equation, Fourier developed the Fourier series. In 1822, he wrote: 'It follows from my research on this subject that even discontinuous arbitrary functions can always be represented by expansions into sines or cosines of multiple arcs . . . A conclusion that the celebrated Euler always rejected.'[26] Leaving aside the question of precisely what is meant by 'discontinuous arbitrary functions', not to mention the inaccurate portrayal of Euler's state of mind, Fourier takes himself to have settled the case in Bernoulli's favour by showing how to generate the coefficients of the required trigonometric expansion:

If we apply the principles that we have just established to the question of the movement of vibrating strings, we can resolve all the difficulties that the analysis employed by Daniel Bernoulli presented. In fact, the solution proposed by this great geometer does not seem at all applicable to the case where the initial figure of the string is that of a triangle . . . The inventors of the analysis of partial differential equations even took this application to be impossible. [Cf. d'Alembert] . . . [These objections] show how necessary it is to demonstrate that any function can always be expanded as a series of sines or cosines of multiple arcs. Of all the proofs of this proposition, the most complete is that which consists of actually resolving an arbitrary function into such a series and assigning the values of the coefficients. . . . the geometers only admit that which they can't dispute.[27]

---

[24] This is Daniel, son of the aforementioned Johann. Euler, by the way, was a student of Johann's. For this anomaly, in addition to Youschkevitch (1976) and Bottazzini (1986), I am indebted also to Hawkins (1970), chs. 1 and 2.

[25] See Truesdell (1960), 261, 277–8, 281–2, 284–5, 297–9.

[26] Quoted by Bottazzini (1986), 72, as translated by Grattan-Guinness.

[27] Quoted ibid. 77, as translated by Grattan-Guinness.

If Fourier is right in his claims, Definabilism could be creditably revived in a form that identifies a function with its Fourier expansion. Given the flexibility of Fourier series, this version may not be subject to the worries that trouble d'Alembert's version.

The situation was clarified by Dirichlet in 1829, when he proved that there is a Fourier series representation for any function with finitely many maxima, minima, and discontinuities (in Cauchy's sense), as long as the behaviour at the discontinuities meets a simple condition. This class of functions includes everything Euler seems to have had in mind, everything involved in the vibrating string and other applications. The terminological confusion of the time precluded a precise restatement of Definabilism in this relaxed and improved form, but the maxim could be regarded as implicitly revived.

But its undisputed status didn't last long; the new detractor was Riemann. In the fall of 1852, Riemann met often with Dirichlet; in 1854, he begins his study with a historical analysis of the situation from d'Alembert to Dirichlet; it concludes:

In fact, [the problem] was completely solved for all cases which present themselves in nature alone, because however great may be our ignorance about how the forces and states of matter vary in space and time in the infinitely small, we can certainly assume that the functions to which Dirichlet's research did not extend do not occur in nature.[28]

This might sound like the end of the story, but Riemann continues:

Nevertheless, those cases that were unresolved by Dirichlet seem worthy of attention for two reasons . . .

The first is that, as Dirichlet himself remarked at the end of his paper, this subject stands in the closest relationship to the principles of the infinitesimal calculus and can serve to bring these principles into greater clarity and certainty. In this connection its treatment has an immediate interest.

But the second reason is that the applicability of Fourier series is not restricted to physical researches; it is now also being applied successfully to one area of pure mathematics, number theory. And just those functions whose representability by a trigonometric series Dirichlet did not explore seem here to be important.

The anomaly for d'Alembert's Definabilism came from physical mechanics, but Riemann is granting that the new Definabilism will not be

---

[28] This quotation and that following are as quoted and translated in Bottazzini (1986), 242.

troubled from that quarter. Rather, his worries are drawn from mathematics itself: functions beyond those authorized by Dirichlet's theorem are needed to settle the foundations of the calculus, and may also be needed in applications of analysis to number theory. This second anomaly for Definabilism is purely mathematical.

Now it is clear that Riemann had a modern notion of function. Even Bottazzini, who also sees the general definition in both Euler and Dirichlet, writes:

> But if for Dirichlet, as had also been the case for Euler, the generality of the definition did not go along with a consistent practice in the study of equally 'general' functions, the opposite is true for Riemann. In his [paper] of 1854 . . . he revealed to the mathematical world a universe extraordinarily rich in 'pathological' functions. (Bottazzini (1986), 217)

Indeed, Riemann describes a range of unusual functions, including many that cannot be represented by Fourier series. And, as he maintained, such functions did play a central role in the eventual founding of the calculus.[29] But the fact remains that he did describe these functions, which leaves the door open to yet another version of Definabilism—a version expanded to allow the various means of definition used by Riemann—and he obviously did not provide a problem case for *this* form of Definabilism.

Nevertheless, Riemann's new approach did encourage a very broad understanding of the nature of functions, an understanding that undermines the spirit of Definabilism. Hawkins describes the situation this way:

> Riemann's memoir passed on to his successors the viewpoint that a function of a real variable is to be regarded as any correspondence $x \rightarrow f(x)$ between real numbers; a function need not possess the properties (e.g., continuity and integrability) usually ascribed to the more familiar examples of functions occurring in analysis, even though, as in his examples, the functions may be represented by an analytical expression. . . . functions as conceived by [Riemann] do not possess general properties. (Hawkins (1970), 29)

Thus, Darboux, in his study of 'the principles on which the integral calculus rests', constructed various unusual functions and employed a new level of rigour because 'Many points, which could rightfully be regarded as evident or which could be conceded in the applications of science to

---

[29] See Hawkins (1970), ch. 2.

the usual functions, must be submitted to a rigorous examination in the statement of propositions relative to more general functions'.[30] In his foundational work, Du Bois-Reymond called these latter 'assumption-less' functions. This move away from old ideas about functions, away from the assumption that they 'possess general properties', gave mathematicians less reason that ever to expect all functions to be definable in any given way, in other words, less reason than ever to suppose any version of Definabilism to be acceptable.

In any case, subsequent development of the function concept led to the classificatory work of Baire, Borel, and Lebesgue mentioned earlier (in I. 4).[31] At this point, around the turn of the twentieth century, set theoretic methods began to infiltrate the study of functions, and Baire begins work, in 1899, with the modern notion of an arbitrary correspondence. Concerned to tame the confusion of discontinuous functions, he constructs the following hierarchy: Baire class 0 consists of continuous functions; Baire class 1 consists of pointwise limits of sequences of Baire class 0 functions; in general, Baire class $\alpha + 1$ functions are pointwise limits of sequences of Baire class α functions.[32] He goes on to argue, on the basis of a cardinality argument, that this hierarchy does not exhaust the discontinuous functions: Cantor has shown that there are more that $2^{\aleph_0}$ functions from reals to reals,[33] but Baire shows that there are only $2^{\aleph_0}$ functions in each of the $\aleph_1$ Baire classes, and hence, only $2^{\aleph_0}$ Baire functions in all.

In 1905, Lebesgue continued this work, directly addressing the question of the definability of these functions. He writes:

Although, since Dirichlet and Riemann, it is generally agreed that there is a function when there is a correspondence . . . without concern for the procedure that serves to establish this correspondence, many mathematicians seem to consider only those established by analytic correspondences as true functions. One might think that this introduces an arbitrary restriction . . . It isn't clear that there are functions that aren't analytically representable; there is thus room to ask if there are such functions.[34]

---

[30] These remarks of Darboux's are as quoted and translated ibid. 27.

[31] My main sources for this discussion are Monna (1972) and Moore (1982).

[32] A function f is the pointwise limit of the sequence $g_0, g_1, g_2, \ldots$ iff for any real $r, f(r)$ is the limit of $g_0(r), g_1(r), g_2(r), \ldots$ (All functions under consideration are from reals to reals.)

[33] Because there are as many functions from reals to reals as there are subsets of $\mathbb{R}$, and by Cantor's Theorem, the cardinality of $\wp(\mathbb{R})$ is greater than the cardinality of $\mathbb{R}$, that is, $2^{\aleph_0}$.

[34] As quoted in Monna (1972), 71, translation mine.

In pursuit of this question, Lebesgue counts a function as analytically representable if and only if it can be expressed using countably many sums, products, variables, constants, and limits, and he shows that a function is analytically representable in this sense if and only if it is in some Baire class. Then, following Baire, he uses a cardinality argument to establish the existence of a non-Baire, and hence, non-analytically representable function.

As it happens, both Baire and Lebesgue were troubled by this cardinality argument, which purports to demonstrate the existence of a non-Baire or non-analytically representable function without defining or specifying it in any way. In a letter of 1898, Baire describes how a non-Baire function can be obtained from a certain partition of the reals,[35] then continues:

> I have not succeeded in *defining* such a partition. Clearly it is a delicate matter not just to answer, but even to pose, such a question. The meaning of the phrase 'to define a set' would have to be made more precise. Yet I am convinced that the act of imposing on a set the condition of being definable must considerably restrict the notion of set. . . . May we not hope to learn how far we are permitted to use the notion of *arbitrary function?*[36]

Lebesgue was similarly ambivalent; he hoped to find some way of defining the non-analytically representable function.

In the aftermath of Zermelo's 1904 proof of the Well-Ordering Theorem, it gradually became clear that Baire's and Lebesgue's discomfort had an identifiable source: their proofs depend in subtle ways on the Axiom of Choice, which asserts the existence of an otherwise unspecified choice set. So, for example, Baire implicitly used the axiom in his proof that there are only $2^{\aleph_0}$ Baire functions—it is needed to show that the union of $\aleph_1$ sets of size $2^{\aleph_0}$ has size $2^{\aleph_0}$—and Lebesgue relied on it in his proof that the analytically representable functions are precisely the Baire functions. In fact, little of the combined theory of real functions developed by Baire, Borel, and Lebesgue would survive without the axiom.[37]

---

[35] Notice, once again, that a question about functions is converted into a question about sets of reals. Cf. I. 4.

[36] As quoted and translated in Moore (1982), 68.

[37] See Moore (1982), §§ 1. 7 and 2. 3. It eventually became clear that this work, along with the rest of descriptive set theory, can be carried out in ZF with a weaker version of choice, the Axiom of Dependent Choices (DC). (DC says: if for every $x \in A$, there is a $y \in A$, such that $x R y$, then there is a sequence $a_0, a_1, a_2, \ldots$ of elements of A such that for every $n \in \omega$, $a_n R a_{n+1}$.)

But despite their unconscious dependence on the axiom, Baire, Borel, and Lebesgue were among its most severe critics. In 1905, in a well-known exchange of letters with Hadamard, the French analysts explain their opposition to Choice in language that returns Definabilism to centre stage. For example, Lebesgue, having overcome his earlier indecision, writes: 'The question comes down to this, which is hardly new: *Can we prove the existence of a mathematical object without defining it?* . . . I believe we can only build solidly *by granting that it is impossible to demonstrate the existence of an object without defining it*' (Baire *et al.* (1905), 314). Embracing this version of Definabilism meant rejecting the Axiom of Choice and its consequences.

Like Zermelo, Hadamard takes the opposing view, answering Lebesgue's question 'in the affirmative' (ibid. 317) and rejecting this new incarnation of Definabilism. In support of this position, Hadamard argues:

I believe that in essence the debate is the same as the one which arose between Riemann and his predecessors over the notion of function. The *rule* that Lebesgue demands [for defining the choice set] appears to me to resemble closely the analytic expression on which Riemann's adversaries insisted so strongly. (Ibid. 318)

He elaborates in a footnote:

I believe it necessary to reiterate this point, which, if I were to express myself fully, appears to form the essence of the debate. From the invention of the infinitesimal calculus to the present, it seems to me, the essential progress in mathematics has resulted from successively annexing notions which, for the Greeks or the Renaissance geometers or the predecessors of Riemann, were 'outside mathematics' because it was impossible to describe them. (Ibid.)

As we've just seen, Hadamard could have included d'Alembert in his list. He is arguing that Definabilism has been a bad methodological maxim in the past, threatening to curtail 'essential progress', and that the case of the Axiom of Choice is no different: for the good of mathematics, Definabilism should be rejected.[38]

Hadamard's opponents, fine mathematicians all, are not immune to this style of argument. For example, Borel writes: 'The results obtained, as far back as the end of the 19th century, have shown superabundantly

---

[38] The argument of this section against $V = L$ was inspired by these remarks of Hadamard.

how simplistic it is to suppose it will be possible to limit the field of Mathematics to one determinate category of functions.'[39] And Moore describes a paper of Lebesgue's from this period, not published till years later, in which he worries that 'in the past those who wished to extend the concept of function [have] always been in the right'.[40] So the supporters of Definabilism realize they are up against another in a series of anomalies for the position. But they are not ready to give it up.

It should be noted that Definabilism arose also in another form in the debate over Zermelo's proof. Poincaré, the central figure here, did not object to the Axiom of Choice (which he regarded as synthetic a priori). He did, nevertheless, reject Zermelo's argument for the Well-Ordering Theorem, on the grounds that it makes use of an impredicative definition.[41] Thus, Poincaré's objection is based on an even stronger version of Definabilism: 'Never consider any objects but those capable of being defined in a finite number of words . . . Avoid non-predicative classifications and definitions' (Poincaré (1909), 63). Zermelo defends the use of impredicative definitions on the grounds that 'proofs that have this logical form are by no means confined to set theory; exactly the same kind can be found in analysis wherever the maximum or the minimum of a previously defined "completed" set of numbers Z is used for further inferences' (Zermelo (1908a), 190–1). Poincaré rejected Zermelo's particular example—a proof of Cauchy's—but as we've seen (in I. 2), subsequent efforts on the part of Russell and Whitehead to found classical mathematics without impredicative definitions did eventually fail. In Gödel's words, Russell and Whitehead's system 'makes impredicative definitions impossible and thereby destroys the derivation of mathematics from logic, effected by Dedekind and Frege, and a good deal of modern mathematics itself' (Gödel (1944), 127). Gödel concludes: 'I would consider this rather as a proof that the vicious circle principle [which rules out impredicative definitions] is false than that classical mathematics is false' (ibid.). In the spirit of Zermelo, but with more information, Gödel rejects this stronger version of Definabilism.

In sum, then, we've seen Definabilism in various forms challenged by a series of anomalies, and in each case, the subsequent practice of mathematics has borne out the fruitfulness of siding with its opponents. Each

---

[39] As quoted in Monna (1972), 74–5, translation mine.

[40] This is Moore's paraphrase of Lebesgue on p. 100 of Moore (1982).

[41] Recall (from I. 2) that an impredicative definition of x defines x in terms of a collection to which x itself belongs.

rejection can, admittedly, be seen as grounds for modifying, rather than rejecting, Definabilism, though this course must naturally seem more threadbare in each succeeding case, especially in the case of the Axiom of Choice, where nothing even resembling a definition was in evidence. The analogy with Mechanism, faced with the ether, is striking. And the analogy can be extended, because there was also a rising alternative maxim: Combinatorialism.

Perhaps the first, and certainly a most compelling statement of Combinatorialism comes in a 1934 lecture of Bernays.[42] Though 'the mathematical sciences are growing in complete security and harmony', Bernays worries 'that objections have been raised . . . [to] certain ways of reasoning peculiar to analysis and set theory. These modes of reasoning were first systematically applied in giving a rigorous form to the methods of the calculus' (Bernays (1934), 258). The use of impredicative definitions and the Axiom of Choice are among the methods Bernays has in mind. His defence begins with a description of Combinatorialism:

[Modern] analysis . . . abstracts from the possibility of giving definitions of sets, sequences, and functions. These notion are used in a 'quasi-combinatorial' sense, by which I mean: in the sense of an analogy of the infinite to the finite.

Consider, for example, the different functions which assign to each member of the finite series 1, 2, . . ., n a number of the same series. There are nn functions of this sort, and each of them is obtained by n independent determinations. Passing to the infinite case, we imagine functions engendered by an infinity of independent determinations which assign to each integer an integer, and we reason about the totality of these functions.

In the same way, one views a set of integers as the result of infinitely many independent acts deciding for each number whether it should be included or excluded. We add to this the idea of the totality of these sets. Sequences of real numbers and sets of real numbers are envisaged in an analogous manner. (Ibid. 259–60)

So, according to Combinatorialism, there is one function from reals to reals for every way of making $2^{\aleph_0}$ independent assignments of a real to a real. These assignments are taken to exist, on analogy with the permutations of 1, 2, . . ., n, regardless of whether or not we have a rule to describe them.

---

[42] My terminology is not quite that of Bernays. He describes a metaphysical view he calls 'platonism' and a set of methodological attitudes which he calls 'quasicombinatorial', and holds that the later are inspired by the former. I use 'Combinatorialism' for the quasi-combinatorial aspect of his thinking; the link with philosophical views like platonism (more or less a synonym for 'mathematical realism') is explored in III. 4.

Combinatorialism stands in explicit opposition to Definabilism when it 'abstracts from the possibility of giving definitions'. In addition, 'The axiom of choice is an immediate application of the [combinatorial] concepts in question' (ibid. 260). A set is constituted by (perhaps infinitely many) independent determinations, so the choice set for a family of disjoint, non-empty sets is constituted by independent determinations selecting one element from each of those non-empty sets. Furthermore, 'A similar case is that of Poincaré's impredicative definitions' (ibid.). As definitions are not required, it follows that specifically predicative definitions are not required. Bernays continues:

> In Cantor's theories, [combinatorial] conceptions extend far beyond those of the theory of real numbers. This is done by iterating the use of the [combinatorial] concept of a function and adding methods of collection. This is the well-known method of set theory . . . The [combinatorial] conceptions of analysis and set theory have also been applied in modern theories of algebra and topology, where they have proved very fertile. (Ibid.)

Finally, he concludes that the use of these methods 'is so widespread that it is not an exaggeration to say that [Combinatorialism] reigns today in mathematics' (ibid. 261). This is at least as true now as it was in 1934.

Historically, then, we see that Definabilism has gone the way of Mechanism, and by a similar route. There was a series of challenging anomalies: Euler's initial conditions and solutions to the wave equation; Riemann's pathologies; Zermelo's choice sets and impredicative definitions. Repeatedly, Definabilism resisted outright refutation by generalizing the allowable means of expression, but these very shifts subtly discouraged the expectation that a stable version of the maxim could be found. But here, as with Mechanism, anomalies and discouragement were not enough to defeat an entrenched methodological maxim. In both cases, this was finally accomplished by the widespread success of a rival maxim. Thus Combinatorialism deposed Definabilism, much as the Field Conception replaced Mechanism.

(iii) Now recall that the construction of L proceeds by adding, at stage $\alpha + 1$, any subset of L_α that can be given by a formula whose quantifiers range over and whose parameters are drawn from L_α, that is, any predicatively definable subset of L_α. The connection between $V = L$ and Definabilism is obvious: the Axiom of Constructibility states that sets are definable in a uniform, indeed, in a predicative, way. In contemporary mathematics, the assumption that $V = L$ appears as a throw-back to an especially strong form[43] of a now-discredited methodological maxim. The well-entrenched successor to the discredited maxim gives no support to the axiom, and history supports the expectation that it would limit the development of mathematics. Under these circumstances, the deep and widespread resistance to adding $V = L$ as a new axiom seems perfectly rational.

The pre-1960s Combinatorialist admits that $V = L$ is flexible enough to handle all the anomalies for previous versions of Definabilism, that it is consistent to assume that all the combinatorially-determined sets will turn up at some stage in the construction of L, but the history of the situation makes her quite properly suspect that new anomalies will arise, that adopting $V = L$ would limit fruitful inquiries. I propose this line of thought as one plausible reconstruction of the case against $V = L$ that lies behind the familiar objection that it is 'restrictive'.

---

[43] Notice that, from the predicativist's point of view, $V = L$ is an axiom divided against itself: the formulas used to define sets at each stage are predicative, but the ordinals that index those stages need not be.

5

Hints of Trouble

In fact, I think this argument has considerable merits (see III. 5. i), but even at that, it is too weak to do justice to the current state of mind concerning $V = L$. Most set theorists today would agree that the axiom is dubious or suspicious, but they would go on to say more: they would reject it outright. An argument that it would be unwise to adopt an axiom just now is not, by itself, an argument for rejecting it once and for all. To mine the full content of the idea that $V = L$ is restrictive, we must take into account that it is inconsistent with the existence of various non-constructible sets, beginning with $0^{\#}$.

To see the role this plays, consider the status of another hypothesis: $V = $ HOD.[1] Call a set x *ordinal definable* if x is definable from a finite collection of ordinals (that is, for some formula ϕ and some ordinals α_0, $\alpha_1, \ldots, \alpha_n$, x is the unique set such that $\phi(x, \alpha_0, \alpha_1, \ldots, \alpha_n)$). A set x is *hereditarily ordinal definable* if its members, the members of its members, and so on, are all ordinal definable.[2] Finally, HOD is the collection of all hereditarily ordinal definable sets. The main difference between HOD and L is that HOD's definitions are not required to be predicative. Like $V = L$, $V = $ HOD is relatively consistent—if ZF + $V = $ HOD implies a contradiction, then so does ZF all by itself—so it would be a safe new axiom.

Now HOD lacks the simplicity and clarity of L, and $V = $ HOD settles fewer questions than $V = L$, both of which make $V = $ HOD in some respects a less attractive axiom candidate. Nevertheless, when it comes to judging which hypothesis might form part of an acceptable theory of sets, $V = L$ is widely rejected, while $V = $ HOD is considered a possibility. As both have a prima facie connection with Definabilism, we need an explanation of this difference.

I think (at least) two quite reasonable factors account for the current

---

[1] I am grateful to Steel for calling attention to HOD in this connection.
[2] That is, every set in x's transitive closure is ordinal definable. See Enderton (1972), 178, for a proper definition of transitive closure.

state of opinion, one that harmonizes well with the present case against $V = L$, and one that points beyond it.[3] The first is simply that the definitions in HOD need not be predicative, which severs $V = $ HOD's connection with the strongest form of Definabilism; from the point of view we've been considering, this difference alone would warrant a less suspicious attitude towards $V = $ HOD. The second is that—so far at least—everything set theorists have come up with is consistent with $V = $ HOD; for example, if ZFC + MC is consistent, then so is ZFC + MC + $V = $ HOD (McAloon (1966)). The fact that $V = L$, but not $V = $ HOD, has actually been shown to be limitative, must go a long way towards accounting for the difference in attitude.

So the full story of the rejection of $V = L$ requires that we take account of such non-constructible items as $0^{\#}$. What follows is perhaps more autobiographical than philosophical, but when I undertook this extension of the argument, I found myself led to worries, even doubts, about my underlying realism. To begin with, among the various justifications proposed for $0^{\#}$ and the rest, the most compelling seem to rest on maximizing principles[4] of a sort quite unlike anything that turns up in the practice of natural science: crudely, the scientist posits only those entities without which she cannot account for our observations, while the set theorist posits as many entities as she can, short of inconsistency. In fact, this very contrast seems to lie behind the poor fit between pure Quinean indispensability and set theoretic practice: Quine counsels us to economize, like good natural scientists, and thus to prefer $V = L$, while actual set theorists reject $V = L$ for its miserliness. This raises questions about the viability of the science/mathematics analogy.

To see the point, or a closely related point, from another angle, suppose a set theorist argues, 'ZFC + MC is preferable to ZFC + $V = L$ because . . .', and then proceeds to list various mathematical attractions of the former theory. From the realist's point of view, it would seem fully rational to respond, 'Yes, I agree with you that ZFC + MC is a very nice theory, but if all sets are constructible, this theory is false, despite its niceness.' From this point of view, the set theorist owes evidence, not that the theory has many virtues, but that it is actually true in the real world of

---

[3] It's also worth noting that $V = $ HOD has none of the inner tensions of $V = L$; it allows impredicativity in its ordinals as well as its defining formulas. In so far as we prefer an axiom candidate with a coherent perspective, we should prefer $V = $ HOD to $V = L$. I don't try to assess this factor here.

[4] I attempt to spell this out in III. 5 and III. 6.

sets. (Recall Einstein and Infeld's dismay that light waves must be trans-versal rather than longitudinal; when we attempt to describe something objective, what we like isn't necessarily what's true.) Yet—and here's the problem—this reply to the set theorist's argument for ZFC + MC seemed to me out of place, out of step with the actual practice of set theory.

Now it must be granted, even in natural science, that some among the various reasons we have for preferring theory T to theory T' may not be fully truth-tracking; for example, we may, all things being equal, prefer a theory whose calculations are easier, though we think this feature has more to do with our cognitive abilities than with the truth. We might try to retain our mathematical realism by assimilating the set theorist's arguments for $0^{\#}$ to reasons of this sort. But I think this approach distorts the situation to an unacceptable degree: the reasons our set theorist gives don't seem to be matters of which theory we happen to find convenient or simple or whatever; rather, they seem to be tracking mathematically important features. It's just that this 'tracking' apparently doesn't oper-ate as it does in natural science.

All this is obviously too vague and imprecise to constitute any serious objection to realism, but these considerations (along with worries associ-ated with the role of continuum mathematics in science)[5] did seem to me cause for concern.[6] Assuming the worst—that set theoretic realism is a not viable account of set theory—then something must be wrong with the reasoning offered in its favour. And this thought leads inevitably to a re-examination of the indispensability arguments.

---

[5] See the material surveyed in II. 6. ii and II. 6. iv.

[6] I'm not the only one. For example, Kitcher writes: 'Can we assume that invoking en-tities that satisfy constraints we favor is a legitimate strategy of recognizing hitherto ne-glected objects that exist independently of us? From a realist perspective, the method of postulating what we want has (in Bertrand Russell's famous phrase) "the advantages of theft over honest toil". If that method is, as Richard Dedekind supposed, part of the honest trade of mathematics, is something wrong with the realist perspective?' ((1989), 564).

6

Indispensability and Scientific Practice

The argument, as we've seen (in II. 2), goes like this. Our best scientific theory of the world makes indispensable use of mathematical things: the temperature of a gas as a function of time, acceleration as a second derivative, Maxwell's equations. (This is taken as an unvarnished fact.) To draw a testable consequence from our theory requires the use of various far-flung parts of that theory, including much mathematics, so the confirmation resulting from a successful test adheres not to individual statements but to large bodies of theory. (This is holism.) Finally, our theory is committed to those things that it says 'there are'. (This is Quine's criterion of ontological commitment.) It follows that our theory, and we who adopt it, are committed to the existence of mathematical things.

To get a feel for the picture of natural science at work here, consider the case of molecular theory. Quine writes:

According to physics my desk is, for all its seeming fixity and solidity, a swarm of vibrating molecules. The desk as we sense it is comparable to a distant haystack in which we cannot distinguish the individual stalks . . . Comparable, but with a difference. By approaching the haystack we can distinguish the stalks . . . On the other hand no glimpse is to be had of the separate molecules of the desk; they are, we are told, too small. (Quine (1955b), 246)

What, then, convinces the physicist that this far-fetched theory is true? According to Quine, molecular theory is supported by 'a convergence of indirect evidence' (ibid.), which he divides into five categories:

One is simplicity: empirical laws concerning seemingly dissimilar phenomena are integrated into a compact and unitary theory. Another is familiarity of principle: the already familiar laws of motion are made to serve where independent laws would otherwise have been needed. A third is scope: the resulting unitary theory implies a wider array of testable consequences than any likely accumulation of separate laws would have implied. A fourth is fecundity: successful further extensions of theory are expedited. The fifth goes without saying: such testable consequences of the theory as have been tested have turned out well, aside from such sparse exceptions as may in good conscience be chalked up to unexplained interferences. (Ibid. 247)

These are the virtues we look for in our scientific theories, though we are sometimes willing to trade off losses in one area against gains in another. Quine considers the worry that the possession of theoretical virtues, though welcome for many reasons, may not be an indicator of truth: perhaps 'the benefits conferred by the molecular doctrine give the physicist good reason to prize it, but afford no evidence of its truth' (ibid. 248); 'The tendency of [these] reflections [is] . . . to belittle molecules and their ilk, leaving common-sense bodies supreme' (ibid. 250). But Quine will have nothing of this way of thinking: 'this invidious contrast is unwarranted. What are given in sensation are variformed and varicolored visual patches, varitextured and varitemperatured tactual feels, and an assortment of tones, tastes, smells and other odds and ends; desks are no more to be found among these data than molecules' (ibid.). This should not be taken as an attack on ordinary objects. Rather,

Having noted that man has no evidence for the existence of bodies beyond the fact that their assumption helps him organize experience, we should have done well, instead of disclaiming evidence for the existence of bodies, to conclude: such, then, at bottom, is what evidence is, both for ordinary bodies and for molecules. . . . the benefits of the molecular doctrine which so impressed us . . ., and the manifest benefits of the aboriginal posit of ordinary bodies, are the best evidence of reality we can ask. (Ibid. 251)

Thus scientific positing is a mere extension of common-sense positing, and mathematical positing a mere extension of scientific:

A platonistic ontology [of sets] . . . is, from the point of view of a strictly physicalistic conceptual scheme, as much a myth as that physicalistic conceptual scheme itself is for phenomenalism. This higher myth is a good and useful one, in turn, in so far as it simplifies our account of physics. Since mathematics is an integral part of this higher myth, the utility of this myth for physical science is evident enough. (Quine (1948), 18)

In his debate with Carnap, we found Quine asserting the continuity of ontology with natural science; here we find him, on the other end of the scale, asserting the continuity of natural science with common sense.[1]

So the Quinean picture of natural science, the picture that underlies the indispensability argument, depends on a number of theses, from holism to the criterion of ontological commitment to a particular account of the theoretical virtues and scientific confirmation. To test this picture

---

[1] Duhem, though the source of Quinean holism, agrees with neither of these instances of Quinean gradualism. See my (199?a).

against the realities of scientific practice, I propose to consider in some detail the actual history of the case Quine raises: molecular (or atomic) theory.[2] I treat this story in (i), then turn to the scientific role of mathematics in (ii). Finally, (iii) and (iv) contain some general conclusions about indispensability and the practice of natural science.

(i) Though the notion that matter is composed of tiny particles goes back to the Greeks, the beginning for the modern atomic hypothesis was Dalton's experimental work in the first decade of the nineteenth century. During this period, Proust experimentally verified the Law of Definite Proportions—the proportions in which two substances combine do not vary continuously—and Dalton added the Law of Multiple Proportions—the definite proportions in which substances combine come in simple integral multiples.[3] Dalton hypothesized that a sample of an elementary substance is actually made up of many tiny identical atoms, that these remain unchanged through chemical reactions, and that a sample of a compound is made of many identical molecules, each composed of an identical combination of atoms from constituent substances. This simple atomic hypothesis explains both laws of proportion.

In the same decade, Gay-Lussac discovered the Law of Combining Volumes: at a given temperature and pressure, the volumes of gases A and B that combine to form a given compound are in simple integral proportions.[4] In 1811, Avogadro theorized that the equal volumes of gas (under similar conditions) contain equal numbers of Dalton's atoms, and that many elementary gases consist of diatomic molecules. This embellishment of atomic theory explains not only the Law of Combining Volumes, but also Boyle's Law of 1662—pressure varies inversely with volume—and Charles's Law—gases expand equally when heated equally.

During the 1820s, various scientists realized that compounds with different chemical properties sometimes analyse into the same elements in the same proportions. An atomic explanation for this 'isomerism', as it is now called, soon followed: the same atoms can combine in different spatial relationships, and those spatial relationships influence the

---

[2] The important structural features of this case were first brought to my attention by Miller (1987), 470–82. My account here is also based on more detailed historical sources: Glymour (1980), Ihde (1964), Nye (1972), and the classic Perrin (1913).

[3] e.g. three grams of carbon combine with four grams of oxygen or with eight grams of oxygen, but no amount in between. And eight is twice four.

[4] e.g. two volumes of hydrogen combine with one volume of oxygen to form two volumes of water.

molecule's chemical behaviour. In the 1830s, Dumas noticed that a compound losing hydrogen while gaining chlorine did so in equal volumes, which led to his Law of Substitution; the notion that the substitution takes place atom-for-atom could scarcely be avoided. Several decades of clues finally came together in the early 1850s, when Frankland added the concept of valence to the developing picture.

Despite this impressive string of successes, atomic theory during the first half of the nineteenth century was plagued by one very serious difficulty: the problem of determining atomic weights. Dalton had chosen hydrogen as his basis and calculated the relative weight of oxygen by measuring the amount of oxygen that combines with a given amount of hydrogen to form water. Obviously, no conclusion can be drawn from these measurements unless the chemical formula for water is already known. Dalton overcame this obstacle by assuming that the most common compound of two elements has a binary molecule, and thus, that water is HO. This simple error points up the problem: atomic weights can be calculated from combining weights and molecular formulas, and molecular formulas can be calculated from combining weights and atomic weights, but the early nineteenth century chemists knew only the combining weights.

Soon after Dalton, Berzelius devised his own table of atomic weights, based on different hypotheses and differing also in the assigned values. By 1820, two new methods were added to this early guesswork: Mitscherlich's Law of Isomorphism—similar crystalline structures result from the same number of atoms in the same arrangement—and Petit and Dulong's Law—the product of the specific heat and the atomic weight is a constant. Petit and Dulong produced another table of atomic weights that differed from those of Berzelius and Dalton. And in 1826, Dumas announced yet another method, based on his measurements of vapour densities, which led to still different results.

The conflicts between the values produced by these various methods led Dumas to conclude that atomic theory should be banished from chemistry. Though he apparently believed in atoms, Dumas came to reject the many hypotheses of atomic theory and to abandon hope that they might produce a table of atomic weights confirmable by independent empirical tests. His dramatic statement reads: 'If I were master, I would erase the word "atom" from science, persuaded that it goes beyond experience; and never in chemistry ought we to go beyond experience.'[5]

---

[5] As quoted and translated in Glymour (1980), 257.

Despite Dumas's stature, this admonition went unheeded. Compounds continued to be analysed, molecular formulas proposed, and atomic weights conjectured.

Finally, in 1858, Cannizzaro did what Dumas had neglected to do: he distinguished carefully between molecule and atom.[6] With this simple clarification, a steadfast reinstatement of Avogadro's hypothesis, and the assumption that the smallest quantity of an element occurring in a molecule of a compound is its atomic weight, Cannizzaro was able to calculate a consistent table of atomic weights using vapour densities. He then compared these results to those achieved via specific heats, with admirable success, thus bringing order to atomic theory after decades of confusion.

Two years later, in 1860, around 140 of the world's most respected chemists convened in Karlsruhe to assess the status of the atomic theory. Cannizzaro presented his results, and reprints of his 1858 paper were distributed. Meyer describes his reaction:

The scales seemed to fall from my eyes. Doubts disappeared and a feeling of quiet certainty took their place. If some years later I was myself able to contribute something toward clearing the situation and calming heated spirits no small part of the credit is due to this pamphlet of Cannizzaro. Like me it must have affected many others who attended the convention. The big waves of controversy began to subside, and more and more the old atomic weights of Berzelius came to their own. As soon as the apparent discrepancies between Avogadro's rule and that of Dulong and Petit had been removed by Cannizzaro both were found capable of practically universal application, and so the foundation was laid for determining the valence of the elements, without which the theory of atomic linking could certainly never have been developed.[7]

Meyer's own contribution began with his influential *Die modernen Theorien der Chemie* of 1864, which contains one of the first hints of the periodic table. In the words of one historian, the solution of the problem of atomic weights brought 'the atom into general acceptance as the fundamental unit of chemistry' (Ihde (1964), 257).

Around this same time, with the rise of the kinetic theory of heat, the influence of atomic thought spread into physics. In the hands of such thinkers as Maxwell and Boltzmann, the kinetic theory flowered, providing, among other things, the first calculations of absolute molecular magnitudes. Perrin's summary gives the flavour of these results:

---

[6] Gaudin had suggested this move back in 1826, but Glymour ((1980), 254) speculates that Dumas overlooked the idea out of distaste for theory.

[7] As quoted and translated in Ihde (1964), 229.

each molecule of air we breathe is moving with the velocity of a rifle bullet; travels in a straight line between two impacts for a distance of nearly one ten-thousandth of a millimetre; is deflected from its course [five billion] times per second . . . There are thirty [billion billion] molecules in a cubic centimetre of air, under normal conditions. Three thousand million of them placed side by side in a straight line would be required to make up one millimetre. Twenty thousand million must be gathered together to make up one thousand-millionth of a milligramme. (Perrin (1913), 82)

By 1900, the atomic theory enjoyed all five theoretical virtues in abundance; its power and usefulness become more obvious with each experimental and conceptual advance.

At this point, history deals a blow to our theory of confirmation: despite the virtues of atomic theory, scientists did not agree on the reality of atoms. So, for example, in an influential textbook of 1904, the chemist Ostwald writes: 'the atomic hypothesis has proved to be an exceedingly useful aid to instruction and investigation . . . One must not, however, be led astray by this agreement between picture and reality and combine the two.'[8] A number of sociological influences can be identified here—from the rise of social and political 'idealism'[9] to Maxwell's success in eliminating the mechanical models he had used to generate his equations—but a good portion of the scepticism was based on considerations even the supporters of atoms considered reasonable. Thus, Perrin writes of his contemporary opponents: 'the sceptical position . . . was for a long time legitimate and no doubt useful' (Perrin (1913), 216). Clearly, this community evaluation of atomic theory involved more than the five theoretical virtues.

A clue to the other factors at work comes from Berthelot; at the 1877 meeting of the French Academy, he posed the rhetorical question, 'who has ever seen a gas molecule or an atom?'[10] Later, Mach was noted for similar remarks.[11] Apart from their concern about various details of atomic theory—for example, the conception of atoms as without parts—these sceptics were fundamentally opposed to positing entities inaccessible to direct experimental testing. And this was how their opponents understood them; speaking of the early sceptics, Perrin writes: 'It appeared to them more dangerous than useful to employ a hypothesis deemed incapable of verification' (Perrin (1913), 15). The virtue closest to what's being asked for is the fifth—agreement with experiment—but

---

[8] As quoted in Miller (1987), 472.   [9] See Nye (1972), 30.
[10] As quoted ibid. 7.   [11] See Bernstein (1983/4) for discussion.

the atomic theory had plenty of that. What it didn't have was some stronger sort of experimental success, something more 'direct', something that more conclusively 'verifies'. The community, as a whole, recognized the need for something beyond the five virtues, something worthy of the phrases 'experimental verification' and 'direct test'. The resolution of this impasse came soon after the comment quoted above from Ostwald's 1904 textbook. Describing the work that led to one of his remarkable series of papers in 1905, Einstein writes:

Not acquainted with earlier investigations of Boltzmann and Gibbs, which had appeared earlier and actually exhausted the subject, I developed the statistical mechanics and the molecular-kinetic theory of thermodynamics which was based on the former. *My major aim in this was to find facts which would guarantee as much as possible the existence of atoms of definite finite size.* (Einstein (1949a), 47, emphasis added)

In his pursuit of a 'guarantee' of the existence of atoms, Einstein makes a series of calculations and concludes that

according to the molecular-kinetic theory of heat, bodies of microscopically-visible size suspended in a liquid will perform movements of such magnitude that they can be easily observed in a microscope . . . If the movement discussed here can actually be observed . . . an exact determination of actual atomic dimension is then possible. On the other hand, [should] the prediction of this movement [prove] to be incorrect, a weighty argument would be provided against the molecular-kinetic conception of heat. (Einstein (1905), 1–2)[12]

He acknowledges that the movement involved in this crucial test might be the so-called Brownian movement, but confesses 'the information available to me regarding the latter is so lacking in precision, that I can form no judgement in the matter' (ibid.).

Meanwhile, thinkers more familiar with Brownian motion were convinced of its relevance. In a series of papers appearing between 1888 and 1895, Gouy argued that Brownian motion was caused by molecular movements and that it offered a potential confirmation of the kinetic theory of heat. In a letter written some years later, he remarks: 'From the historical point of view, one wonders today how the great founders of kinetic theory . . . have not been able to see that Brownian movement

---

[12] In the final sentence, I have substituted 'should' for 'had' and 'prove' for 'proved', so that the forward-looking final clause will match the rest of the sentence. (For the German, see Nye (1972), 139.) When this passage was written, the prediction had not yet been tested, and Einstein's later correspondence with Perrin suggests that Perrin's experiments displayed a level of precision Einstein had not thought possible (see Nye (1972), 147).

places under the eyes the realisation of all their hypotheses!'[13] The phrase 'under the eyes' is especially conspicuous when compared with Ostwald's complaint, published in the same year as Gouy's last paper, against the atomists's practice of 'disturbing us with forces, the existence of which we cannot demonstrate, acting between atoms which we cannot see'.[14]

At an international Congress in 1904, Poincaré, another opponent of atomic theory, commented on the potential significance of Gouy's work: 'If this be so, we no longer have need of the infinitely subtle eye of Maxwell's demon; our microscope suffices us.'[15] And Born, writing much later, uses the same terms to describe Einstein's work: 'The fundamental step taken by Einstein was the idea of raising the kinetic theory of matter from a possible, plausible, useful hypothesis to a matter of observation, by pointing out cases where the molecular motion and its statistical character can be made visible' (Born (1949), 165). Thus there was agreement on all sides that the longed-for direct verification might be found in the phenomenon of Brownian motion, but the obstacles to experimental confirmation were tremendous.[16]

This task was undertaken by Perrin:

However seductive the hypothesis may be that finds the origin of the Brownian movement in the agitation of the molecules, it is nevertheless a hypothesis only . . . I have attempted to subject the question to a definite experimental test that will enable us to verify the molecular hypothesis as a whole. (Perrin (1913), 88–9)

Perrin based his first experiment on fairly transparent reasoning. Gas contained in a vertical column is more compressed lower down and more rarefied higher up, simply due to gravity; the density of oxygen, for example, at 0° centigrade, will be reduced by half at a height of five kilometres. Using experimental techniques of unprecedented accuracy, Perrin measured the rate of rarefication of tiny manufactured particles subject to Brownian movement in a dilute emulsion. He writes:

Thus, once equilibrium has been reached between the opposing effects of gravity, which pulls the particles downwards, and of the Brownian movement, which tends to scatter them, equal elevations in the liquid will be accompanied by equal rarefactions. But if we find that we have only to rise 1/20 of a millimetre, that is, 100,000,000 times less than in oxygen, before the concentration of particles be-

---

[13] As quoted ibid. 21. [14] As quoted ibid. 28.
[15] As quoted ibid. 38.
[16] As noted earlier, Einstein seemed to think the experiments too difficult.

comes halved, we must conclude that the effective weight of each particle is 100,000,000 times greater than that of an oxygen molecule. *We shall thus be able to use the weight of the particle, which is measurable, as an intermediary or connecting link between masses on our usual scale of magnitude and the masses of the molecules.* (Ibid. 93–4, emphasis in the original)

Perrin and his co-workers carried out experiments of this sort on particles of various sizes and compositions, suspended in various liquids, in various concentrations, and at various temperatures, and the number obtained for the absolute atomic weights and for Avogadro's number varied only slightly (e.g. between 65×10^{22} and 72×10^{22} for Avogadro's number).

In a section headed 'A Decisive Proof', Perrin describes these results and relates that

It was with the liveliest emotion that I found, at the first attempt, the very numbers that had been obtained from the widely different point of view of the kinetic theory . . . *Such decisive agreement can leave no doubt as to the origin of the Brownian movement* . . . The objective reality of the molecules therefore becomes hard to deny. At the same time, molecular movement has not been made visible. The Brownian movement is a faithful reflection of it, or, better, it is a molecular motion in itself, in the same sense that infra-red is still light. (Ibid. 104–5, emphasis in the original)

Perrin went on to verify the rest of Einstein's predictions in a series of equally well-made experiments.

Perrin's results were published between 1908 and 1911, followed by his masterful popular exposition in *Atoms*, first published in 1913. His conclusions were quickly accepted. To cite only the more dramatic reversals, in the 1908 preface to the fourth edition of his textbook, Ostwald writes:

I have satisfied myself that we arrived a short time ago at the possession of experimental proof for the discrete or particulate nature of matter—proof which the atomic hypothesis has vainly sought for a hundred years, even a thousand years. The isolation and measurement of gases on the one hand, which the lengthy and excellent works of J. J. Thomson have crowned with complete success, and the agreement of Brownian movement with the demands of the kinetic hypothesis on the other hand, which have been proved through a series of researches and at last most completely by J. Perrin, entitle even the cautious scientist to speak of an experimental proof for the atomistic constitution of space-filled matter.[17]

---

[17] As quoted in Nye (1972), 151.

And commenting at the conclusion of a 1912 conference, Poincaré declares:

> the long-standing mechanistic and atomistic hypotheses have recently taken on enough consistency to cease almost appearing to us as hypotheses; atoms are no longer a useful fiction; things seem to us in favour of saying that we see them since we know how to count them . . . The brilliant determination of the number of atoms made by M. Perrin have completed this triumph of atomism . . . The atom of the chemist is now a reality.[18]

Mach and Duhem, who both died in 1916, remained opposed to atomism despite the general trend of opinion, a fact for which their admirers are still apologizing.[19]

Thus the actual behaviour of the scientific community in this case does not square with the Quinean account of confirmation:[20] atomic theory around the turn of the twentieth century was well-endowed with the five theoretical virtues, but it was not accepted as true until it had passed a further test. That further test was sometimes described in terms of 'seeing' or 'observing', other times in vaguer terms of 'direct testing' or 'experimentally verifying'.[21] I won't attempt to analyse this notion; for our purposes the salient point is that scientists do not, in practice, view the overall empirical success of a theory as confirming all its parts. In some cases, a central hypothesis of an empirically successful theory will continue to be viewed as a 'useful fiction' until it has passed a further, more focused, and more demanding test.

This suggests that there is something wrong with the Quinean premisses. One way to see the problem is to hold holism responsible, to conclude that the holistic notion of a homogeneous scientific theory,

---

[18] As quoted ibid. 157.

[19] See e.g. de Broglie (1954) or Bernstein (1983/4).

[20] As Miller (1987) notes, Quine's account of confirmation is not the only one in trouble; most general accounts have an equally difficult time distinguishing the situation in 1860, when the atom became 'the fundamental unit of chemistry', and that in 1913, when it was accepted as real. For example, if scientific theories are confirmed by inference to the best explanation, it is hard to see why the wide range of explanations it provided in 1860 wasn't enough, or why the addition of an explanation for a single extra phenomenon, Brownian motion, should make such a dramatic difference. Or e.g. if a theory is confirmed when it affords many different means of calculating a single number that all agree, as in Perrin's work on Avogadro's number, why wasn't Cannizzaro's similar feat with atomic weights decisive?

[21] The evolution of the scientific use of 'observation' and related terms is a fascinating subject in its own right. It seems that in the theory of elementary particles, scientists still insist on 'seeing' in some sense; e.g. Hacking ((1983), 182) quotes a scientific report that 'Of these fermions, only the *t* quark is yet unseen'.

confirmed by experience as a unit, is oversimplified as a picture of how natural science is in fact conducted. Or, to view the matter from another angle,[22] we might place blame on the criterion of ontological commitment; we might deny that we are committed to everything our theory says 'there is'. Perhaps the notion that all existence claims are on the same footing—the 'univocality of "there is"' as Quine calls it—is inaccurate as a reflection of the function of scientific language: if the 'there is' of the pre-Perrin 'there are atoms' is viewed fictionally, rather than literally, then we could take the whole theory to be confirmed as a unit; the trick would then be to explain how Perrin's experiments license a switch from that theory to one with a literal 'there are atoms'. Either way, we are forced to examine the detail of scientific theorizing; attention to a general and undifferentiated 'theory *T*' is not enough.

(ii) However we parse the problem, the case of atoms makes it clear that the indispensable appearance of an entity in our best scientific theory is not generally enough to convince scientists that it is real. If we still hope to draw conclusions about the existence of mathematical things from the application of mathematics in science, we must be more attentive to the details of how mathematics appears in science and how it functions there. Given our ultimate concern with the independent questions of set theory, we should focus attention on the use of the real numbers, functions from reals to reals, and the calculus and higher analysis, that is, on the mathematics of the continuum.

If we open any physics text with these questions in mind, the first thing we notice is that many of the applications of mathematics occur in the company of assumptions that we know to be literally false. For example, we treat a section of the earth's surface as flat, rather than curved, when we compute trajectories; we assume the ocean to be infinitely deep when we analyse the waves on its surface; we use continuous functions to represent quantities like energy, charge, and angular momentum, which we know to be quantized; we take liquids to be continuous substances in fluid dynamics, despite atomic theory. On the face of it, an indispensability argument based on such an application of mathematics in science would be laughable: should we believe in the infinite because it plays an indispensable role in our best scientific account of water waves?

Of course, what's at work in these examples is the familiar phenome-

---

[22] The case of the holist Duhem encourages this perspective. See my (199?a) for discussion.

non of scientific idealization, an umbrella term under which we collect a wide variety of different techniques.[23] For example, Galileo's revolutionary contribution to scientific method might be called idealization by causal isolation. The Aristotelian method was to approach nature in its full complexity, to attempt to describe and explain the motions that actually occur. Galileo instead proposed to study, for example, that aspect of an object's downward motion which is due to gravity, ignoring disturbances like air resistance, or, to put it another way, the motion of a body falling in a vacuum.[24] Aristotle would have protested that air resistance is always a factor, that a vacuum is impossible, that the imagined motion of an object in a vacuum bears no calculable relation to the real motion of objects in the world. Galileo insisted, on the contrary, that there is such a calculable relation, that the behaviour of an object falling in a vacuum is a limiting case, that we can determine what happens in 'space entirely devoid of air' by observing what happens 'in the thinnest and least resistant media' and 'comparing this with what happens in others less thin and more resistant'.[25] What happens in ideal circumstances can be extrapolated from what happens in real circumstances by gradually minimizing the disturbing causal factors.

Though many well-known idealizations—like the famous frictionless plane—work by causal isolation, this is not the only variety. Consider, for example, what we might call simplifications: to take a bit of the earth's surface to be flat or the ocean to be infinitely deep is to simplify, not to causally isolate. These examples are simplifications of the actual physical situation, before any mathematics is introduced, but they are performed (at least in part) in the interests of the mathematics that will eventually be introduced, in order to make it more tractable. There are also simplifications performed directly on the mathematics itself, for example, when an elliptical orbit, already an idealization, is replaced by a circle. Finally, as this last example shows, there is also the category of mathematizations—when a mathematical object represents or replaces a physical one—and these are often accompanied by simplifications performed either before or after. When mathematization takes place in measurement contexts, there is often no explicit simplification involved, though the limits of accuracy of our measuring devices introduce approximations.

---

[23] The following remarks on the varieties of scientific idealization are much influenced by McMullin (1985) and Cartwright (1989), ch. 5.

[24] In Galileo's words, the 'downward tendency which (body) has from its own heaviness' (McMullin (1985), 267).

[25] As quoted ibid. 267.

Given the ubiquity of idealizations of various forms in the practice of science, it should not be supposed that Quine ignores the topic. His thought is that idealizations in science can be understood along the same lines as infinitesimals in mathematics; much as Weierstrass replaced talk of infinitesimals by talk of εs and δs, Quine proposes to replace talk of idealized objects by Galilean paraphrases. So, for example, a statement about the frictionless plane is paraphrased as a claim about the behaviour of actual planes as friction is gradually reduced to a minimum. For Galileo, this limiting process describes the epistemic connection between facts about actual planes and facts about frictionless planes; for Quine, it provides a more accurate statement, or perhaps a meaning analysis:

Hold, if you will, that the myth of ideal objects is merely convenient and not quite true, and that the paraphrase is what is true; or hold, if you will, that the myth of ideal objects is strictly true by virtue of having the paraphrase as its true meaning. Either of these philosophies is acceptable. (Quine (1960), 250)[26]

Either way, Quine finds a literally true theory behind the surface idealization.

The trouble with this Quinean account is that it only seems suited to idealizations for causal isolation, the sort of idealization Galileo had in mind when he proposed the paraphrase in the first place. In contrast, consider the ideal fluids of fluid dynamics, which are simplifications introduced prior to mathematization, not idealizations for causal isolation. On Quine's principles, a claim about a continuous ideal fluid would be replaced by, or translated as, a claim about what happens to actual fluids as they approximate ever more closely to ideal fluids, that is, I suppose, as their molecules become ever more tightly packed together, approximating continuous matter. But this is all wrong. If the molecules of an actual fluid are packed tightly enough, it stops being a fluid, and even if it didn't, the best we could approximate in this way would be density, not full continuity. The real point is that fluid dynamics isn't more applicable to one fluid than another, depending on how closely that fluid approximates a continuum; rather, it provides a workable account of any fluid. Examples could be multiplied, but I think it is clear that the method of Quinean paraphrase will not successfully eliminate idealizations from natural science.

---

[26] In fact, for Quine, they are the same. The quotation continues: 'as long as both are recognized as loose formulations of one and the same situation; that they seem opposed is due to fancying, in "true meaning", a more than impressionistic manner of speaking'.

Given that science abounds with idealizations, and given that we are not justified in drawing ontological conclusions from an application of mathematics that occurs in such a context, we should turn our attention to the role of mathematics outside explicit idealizations. Given that our primary interest is in continuum mathematics, we might begin with one of the most common and most powerful mathematizations in all of science: the representation of phenomena by differential equations. For such equations to be literally true, the physical phenomenon in question must be truly continuous, which would be enough to give truth-values to the independent questions of descriptive set theory, if not the CH itself.[27]

Let me begin this enquiry with a look at a suggestive discussion from Feynman's introductory physics lectures. Here Feynman is meditating on the fact that the differential equation developed for electrostatics also turns up in the analyses of heat flow, distortions of a stretched membrane, diffusion of neutrons, irrotational fluid flow, and uniform illumination of a plane. He notes that one of these applications clearly involves a simplifying idealization:

The equation we found for neutron diffusion is only an approximation that is good when the distance over which we are looking is large compared with the mean free path. If we look more closely, we would see the individual neutrons running around. Certainly the motion of an individual neutron is a completely different thing from the smooth variation we get from solving the differential equation. The differential equation is an approximation because we assume that the neutrons are smoothly distributed in *space*. (Feynman, Leighton, and Sands (1964), 12–12)

This idea of smooth distribution in space explains why this particular equation is a good approximation in so many different kinds of cases:

As long as things are reasonably smooth in space, then the important things that will be involved will be rates of change of quantities with position in space. That is why we always get an equation with a gradient. The derivatives *must* appear in the form of a gradient or a divergence; because the laws of physics are *independent of direction*, they must be expressible in vector form. The equations of electrostatics are the simplest vector equations that one can get which involve only the spacial derivatives of quantities. Any other *simple* problem—or simplification of a

---

[27] Presumably the definable subsets of the continuum exist if the continuum does, so there should be a fact of the matter about their Lebesgue measurability, etc. CH is a more delicate matter; if there is a physical continuum in the full second-order sense of Dedekind, then CH is also either true or false.

complicated problem—must look like electrostatics. What is common to all our problems is that they involve *space* and that we have *imitated* what is actually a complicated phenomenon by a simple differential equation. (Ibid.)

In other words, many phenomena can be simplified in such a way as to allow mathematization by the electrostatics equations. Obviously, none of these phenomena involve candidates for literal continua.

But this still leaves electrostatics itself. Feynman asks:

Are [the electrostatic equations] also correct only as a smoothed-out imitation of a really much more complicated microscopic world? Could it be that the real world consists of little X-ons which can be seen only at *very* tiny distances? And that in our measurements we are always observing on such a large scale that we can't see these little X-ons, and that is why we get the differential equations? (Ibid.)

Feynman concludes his discussion with this cryptic remark looking forward to electrodynamics:

Our currently most complete theory of electrodynamics does indeed have its difficulties at very short distances. So it is possible, in principle, that these equations are smoothed out versions of something. They appear to be correct at distances down to about 10^{-14} cm, but then they begin to look wrong. It is possible that there is some as yet undiscovered underlying 'machinery', and that the details of any underlying complexity are hidden in the smooth-looking equations—as is so in the 'smooth' diffusion of neutrons. (Ibid. 12–12, 12–13)

But he admits that 'no one has yet formulated a successful theory that works that way' (ibid. 12–13).

The 'difficulties' Feynman refers to only become clear many chapters later, when he reaches electromagnetism. There he writes:

Now we want to discuss a serious trouble—the failure of the classical electromagnetic theory. . . . the concepts of electromagnetic momentum and energy, when applied to the electron or any charged particle . . . are in some way inconsistent . . . There is an infinite amount of energy in the field surrounding a point charge . . . the electromagnetic mass—goes to infinity. And we can see that the infinity arises because of the force of one part of the electron on another—because we have allowed what is perhaps a silly thing, the possibility of a 'point' electron acting on itself. (Ibid. 28–1, 28–2, 28–6)

Feynman then describes, in some detail, a number of ingenious attempts to modify Maxwell's theory to avoid this absurdity, all of which fail.

Of course, all our classical theories fail at some point, but this is a failure of a different sort: 'You can appreciate that there is a failure of all classical physics because of the quantum-mechanical effects. Classical mechanics is a mathematically consistent theory; it just doesn't agree with experience. It is interesting, though, that classical theory of electromagnetism is an unsatisfactory theory all by itself' (ibid. 28–1). Still, it is possible that the introduction of quantum mechanical considerations into classical electromagnetism will dissolve the difficulties. Unfortunately, 'The Maxwell theory still has the difficulties after the quantum mechanics modifications are made. . . . the quantized theory of Maxwell's electrodynamics gives an infinite mass for a point electron' (ibid. 28–10). And the modified theories do no better:

It turns out . . . that nobody has ever succeeded in making a *self-consistent* quantum theory out of *any* of the modified theories . . . We do not know how to make a consistent theory—including the quantum mechanics—which does not produce an infinity for the self-energy of an electron, or any point charge. And at the same time, there is no satisfactory theory that describes a non-point charge. (Ibid. 28–1)

He concludes, quite simply, 'It's an unsolved problem' (ibid.).

This stark conclusion sounds odd in light of the fact that there is a well-known theory of quantum electrodynamics—fondly called QED—and even odder in light of the fact that Feynman himself helped invent that theory in 1948, years before he gave the lectures that became the above passage. Describing the breakthrough that makes this theory possible, Feynman writes: 'it turns out that it is possible to sweep the infinities under the rug, by a certain crude skill, and temporarily we are able to keep on calculating' (Feynman (1967), 156). As it happens, predictions made using this 'crude skill' have been amazingly accurate:

To give you a feeling for the accuracy of these numbers, it comes out something like this: If you were to measure the distance from Los Angeles to New York to this accuracy, it would be exact to the thickness of a human hair. That's how delicately quantum electrodynamics has, in the past fifty years, been checked—both theoretically and experimentally. (Feynman (1985), 7)

Feynman adds, jokingly, that 'These numbers are meant to intimidate you into believing that the theory is probably not too far off!' (ibid.). But, in fact, though he won a Nobel Prize for devising the 'crude skill' that makes these calculations possible, Feynman does not consider the method acceptable:

Schwinger, Tomonaga and I independently invented ways to make definite calculations . . . (we got prizes for that) . . . The shell game we play . . . is technically called 'renormalization'. But no matter how clever the word, it is what I would call a dippy process! Having to resort to such hocus-pocus has prevented us from proving that the theory of quantum electrodynamics is mathematically self-consistent. It's surprising that the theory still hasn't been proved self-consistent one way or the other by now; I suspect that renormalization is not mathematically legitimate. What *is* certain is that we do not have a good mathematical way to describe the theory of quantum electrodynamics; such a bunch of words . . . is not good mathematics. (Ibid. 128–9)

The situation has not improved since Feynman wrote this passage.

What's important here for our purposes is Feynman's diagnosis of the underlying problem. The challenge is to combine the electromagnetic field with the probabilities of quantum mechanics. Of the latter, he writes:

Probability amplitudes are very strange, and the first thing you think is that the strange new ideas are clearly cock-eyed. Yet everything that can be deduced from the ideas of the existence of quantum mechanical probability amplitudes, strange though they are, do work, throughout a long list of strange particles, one hundred per cent. Therefore I do not believe that when we find out the inner guts of the composition of the world we shall find these ideas are wrong. (Feynman (1967), 166)

So the problem must be on the other side, in the electromagnetic field, spread out in continuous space: 'On the other hand, I believe that the theory that space is continuous is wrong, because we get these infinities and other difficulties . . . I rather suspect that the simple ideas of geometry, extended down into infinitely small space, are wrong' (ibid. 166–7). This, finally, is the thought behind the original hint that the differential equations of electrodynamics might be 'smoothed out' versions of some underlying complexity, in other words, they may be idealizations, as in the case of neutron diffusion.

Now electromagnetism is not the only force that needs to be squared with quantum mechanics. Davies describes the situation after the discovery of QED:

When I was a student in the 1960s particle physics was in a mess . . . The four fundamental forces of nature that act on these particles—electromagnetism, gravitation, and the weak and strong nuclear forces—were . . . ill-understood at the quantum . . . level. Only one of these forces, electromagnetism, had a consistent theoretical description. The weak force could not be properly understood, and many calculations of its effects gave manifest nonsense . . . The strong force appeared to be not a single force at all, but a complex tangle of perplexing interactions that seemed to have no simple underlying form. Gravitation was dismissed as irrelevant to particle physics, and the most strenuous attempts at providing it with a quantum description gave mathematical rubbish for almost all predictions. (Davies (1989a), 1)

Matters improved dramatically thereafter, due to two breakthroughs of the 1960s: the development of quark theory and the study of gauge symmetries.[28] With the new understanding of gauge symmetries, Salam and Weinberg combined the weak force with electromagnetism as the electroweak force, much as Maxwell had previously combined electricity and magnetism, and produced a renormalized theory of this new combination. Using similar gauge methods, the strong force was then understood as a force between quarks, which led to its treatment in the theory of quantum chromodynamics, or QCD.

At that point, Davies continues:

With promising theories of three out of the four of nature's forces 'in the bag' the conspicuous odd man out is gravitation. Gravitation was the first of nature's forces to receive a systematic mathematical description (by Newton), but it continues to resist attempts to provide it with a quantum field description, in spite of its gauge nature. Direct attempts to quantise gravity in analogy with QED soon run into insuperable mathematical problems associated with the appearance of infinite terms in the equations. These 'divergences' have plagued all quantum field theories over the years, but the gauge nature of the other forces enables the divergences in their theories to be circumvented. (Ibid. 3)

Circumvented by renormalization, that is: the quantum theories of the electroweak (that is, electromagnetic plus weak) force and the strong force can be renormalized, but the analogous quantum theory of gravity cannot. Davies concludes that 'So long as gravity remains an unquantised force there exists a devastating inconsistency in the heart of physics' (ibid.). Here not even the 'shell game' can 'sweep the infinities under the rug'.

Here again, what interests us is in the diagnosis. Why is it especially difficult to harmonize quantum mechanics with gravity? Isham sees conflicting pictures of space-time as the underlying problem: 'gravitational effects are regarded as arising from a *curvature* in spacetime, and it is the reconciliation of this dynamical view of spacetime with the passive role it

---

[28] e.g. to define the electric potential of a test charge, we chose an arbitrary reference point and assign an arbitrary value to the potential of the test charge at that point. Because these choices are arbitrary, they can be changed without affecting the physics of the situation, that is, the system displays a gauge symmetry, because it can be re-gauged. (For a textbook treatment, see Halliday and Resnick (1974), 593.)

plays in quantum theory that constitutes the primary obstruction to the creation of a satisfactory quantum theory of gravity' (Isham (1989), 70). He goes on to develop this point:

It must be admitted that, at both the epistemological and ontological levels, our current understanding of space and time leaves much to be desired. In a gross extrapolation from daily experience, both special and general relativity use a model for spacetime that is based on the idea of a continuum, i.e. the position of a spacetime point is uniquely specified by the values of four real numbers (the three space, and one time, coordinates in some convenient coordinate system). But the construction of a 'real' number from integers and fractions is a very abstract mathematical procedure, and there is no *a priori* reason why it should be reflected in the empirical world. Indeed, from the viewpoint of quantum theory, the idea of a spacetime point seems singularly inappropriate: by virtue of the Heisenberg uncertainty principle, an *infinite* amount of energy would be required to localise a particle at a true point; and it is therefore more than a little odd that modern quantum field theory still employs fields that are functions of such points. It has often been conjectured that the almost unavoidable mathematical problems arising in such theories (the prediction of infinite values for the probabilities of physical processes occurring, and the associated need to 'renormalise' the theory . . .) are a direct result of ignoring this internal inconsistency. Be that as it may, it is clear that quantum gravity, with its natural Planck length, raises the possibility that the continuum nature of spacetime may not hold below this length, and that a quite different model is needed. (Ibid. 72)

Given this analysis, it is worth returning to Einstein's remark on his own use of the continuum in general relativity: 'Adhering to the continuum originates with me not in a prejudice, but arises out of the fact that I have been unable to think up anything organic to take its place' (Einstein (1949b), 686). Thus, even the inventor of gravitational theory sees no compelling evidence for the continuity of its underlying space-time.

We've seen, at some length, how difficulties in theories ranging from classical electrodynamics to quantum gravity have been traced to the assumption that space-time is continuous. Under the circumstances, it seems the question of the continuity of space-time must be considered open. Most generally, we have been asking if science tells of any physical continuum, if there are any applications of continuum mathematics that are not idealizations. Space-time presents itself as the most likely candidate,[29] but there remain many other applications of continuum mathe-

---

[29] Though I have consistently phrased this as a question about space-time, some prefer to speak of the electromagnetic field itself. For example, Malament ((1982), 532), speaking of Field (1980), writes: 'Field here construes an electromagnetic field as "an assignment of

matics in science. Nothing short of an exhaustive survey of all these applications would clinch the case—a survey I am unfortunately not
equipped to conduct—but I think what we've seen here is enough to cast
serious doubt on the existence of any physical phenomena that are literally continuous.

(iii) So, what is the upshot of all this for the indispensability arguments?
First, we've seen that scientists do not take the indispensable appearance
of an entity in our best scientific theory to warrant the ontological conclusion that it is real; for this conclusion, the appearance must be in a hypothesis that is not legitimately judged a 'useful fiction', in other words,
in one that has been 'experimentally verified' (see (i)), and it must be in
the context that is not an explicit idealization (see (ii)). So strong uses of
indispensability—uses that do not recognize these subtleties—are in
conflict with the practice of science. Second, we've seen that the status of
some applications—like the use of continuous spacetime—are as yet unsettled, and that it could turn out that all applications of continuum
mathematics in natural science are actually instances of idealization. So
it isn't clear that responsible uses of indispensability—those which do
recognize the subtleties involved—can currently be taken to warrant an
ontological commitment to continuum mathematics.

For the record, we should consider how much mathematics does appear in unproblematically literal applications. Simple uses of the small finite would seem to be straightforward: there are nine planets orbiting the
our sun; there are three atoms in a water molecule.[30] Though we may
simplify by regarding the sun and the planets as geometric spheres, or
even by regarding them as entities with any geometrically sharp boundaries at all, it still seems proper to say that there literally is or isn't a planet

---

properties to points or regions of space-time." I suppose one can characterize a field this
way, but then one could characterize a sofa similarly. The important thing is that electromagnetic fields are "physical objects" in the straightforward sense that they are repositories
of mass-energy. Instead of saying that space-time points enter into causal interactions and
explaining this in terms of the "electromagnetic properties" of those points, I would simply say that it is the electromagnetic field itself that enters into causal interactions.
Certainly this is the language employed by physicists.' From this point of view, our question is about the literal continuity of the electromagnetic field, and the same issues arise.
See Field (1985), § 3, for further discussion.

[30] In my (1990a), I argue that we have perceptual access to simple numerical facts like
'there are three apples on the table'. I see no need to retract that claim here, but the further
claim—that these facts are facts about sets—is the one central to the realism of (1990a),
and it depends on an indispensability argument (see pp. 60–2) that I do now reject.

in a certain general area of space, and to say that nine such planets literally are generally in orbit around the general area of the sun. The same goes for the atoms. Of course, such locutions can be parsed as purely logical claims,[31] so it isn't clear that they commit us to numbers. The case is even less clear for the large finite, as our current theories suggest that there may be an upper bound on the number of particles in the universe.

The traditional debate over the presence of geometric figures in nature focused on whether or not the 'lines' in nature are perfectly straight or the 'spheres' in nature perfectly spherical. For example, one of Galileo's critics insisted that an actual ball will not meet a flat table at a single point, as a true sphere would meet a true plane, because of 'the impediments of matter': the ball will flatten slightly where it rests on the table. Galileo, of course, agreed, but he argued that the shape of the ball is so close to that of a true sphere that we can apply the geometric theorems and take the resulting errors into account afterwards. But this Galilean point is not the one that confronts us here: we want to know if there are any geometric figures, perfect or otherwise, in nature. Here the problem of vague boundaries becomes acute: it isn't that physical objects rarely, if ever, possess perfect geometric shapes, but that they possess no precise shapes at all, perfect or otherwise. No geometric figures occur in nature as boundaries of our vaguely defined objects.

Of course, if space-time is a continuum, there are enough space-time points to instantiate even the uncountable infinite, so the countable and the large finite would also appear in nature. And geometric objects of all sorts, perfect and otherwise, would exist as collections of points, even if there were no distinctive physical phenomenon occupying precisely those points and no others. But we've seen that a space-time continuum is not something we can take as established.

So the upshot of our discussion so far is this: given the state of current natural science, a responsible indispensability argument—one that recognizes the subtleties we've been exploring—seems unlikely to support the existence of more than a few (if any) mathematical entities,[32] and these few cannot be expected to guarantee determinate truth-values

---

[31] e.g. 'there are x, y, and z, all distinct from one another, all atoms in this water molecule, and every such atom is either x, y, or z'.

[32] Resnik (1995) presents a 'pragmatic indispensability argument', which he contrasts with a more familiar 'confirmational indispensability argument'; he argues that the former is immune to criticisms of the latter lodged by Sober (1993) and myself. (I remain unconvinced, but the reader will judge for herself.) For a modal–structuralist defence of indispensability arguments, see Hellman (199?).

to the independent questions of set theory. This conclusion could change with the progress of science, but for now, it casts serious doubt on the notion that a version of mathematical realism based on a responsible version of indispensability can provide the sort of methodological punch that Gödel and the set theoretic realist had hoped to gain.

This is a sorry conclusion, but in fact I think it still gives too much weight to indispensability considerations. So far, we have doubted that indispensability can support enough mathematical entities to do the desired job, but we have not doubted the assumption that underlies the cogency of the inference itself, the assumption that the interaction of mathematics with natural science is the proper arbiter of mathematical ontology. But it seems to me that this whole approach to the assessment of mathematical existence claims is called into doubt by a closer look at the way science and mathematics are actually practiced. In (iv), I sketch this case from the point of view of scientific practice; mathematical practice is the subject of II. 7.

(iv) The worry I want to raise could be put this way: science seems not to be done the way it would be done if the interrelations of mathematics and science were as the indispensability argument requires; in particular, science seems not to be done as it would be done if it were, in fact, the arbiter of mathematical ontology. We've seen that the continuous structure of space-time is under pressure from a series of anomalies, beginning in classical electrodynamics, but I'd like to illustrate the problem here by returning to simpler times, before this use of continuum mathematics was called into question. To do this, I make one last foray into the Feynman lectures, this time to their earliest pages.

In a chapter called 'Time and Distance', Feynman introduces the topic of motion. He reminds his students that modern science, based on observation, is thought to have begun with Galileo's quantitative experiments:

> Until that time, the study of motion had been a philosophical one based on arguments that could be thought up in one's head . . . Galileo was skeptical, and did an experiment on motion which was essentially this: He allowed a ball to roll down an inclined trough and observed the motion. He did not, however, just look; he measured *how far* the ball went in *how long a time*. (Feynman, Leighton, and Sands (1963), 5–1)

Feynman tells the story, perhaps apocryphal, of how Galileo thought to use the regular beating of his own pulse to measure intervals of time, and he goes on to describe the subsequent development of more and more refined clocks, down to an accuracy of 10^{-24} of a second. He then asks: 'What about still smaller times? Does "time" exist on a still smaller scale? Does it make any sense to speak of smaller times if we cannot measure—or perhaps even think sensibly about—something which happens in a shorter time? Perhaps not' (ibid. 5–3). And he tells his beginning students: 'These are some of the open questions which you will be asking and perhaps answering in the next twenty or thirty years' (ibid.). The question of the fine structure of time is left firmly unresolved.

What's important for our purposes is what happens a few chapters later, under the heading 'Description of motion'. There Feynman describes how the motion of a car along a road can be represented by a table of times and positions, by a graph of positions at times, and finally, by a function from real numbers to real numbers. The odd thing is that this final representation presupposes that time is infinitely divisible—in mathematical terms, that it is not only dense,[33] but continuous—in other words, it presupposes a fine structure for time that is far more detailed than the question that was left open only a few pages earlier. But shouldn't the question of the fine structure of time be settled first, before this representation of motion is adopted? Feynman doesn't seem to think so; he proposes the functional representation despite his earlier remarks on time, and such reservations as he does express centre on his neglect of the curvature of space-time and the quantum-mechanical prohibitions on simultaneous position and momentum, not on his previous worries about the density or continuity of time, and not on any more subtle considerations along these lines.

It might be tempting to dismiss this way of proceeding as a forgivable short-cut in an introductory text, but in fact I think it is a much more pervasive phenomenon than that. As a rule, physicists seem happy to use any mathematics that is convenient and effective, without concern for the mathematical existence assumptions involved (e.g. the real numbers in Feynman's case), and—even more surprising—without concern for the physical structural assumptions presupposed by that mathematics (e.g. that time is continuous, in Feynman's case).[34] This lack of concern shows itself in two complementary ways, as can be seen by a contrast with the case of atoms.

---

[33] e.g. the rational numbers are dense—between any two rationals, there is another—but they are not continuous.

[34] For similar sentiments, see Burgess (199?).

On the one hand, the mathematical existence assumptions and the physical structural assumptions underlying the application of the mathematics are not held to the same epistemic standard as ordinary physical assumptions. As we've seen, before Perrin, the assumption of the existence of atoms was hotly debated, experimental verification was demanded, and some argued for the elimination of atoms from science unless and until that verification was forthcoming; in contrast, until troubled by the anomalies, no one worried about the assumption that time is continuous, no one demanded a direct test,[35] and no one called for reform. On the other hand, the success of a theory involving certain mathematical existence assumptions and corresponding physical structural assumptions is not regarded as confirming evidence for those assumptions. In the case of atoms, their central role in the pre-Perrin theory was counted as evidence in their favour, though further confirmation was required; in the case of time, despite the equally central role of continuum mathematics in the physical theory of motion, Feynman considers the question of the actual fine structure of time to remain wide open.

In short, mathematical existence assumptions in science, and their accompanying assumptions about the structure of physical reality, are not treated on an epistemic par with ordinary physical assumptions: the standards for their introduction are weaker, and their role in successful theory lacks confirmatory force; they are at once favoured and trivialized. The trouble is that this epistemic disanalogy undermines the groundwork of the original Quinean argument.

Recall that Quine argued for our commitment to mathematical things by noting that the type of evidence available for atoms (the five theoretical virtues) is the same as the type of evidence available for ordinary physical objects, by concluding that this type of evidence is simply what evidence *is*, and, finally, by construing our evidence for applied mathematical things as the very same type of evidence. But we've now seen that the actual evidence for atoms is different from what Quine identified, stronger than the five theoretical virtues. I think it is fair to say that our evidence for ordinary physical objects is the same as this stronger evidence—if the existence of tables and trees isn't directly verified, what is?—but we've just finished recognizing that the evidence for mathemati-

---

[35] Some would object that the continuity of space-time is not the sort of thing that can be directly tested—as no measurement can be made to more than rational accuracy—but notice that a similar protest might have been made concerning atoms—as it is impossible to observe what is unobservable.

cal objects is not like this, is not the same as the evidence for either atoms or ordinary physical objects. So the Quinean refrain that the evidence we have for atoms and ordinary physical objects is simply what evidence *is*— this refrain has no application to the case of mathematical things, and the whole strategy of arguing for their existence on the basis of their role in science breaks down.

This is what I mean by saying that science seems not to be done as it would have to be done if it were in the Quinean business of assessing mathematical ontology. If it were in that business, it would treat mathematical entities on an epistemic par with the rest, but our observations clearly suggest that it does not.

Indispensability and Mathematical Practice

In II. 6. iii, I sketched my reasons for thinking that a responsible indispensability argument—one that acknowledges the facts explored in II. 6. i and II. 6. ii—may well not support the existence of a continuum. This is a doubt about the scope of indispensability considerations. Worse, I've drawn attention (in II. 6. iv) to features of scientific confirmation that threaten the very cogency of the inference from indispensability to mathematical existence. These together are more than enough to seriously undermine the foundations of set theoretic realism, but for the sake of completeness, we should also evaluate indispensability from the standpoint of mathematical practice.

We saw early on (in II. 2) that pure Quinean indispensability does not square well with the methods mathematicians actually use; we introduced (in II. 3) a modified use of indispensability considerations in the hope of correcting this problem. Unfortunately, I think the problem is still with us, though in a more subtle form. To see this, suppose, with the modified and responsible indispensability theorist, that fundamental mathematical ontology is properly assessed by the role of mathematics in literal applications. Then the question of whether or not the independent questions of set theory have determinate answers depends on the question of the literal application of continuum mathematics in natural science, a question we take to be as yet unsettled. If there should turn out to be a literal application, then the open questions have answers; if not, if all applications of continuum mathematics turn out to be idealizations, then the realist's case collapses, and there is no fact of the matter. This is the position of our indispensability theorist.

If there is a fact of the matter, as the realist hopes, then the set theorist can legitimately pursue this fact, regardless of its independence of ZFC. If there is no such fact, then we are faced with the response of the Glib Formalist (see I. 4): every (relatively) consistent extension of ZFC is as good as any other. Now Glib Formalism does not square with the practice of those set theorists who in fact pursue the search for new axioms; those set theorists obviously do not consider the choice between $V = L$ and MC a matter of indifference (see I. 5 and I. 6). But even if we reject Glib Formalism, it seems that the proper methods for set theorists to use to decide between various extensions of ZFC would depend on whether or not there is a pre-existing fact of the matter; in II. 5, I sketched what I take to be an example of this sort of dependence. So, if our indispensability theorist is right, it seems proper methodology in set theory depends on developments in physics; in particular, on how the question of the literal application of continuum mathematics is resolved.

If this were correct, one would expect set theorists to be vitally interested in the implications of renormalization in quantum field theories, in developments in quantum gravity, in assessments of the literalness of other applications of continuum mathematics in natural science, for the propriety of their very methods would hang in the balance. The trouble is that, as far as I can tell, set theorists are not attentive to these matters, or no more attentive than any other neutral bystander might be. Perhaps this is because they are unaware of the relevance of these matters to their undertakings; perhaps they are unaware that there is any doubt as to the literalness of scientific applications of continuum mathematics. But I doubt that this is the explanation of their indifference.

My guess is that the practice of set theory, the methods set theorists actually use to pursue the independent questions, would be unaffected, no matter how these issues in natural science might turn out. In other words, the vicissitudes of applied mathematics do not seem to affect the methodology of mathematics in the way that they would if applications were in fact the arbiters of mathematical ontology. And this means that mathematics, like natural science, seems not to be conducted as it would be conducted if the presuppositions of our indispensability theorist were correct.

In sum, then, I've raised doubts about the scope of indispensability arguments, and I've suggested that neither science nor mathematics is carried on in ways consistent with the cogency of indispensability arguments. I take these objections to warrant rejection of the set theoretic realism described in II. 3, but notice: all these worries are predicated on conflicts with the actual practice of mathematics and natural science, so a philosopher wedded to realism, or unshakably convinced by the original Quinean considerations, could conclude instead that mathematicians and scientists are in error, that they should correct their methods and procedures in light of these various philosophical insights. My own inclination—and here I follow Quine himself (see III. 3)—is to reject such moves. This simple inclination lies at the heart of naturalism.

III

NATURALISM

The term 'naturalism' is used in a variety of ways in the philosophical literature, but here I hope to develop the hint to which we were led at the end of Part II: if our philosophical account of mathematics comes into conflict with successful mathematical practice, it is the philosophy that must give. This is not, in itself, a philosophy of mathematics; rather, it is a position on the proper relations between the philosophy of mathematics and the practice of mathematics. Similar sentiments appear in the writings of the many philosophers of mathematics who hold that the goal of philosophy of mathematics is to account for mathematics as it is practiced, not to recommend reform. I use the term 'naturalism' because the position I eventually describe (in III. 4) owes so much to Quinean naturalism (see III. 3), but another appropriate term might be 'philosophical modesty'.

The goal of this part is to motivate this version of naturalism, to develop its outlines, and to draw out its consequences. In III. 1 and III. 2, I trace (perhaps unlikely) foreshadowings in Wittgenstein[1] and Gödel; III. 3 describes the Quinean naturalism of which the mathematical naturalism of III. 4 is a variation. With naturalism as a guide, I return to the central set theoretic problem in III. 5 and III. 6.

---

[1] Some philosophers, especially those with a technical bent, tend to be unsympathetic to the style and content of the late Wittgenstein. I encourage such Wittgenstein-phobes to skip over III. 1, and subsequent references back. Nothing essential will be lost.

1

Wittgensteinian Anti-Philosophy

To get a sense of how Wittgenstein's late thinking about philosophy might be relevant to our situation, let's review for a moment. We began with a problem in set theory: there are statements that cannot be decided on the basis of our current axioms; we want to know—are they legitimate mathematical questions?—and if so—how are they to be settled? As Gödel shows, philosophical realism presents an appealing way out of these difficulties; it tells us that the independent questions are legitimate—they are either true or false in the objective world of sets—and they are to be settled by identifying powerful new axiom candidates and adopting the ones that are objectively true.

Set theoretic realism is designed to follow this lead. Sets exist in the same sense as the entities of physics, like atoms. This sort of reality has methodological consequences in science: for example, as early as 1820, Berzelius reasoned that if chemical substances really are composed of molecules, if molecules are not just useful fictions, then the atoms that make up the molecules must occur in definite spatial arrangements, and thus, in sufficiently complex cases, the same number of atoms might be combined in different spatial arrangements, which would produce different chemical properties; this was his explanation of isomers. Similarly, if sets are real in the same sense as atoms and molecules, the set theorist might reason that Σ_2^1 sets of reals either are or aren't Lebesgue measurable, there either are or aren't infinite sets of reals of intermediate size, and thus, that CH and the questions of descriptive set theory have answers despite their independence of ZFC, and thus, that we should search for new true axioms to settle them. This is how philosophical realism is to produce methodological consequences in mathematics.

But we then see that the methods realism recommends don't always harmonize with the actual methods of set theory. The set theorist argues against $V = L$ on the grounds that $V = L$ is restrictive and, presumably, goes on to explain why restrictive theories are unwelcome. But how can this be enough to show that $V = L$ is false in the objective world of sets? The pre-Perrinian physicist could have argued for atoms on analogous grounds—atoms produce good theories—but this was not enough. If it is legitimate, in the set theoretic case, to argue from 'this theory has properties we like' to 'this theory is true', if this is not just a form of wishful thinking, then it appears that we are free to extend our set theory in any way that suits our needs, and it is hard to see how a realm of sets, existing as objectively as the world of atoms, would permit us this degree of latitude. A staunch realist seems forced to allow the rejoinder—'yes, the theory has properties we like, but it still may not be true'—and thus to recommend a method that clashes with practice, offending against our hint of incipient naturalism.

So what are we to do? The philosopher's first thought is likely to be: we need to find a new metaphysics, one that underwrites our belief that the independent questions are legitimate and which provides more palatable and effective guidance on how to settle them. We might think of some form of Conceptualism or Fictionalism, and begin to worry over deep ontological and epistemological questions, much as we did in the case of Realism.

This is the point at which Wittgenstein intrudes. As soon as we undertake the task of finding a suitable replacement for realism, 'The decisive movement in the conjuring trick has been made, and it was the very one that we thought quite innocent' (Wittgenstein (1953), § 308). We think we are making things better by looking for a new metaphysics after rejecting our realism, but in fact, we are making them worse. In Wittgenstein's memorable image, we are trapped, like bugs, and his 'aim in philosophy . . . [is] to shew the fly the way out of the fly-bottle' (ibid. § 309). The key is understanding Wittgenstein's notion of 'philosophy'.[1]

He begins with something very like our embryonic naturalistic sentiment: 'Philosophy may in no way interfere with the actual use of language . . . It leaves everything as it is. It also leaves mathematics as it is' (ibid. § 124). But Wittgenstein goes further: 'Philosophy simply puts everything before us, and neither explains nor deduces anything. . . . If one tried to advance *theses* in philosophy, it would never be possible to question them, because everyone would agree to them . . . Philosophy only states what everyone admits' (ibid. §§ 126, 128, 599). This is what I call 'anti-philosophy', in the sense that modern novels have anti-heroes: an anti-hero is a protagonist who lacks the traditional virtues of nobility, strength, courage, etc.; anti-philosophy is work done by professional

[1] I doubt that there is actually a unique, correct understanding of Wittgenstein's position; for more on the line I follow here, see my (1993b).

philosophers that lacks the traditional theories, controversies, and re- commendations for reform.

On the face of it, the very claim that philosophy makes no controver- sial claims would seem to be a controversial philosophical claim, but what Wittgenstein gives is actually just a description of an activity he proposes to engage in, namely, anti-philosophy. This activity is not theoretical— not a process of explaining or deducing—it isn't even purely descriptive, in any scientific sense of description. Rather, it is akin to Freudian psy- chology, as Wittgenstein understands it:

Take Freud's view that anxiety is always a repetition in some way of the anxiety we felt at birth. He does not establish this by reference to evidence—for he could not do so. But it is an idea which has a marked attraction. It has the attraction which mythological explanations have, explanations which say that this is all a repetition of something that has happened before. When people do accept or adopt this, then certain things seem much clearer and easier for them. (Wittgenstein (1938/46), 43)

This is not a scientific claim, but a 'speculation—something prior even to the formation of an hypothesis' (ibid. 44). The aim is not scientific truth, but a certain benefit to the person who accepts the speculation: 'It is something which people are inclined to accept and which makes it easier for them to go certain ways: it makes certain ways of behaving and think- ing natural for them. They have given up one way of thinking and adopted another' (ibid. 44–5). Wittgenstein's anti-philosophy works sim- ilarly:[2] confronted with a philosophical problem, he presents some spec- ulations, which, if accepted, will change people's ways of thinking and dissolve the problem. His statements about anti-philosophy—what seemed a moment ago to constitute a meta-philosophy—are generaliza- tions from the particular cases he has treated, generalizations about what he takes to be effective ways of anti-philosophizing: 'There is not *a* philo- sophical method, though there are indeed methods, like different thera- pies' (Wittgenstein (1953), § 133).

One central such generalization is the notion that philosophical prob- lems arise out of linguistic confusion. We begin with ordinary forms of expression, which work perfectly well in their ordinary context, and we attempt to apply them outside that context in an idealized, context-free, 'philosophical' sense. In doing so, we remove the contextual backing that made those forms of expression work in the first place: 'philosophical

---

2 Wittgenstein described himself as 'a disciple of Freud' (Wittgenstein (1938/46), 41).

problems arise when language *goes on holiday* . . . when language is like an engine idling, not when it is doing work' (ibid. §§ 38, 132). When we try to apply these expressions without the proper context, we are naturally lost: 'A philosophical problem has the form: "I don't know my way about"' (ibid. § 123). This very disorientation produces the sensation of depth and sends us off on the misguided business of formulating and debating controversial philosophical theses:

> The problems arising through a misinterpretation of our forms of language have the character of *depth*. They are deep disquietudes; their roots are as deep in us as the forms of our language and their significance is as great as the importance of our language. . . . that is what the depth of philosophy is. (Ibid. § 111)

Note the affinity with Carnap's notion of external questions (from II. 2): these are questions raised outside the linguistic framework that gives them sense; we are at a loss, because we have no epistemic standards to apply; we have the impression of deep, fundamental problems, but they are really only pseudo-problems.

The goal of anti-philosophy, then, is to undo this distorting elevation of perfectly good ordinary expressions: 'What *we* do is to bring words back from their metaphysical to their everyday use' (ibid. § 116). Assuming Wittgenstein's diagnosis, we see how this will remove philosophical problems, but it isn't clear that it 'leaves everything as it is'. In fact, it doesn't; it leaves the working parts of language—'the actual use of language'—in place, but it removes the 'idling' pockets of confusion: 'the clarity we are aiming at is indeed *complete* clarity. But this simply means that the philosophical problems should *completely* disappear' (ibid. § 133). When the philosophy is excised, ordinary language—and ordinary mathematical practice along with it—remain unchanged, as promised. These working practices do not force us into philosophy; only a linguistic error does that, the very sort of error the anti-philosopher strives to eliminate. On this view of philosophy, our impulse to replace a defunct metaphysics with a new one is obviously counterproductive; we would be exacerbating rather than improving the situation.

The questions that remain after the excision of philosophy will be legitimate ones, ones that can and should be settled on the basis of the ordinary evidential standards of the ordinary practice. When we philosophized, the very expressions of these legitimate questions were lifted into the context-free realm, at which point the ordinary evidential standards seemed too mundane and colourless to be relevant:

> If I am inclined to suppose that a mouse has come into being by spontaneous

generation out of grey rags and dust, I shall do well to examine those rags very closely to see how a mouse may have hidden in them, how it may have got there and so on. But if I am convinced that a mouse cannot come into being from these things, then this investigation will perhaps be superfluous. (Ibid. § 52)

If we are convinced that our question is beyond the reach of our ordinary standards, we won't bother to examine the details of our everyday practice in our efforts to answer it. The anti-philosopher aims to return the question to its context, and thus, to encourage close examination of the 'grey rags and dust'.

The next step is to apply this anti-philosophical method to the case of mathematics. At first glance, it might seem that philosophical confusions could be eliminated from mathematics by the simple expedient of ignoring what philosophers have to say and retaining only the talk of working mathematicians, but in fact, even mathematicians are not immune to the temptations of linguistic error: 'what a mathematician is inclined to say about the objectivity and reality of mathematical facts, is not a philosophy of mathematics, but something for philosophical *treatment*' (ibid. § 254). What's needed is an analysis of mathematical discourse that separates the actual mathematics from the empty talk: 'what is caused to disappear by such a critique are names and allusions that occur in the calculus, hence what I wish to call *prose*. It is very important to distinguish as strictly as possible between the calculus and this kind of prose' (Wittgenstein (1929/32), 149). When the prose is eliminated, the philosophical pseudo-questions will go with it.

The prose, the fog, the mistaken philosophical theorizing that Wittgenstein undertakes to excise from mathematical discourse is platonism: the view that mathematics is the study of a non-spatio-temporal realm of abstract entities.[3] Here, according to Wittgenstein, 'reality', 'correspondence', and related expressions have been removed from their proper context—natural science—and transplanted into mathematical discourse:

'To mathematical propositions there corresponds . . . a reality' . . . [Y]ou forget where the expression 'a reality corresponds to' is really at home . . . What is 'reality'? We think of 'reality' as something we can *point* to. It is *this*, *that* . . . Professor Hardy is comparing mathematical propositions to the propositions of physics. This comparison is extremely misleading. (Wittgenstein (1939), 239–40)

---

[3] Most of the realistic views described in Part II serve as examples.

Hardy's misleading picture of mathematics as 'the natural history of mathematical objects' (Wittgenstein (1933/44), II, § 40) leads us to worries about the nature of these objects and 'their queer properties' (ibid. V, § 5). In no time, we are faced with a series of deep philosophical questions, like Benacerraf's worry about our epistemological access to non-spatio-temporal, acausal things. But Wittgenstein insists that 'the feeling of something *queer* here comes from a misunderstanding' (ibid. V, § 6). The misunderstanding, of course, is the assumption that we can transfer talk of 'reality', 'objects', and so on, from natural science to mathematics without robbing it of its sense.

To dissolve the resulting deep philosophical questions, the anti-philosopher must prevent the illicit move that produced them, and to do this, he must ask what motivated that move in the first place. Wittgenstein's idea is that the trouble starts from a concern over the interest or importance of mathematics: 'What I am doing is, not to shew that calculations are wrong, but to subject the *interest* of calculations to a test' (ibid. II, § 62). Now it's easy to say what is interesting or important about applied mathematics—it is used to great effect in science—but the importance of unapplied mathematics is less clear. In an attempt to answer this question, the pure mathematician is drawn to the notion of a mathematical realm: 'One would like to say of it [a bit of pure mathematics], e.g.: it introduces us to the mysteries of the mathematical world. *This* is the aspect against which I want to give warning . . . When it looks as if . . ., we should look out' (ibid. II, §§ 40–1). Wittgenstein warns us against this illusory application: '*what* mathematicians take for their application—is quite fantastic . . . So that . . . one is doing a branch of mathematics of whose application one forms an entirely false idea . . . What we have then is the imaginary application. The fanciful application' (ibid. V, §§ 5, 29). To derail the mathematician's linguistic error, the anti-philosopher returns to the ordinary question that generated it: what is the interest or importance of (some bit of) pure mathematics?

Now there's nothing wrong with this ordinary question as it stands, in the context of mathematical practice. In that context, questions of this sort have perfectly good answers: this theorem is important because it draws all these previous results into one and displays their interconnections; this proof is interesting because it lays out the underlying symmetry responsible for the result; this mathematical object is interesting because it has enough structure to generate a rich theory, but is general enough to have wide application; and so on. These answers may lack the thrill of 'it introduces us to the mysteries of the mathematical world', but they have the advantage of being grounded in real practices. They emerge from a careful examination of the 'grey rags and dust'.

The final question must be: why do mathematicians so often give the philosophical, rather than the legitimate answer; why do they tend to ignore the 'grey rags and dust'? Wittgenstein's own answer is clear: 'I want to say: it is essential to mathematics that its signs are also employed in *mufti* . . . It is the use outside mathematics, and so the *meaning* of the signs, that makes the sign-game into mathematics' (ibid. V, § 2). In other words, for Wittgenstein, the only meaningful mathematics is applied mathematics; unapplied mathematics is just a meaningless sign-game, 'a piece of mathematical architecture which hangs in the air, and looks as if it were, let us say, an architrave, but not supported by anything and supporting nothing' (ibid. II, § 35). If this is right, then none of the ordinary justifications just sketched will succeed in giving interest to pure mathematics, and thus, the pure mathematician, faced with a question about his work, has no reply within the ordinary context. This, according to Wittgenstein, is the force behind the linguistic error that produces the 'prose' of mathematical platonism.

This Wittgensteinian line of thought has damaging consequences for set theory. As a part of pure mathematics, it is of interest to us only because we are deceived about its applications: 'The misunderstandings we are going to deal with [e.g. platonism] are misunderstandings without which the calculus [e.g. set theory] would never have been invented, being of no other use, where the interest is centered entirely on the words which accompany the piece of mathematics you make' (Wittgenstein (1939), 16–17). In a discussion of Cantor's Theorem, he speaks of 'the pleasant feeling of paradox': 'If you can show there are numbers bigger than the infinite, your head whirls. This may be the chief reason this was invented' (ibid. 16). This isn't to say that Cantor's Theorem is false, but that it lacks real interest:

this doesn't mean that certain mathematical propositions are *wrong*, but that we think their interest lies in something in which it does not lie. I am *not* saying transfinite propositions are *false*, but that the wrong pictures go with them. And when you see this the result may be that you lose your interest. (Ibid. 141)

To Hilbert's famous cry—'No one shall drive us out of the paradise which Cantor has created for us!' (Hilbert (1926), 191)—Wittgenstein replies:

I would say, 'I wouldn't dream of trying to drive anyone out of this paradise.' I would try to do something quite different: I would try to show you that it is not a paradise—so that you'll leave of your own accord. I would say, 'You're welcome to this; just look around you.' (Wittgenstein (1939), 103)

He predicts that 'mathematicians of the future' will have a 'greater sensitivity', which will lead them out of set theory, and in effect 'prune mathematics' (Wittgenstein (1932/4), 381).

It's important to bear in mind that Wittgenstein, the anti-philosopher, is not directly criticizing set theoretic practice; rather, he advocates the removal of the surrounding prose, and he merely predicts that the result will be a change in the practice of mathematics. In this sense, his anti-philosophy 'leaves mathematics as it is'. Our embryonic hint of naturalism is preserved—in a conflict between philosophy and practice, practice wins—by the extreme measure of eliminating philosophy altogether. In fact, the force of Wittgenstein's prediction can be put this way: extraneous philosophy has been wrongly influencing the practice of mathematics; when it is removed, that practice will grow in stronger, healthier directions. 'Philosophical clarity will have the same effect on the growth of mathematics as sunlight has on the growth of potato shoots. (In a dark cellar they grow yards long.)' (Wittgenstein (1932/4), 381.) This horticultural image is the source of the 'pruning' prediction.

It will surely come as no surprise that I think no such beneficial pruning would remove set theory, or pure mathematics generally, from the body of mathematics. Even on the Wittgensteinian line rehearsed here, there is no suggestion of this until we reach the final question: what drives mathematicians to platonism? This is where Wittgenstein invokes his deep distinction between applied and unapplied mathematics, and paints the latter as without legitimate interest or importance. The 'head whirling' and 'sense of paradox' are seen as the motivation for Cantor's Theorem.

Now we saw early on (in I. 1) that Cantor's development of his theory of sets of real numbers, his enquiry into their size, and his ultimate discovery of Cantor's Theorem, grew out of ordinary mathematical practice, motivated by ongoing mathematical concerns, and histories of the subject tell the same story in more compelling detail.[4] Similarly, set theory since Cantor has developed by pursuing its own mathematical questions and goals (see e.g. I. 2, I. 4, I. 5), and not (or not merely) for the sake of some giddiness it may produce.[5] In Wittgensteinian terms, I suggest that there is more to the grey rags and dust of set theoretic practice

---

[4] e.g. see Dauben (1979).
[5] e.g. see Kanamori (1994).

than Wittgenstein himself has noticed, and I hope to substantiate this claim further in III. 5 and III. 6.

If I am right, then the mathematician's move to platonism is not forced by the dearth of ordinary justifications for his practice, and the final question remains unanswered: why the temptation to platonism? One partial answer is that a legitimate assessment of the interest of a bit of mathematics, couched in terms of its actual merits within mathematical practice, requires a detailed look at the bit of mathematics in question and its interrelations with other bits of mathematics, an undertaking that requires considerable patience and sensitivity; it should not surprise us if mathematicians tend to shrink from the task (especially in conversation with philosophers). And even if a significant number of mathematicians mistakenly suppose that the interest and importance of their work lies in its insights into a platonistic realm, it needn't follow that the work is in fact unjustified by ordinary mathematical considerations. (I come back to this point in III. 4.)

It is worth noting that the mathematician's tendency towards platonism has many causes, of which the interest and importance issue is just one. As it happens, Wittgenstein himself describes several of these quite well:

'To mathematical propositions there corresponds a reality' . . . [To] say this may mean: these propositions are *responsible* to a reality. That is, you can't say just anything in mathematics, because there's this reality. This comes from saying that propositions of physics are responsible to the apparatus—you can't say any damned thing.

It is almost like saying, 'Mathematical propositions don't correspond to *moods*; you can't say one thing now and one thing then.' Or again it's something like saying, 'Please don't think of mathematics as something vague which goes on in the mind.' Because that has been said. Someone may say that logic is a part of psychology: logic treats of laws of thought and psychology deals with thought. You could get to the idea of logic as extremely vague, as psychology is so extremely vague. And if you want to oppose this you are inclined to say 'a reality corresponds'. (Wittgenstein (1939), 240)

Here Wittgenstein is describing, among other things, a phenomenon we noted earlier (in the introduction to Part II): how the experience of doing mathematics—the sense of constraint—is sometimes explained by appeal to mathematical reality. For our purposes here, the important point is that the inclination to platonism has many sources; we needn't posit a fundamental failure of pure mathematics to account for it.

What, then, should we carry away from this brief look at Wittgenstein? The hint of naturalism at the end of Part II was this: if philosophy conflicts with successful practice, the philosophy must give. So, for example, if philosophers argue that classical mathematics must undergo a wholesale change on the grounds of a purely philosophical intuition, as did Goodman and Quine in (1947) (see II. 2), then the naturalist rebels: philosophy is not in the business of criticizing and recommending reform of good mathematics on extra-mathematical grounds. Wittgenstein, the anti-philosopher, takes us further by advocating the excision of all traditional philosophy, and in its place, recommending careful attention to the details of the practice itself. This is the clue I hope to pick up in what follows, but first, another look at Gödel.

2

A Second Gödelian Theme

The line of Gödelian thinking traced in II. 1 presents yet another motivation for platonism: the desire to establish the legitimacy of the independent questions of set theory. A Wittgensteinian anti-philosopher would hold that platonism cannot bear this weight, that support for this view of the independent questions can only come from within the practice of set theory. At this point, I propose to revisit Gödel's writings on the subject and to draw attention to a second line of thought contained there, a line more congenial to our nascent naturalistic leanings.

For the beginnings, we return to Russell. One of the pillars of *Principia Mathematica* that went (nearly) unmentioned in I. 1 is Russell's famous no-class theory: 'classes, so far as we introduce them, are merely symbolic or linguistic conveniences, not genuine objects' (Russell and Whitehead (1910), 72). The idea is that class terms are 'incomplete symbols', that is, they can be translated away in any context where they occur. So, for example, a statement about $\{x \mid x$ has $\phi\}$ is a definitional abbreviation of a statement about the propositional function $\phi(x)$. The fundamental ontology of *Principia* admits only propositional functions, not classes.

Gödel describes the no-class theory like this: 'classes and concepts were to be introduced as a *façon de parler*. . . . the rules for translating sentences containing class names or the term "class" into such as do not contain them were stated explicitly' (Gödel (1944), 131–2). He sees the no-class theory as one of a range of similar undertakings: 'This whole idea of the no-class theory is of great interest as one of the few examples, carried out in detail, of the tendency to eliminate assumptions about the existence of objects outside the "data" and to replace them by constructions on the basis of these data' (ibid.). As we've seen, the project of *Principia* (without the Axiom of Reducibility) must be counted as a failure, and the no-class theory along with it: 'The result has been in this case essentially negative; i.e., the classes and concepts introduced in this way do not have all the properties required for their use in mathematics' (ibid.). This Gödel takes as support for his realism: 'All this is only a verification of the view defended above that logic and mathematics (just as physics) are built up on axioms with real content which cannot be "explained away"' (ibid.). Note the recurrence of the science/mathematics analogy.

Filling in the details of this analysis, we are pressed to compare the no-class theory with some analogous 'tendency' in natural science. The obvious candidate is phenomenalism,[1] the view that a statement about a physical object can be translated into a statement that one would have certain experiences under certain conditions. Thus, the phenomenalist attempts to construct physical objects from sense impressions; the no-class theorist attempts to construct sets from 'logic without the assumption of the existence of classes' (Gödel (1944), 132). And both attempts fail.

Phenomenalism fails because it turns out to be impossible to devise the required language of sensory experience; any effort to translate a physical object statement into a statement of precisely what experiences I would have on various occasions seems to fall back on untranslated claims about the physical context. So the phenomenalist cannot, in fact, produce a theory referring only to sense experiences that explains and predicts further sense experience as well as our ordinary theory of physical objects:

> The physical conceptual scheme simplifies our account of experience because of the way myriad scattered sense events come to be associated with single so-called objects; still there is no likelihood that each sentence about physical objects can actually be translated, however deviously and complexly, into the phenomenalistic language. (Quine (1948), 17–18)

The general form of this failure is: our theory of objects outside the data simplifies our account of (or explains) the data in a way that the proposed phenomenalistic theory, which attempts to construct those objects out of the data, cannot. The corresponding objection to the no-class theory, then, would be that it cannot account for 'logic without the assumption of the existence of classes' (the data) as well as set theory does.

But this is not what Gödel says. His objection to no-class theory (without the Axiom of Reducibility) is that 'the classes . . . introduced in this way do not have all the properties required for their use in mathematics' (Gödel (1944), 132). For example, 'the theory of real numbers in its present form cannot be obtained' (ibid. 134). In other words, Gödel's

---

[1] Cf. Parsons (1990), 112.

objection is not that no-class theory is inadequate to account for some weak logical 'data', but that it is inadequate to the needs of classical mathematics. Here the support for the assumption of the existence of sets lies not in a mathematical analogue to sense perception, not in a strict analogy between mathematics and science, but in the requirements of ordinary mathematical practice. We begin to suspect a second line of thought in Gödel's writings, one not so easily fitted to the philosophical realism described in II. 1.

This suspicion is encouraged by a look at Gödel's discussion of Russell's vicious circle principle. Recall his analysis (from I. 1):

> It is demonstrable that the formalism of classical mathematics does not satisfy the vicious circle principle . . . since the axioms imply the existence of real numbers definable in this formalism only by reference to all real numbers. Since classical mathematics can be built up on the basis of *Principia* (including the axiom of reducibility), it follows that even *Principia* . . . does not satisfy the vicious circle principle. (Ibid. 127)

From this fact, Gödel immediately concludes, 'I would consider this rather as a proof that the vicious circle principle is false than that classical mathematics is false' (ibid.). In other words, a claim about the nature of collections, the vicious circle principle, is false because it does not allow the derivation of classical mathematics. What stands out, for our purposes, is that the argument does *not* run: the VCP is an Anti-realist claim; Realism is correct for reasons x, y, and z; therefore, the VCP is false. Rather, the argument goes straight from mathematical actualities to the falsity of the VCP, without any detour through philosophy. The philosophical theorizing begins only *after* the conclusion against the VCP has been drawn. At that point, Gödel remarks that the falsity of the VCP is 'indeed plausible also on its own account' (ibid.). He goes on to note that the VCP applies only from a 'constructivistic (or [anti-realist]) standpoint' (ibid. 128), and only then argues that realism is more satisfactory.

The same order of argument appears even in Gödel's paper on the continuum hypothesis. Our previous reading traced an argument along this outline: there is an objective world of sets in which CH is either true or false; therefore, CH is a meaningful question, worthy of mathematical pursuit, despite its independence of ZFC. As we've seen, the text undeniably begins that way:

> the undecidability of Cantor's conjecture from the accepted axioms of set theory . . . would by no means solve the problem. For if the meanings of the

primitive terms of set theory . . . are accepted as sound, it follows that the set-theoretical concepts and theorems describe some well-determined reality, in which Cantor's conjecture must be either true or false. Hence its undecidability from the axioms being assumed today can only mean that these axioms do not contain a complete description of that reality. (Gödel (1964), 260)

But the next sentence reads: 'Such a belief [in the well-determined reality of sets] is by no means chimerical, since it is possible to point out ways in which the decision of a question, which is undecidable from the usual axioms, might nevertheless be obtained' (ibid.). Gödel goes on to discuss purely mathematical matters: how the axioms of set theory can be extended in mathematically natural ways; how axioms can be justified by their consequences even if they are not entirely natural. Notice what's happened here: the mathematical considerations are used to support the claim that CH might be settled in mathematically appropriate ways; this claim then implies, *ipso facto*, that CH is a legitimate mathematical question; and finally, this conclusion is used to support our belief in an objective reality of sets. In other words, the mathematics, not the philosophy, is doing the work of establishing the legitimacy of the independent question.

The irrelevance of philosophical realism to Gödel's real concerns is most explicit in a passage late in the Cantor paper, just after the intensely philosophical discussion of 'the "given" underlying mathematics' (ibid. 268). Beginning a new paragraph, he writes:

However, the question of the objective existence of the objects of mathematical intuition . . . is not decisive for the problem under discussion here [i.e. the meaningfulness of the continuum problem]. The mere psychological fact of the existence of an intuition which is sufficiently clear to produce the axioms of set theory and an open series of extensions of them suffices to give meaning to the question of the truth or falsity of propositions like Cantor's continuum hypothesis. (Ibid.)

He goes on to cite the relevance of such new axioms to questions of finitary number theory and the previously mentioned possibility of verifying axioms by their consequences. Here, quite explicitly, it is the mathematical considerations, not the philosophical ones, that are decisive.

In these passages, Gödel is not producing an argument for mathematical realism based on a strong analogy between mathematics and natural science. Rather, his concerns are particular issues in the actual practice of mathematics—should we apply the VCP? Is CH worthy of pursuit?—and his arguments ultimately rest on considerations also drawn from within the practice—the requirements of the classical theory of real numbers, the possibilities for solving the continuum problem on the basis of new axioms. In so far as philosophical claims enter the discussion at all, they appear as secondary conclusions: such-and-such is a good way of doing mathematics; therefore Realism is a better philosophical view than Constructivism or Anti-realism.[2]

On this reading of Gödel, his argument for the legitimacy of CH actually bypasses his philosophical realism altogether; its working parts are all drawn from mathematics itself. If a Wittgensteinian anti-philosopher were to 'treat' Gödel's discussion by excising the 'misguided' philosophy, nothing essential would be lost; the residue would be an inventory of ordinary mathematical considerations, just the sort of thing the anti-philosopher recommends to our attention. Our budding naturalist is tempted to draw a moral: if you want to decide a matter of mathematical methodology—e.g. whether or not to pursue CH—look not to philosophy, but to mathematics. But no form of naturalism can be described before discussion of the fundamental Quinean form.

---

[2] For related readings of Gödel, see Parsons (1990), 107, and Shapiro (1994), 154–5.

3

Quinean Naturalism

Recall (from II. 2) how Quine's views developed out of his interactions with Carnap. Carnap held that science constitutes a linguistic framework with its own evidential rules; that the decision to adopt this framework is pragmatic, not theoretical; that philosophers who attempt to ask a prior ontological question about the existence of the things involved in the framework do so without an evidential context to give their question meaning, and thus ask only a pseudo-question. Quine agrees that the ontological questions are decided on pragmatic grounds, but denies that these standards differ from the evidential rules of science itself. Thus Quine converts philosophical questions into scientific ones.

But if Quine rescues some philosophical questions from Carnap's positivistic junk-heap, he does not rescue them all; comforted as philosophers may be by the notion that 'philosophy is continuous with science', it must be noted that not all traditional philosophy qualifies. In so far as a philosophical question insists on a properly philosophical solution, on the use of a properly philosophical method, Quine's move against Carnap is no help. The only methods Quine ratifies are the methods of science.

To illustrate, consider the position recently urged by van Fraassen (in (1980)): we have good reason to believe in observable things, but also good reason to refrain from belief in unobservable things (like atoms). Given that scientists since Perrin's day do believe in atoms, this sounds like a philosophical intrusion into scientific practice, but van Fraassen insists that it is not: he does not advocate the elimination of unobservables from science; he even allows that it may be good scientific practice to believe in them: 'in that case even the anti-realist, when asked questions about *methodology* will *ex cathedra* counsel [realism]! We might even suggest a loyalty oath for scientists, if realism is so efficacious' (van Fraassen (1980), 93). The trick is that 'the interpretation of science, and the correct view of its methodology, are two separate topics' (ibid.). So 'To someone immersed in [science], the distinction between *electron* and *flying horse* is as clear as between *racehorse* and *flying horse*: the first corresponds to something in the actual world, and the other does not' (ibid. 82). As far as scientific practice—methodology—is concerned, van Fraassen is happy to affirm the existence of atoms; it is only at the level of 'interpretation'—when we are 'stepping back for a moment' (ibid.)— that he recommends agnosticism.

Now those who believe in atoms, upset by van Fraassen's rejection of their belief, are often tempted to reply, to argue that atoms do indeed exist. The trouble is that such a defender of the atomic hypothesis cannot appeal to the various detailed theoretical and experimental grounds described in II. 6; van Fraassen has conceded that these scientific grounds make it good scientific policy to believe in atoms, while doing science. Frustrated atomists are likely to find themselves reduced to declaring that atoms *really* exist, perhaps accompanied by an ineffectual foot stomp.

What's happened here is that van Fraassen has moved the debate outside science, to an arena where scientific methods are irrelevant. The question van Fraassen is debating with his excitable opponent can only be addressed by some higher standards, the standards of the level of 'interpretation', the standards to which we 'step back'. This sort of philosophical question is immune to the Quinean anti-body; it cannot be saved by classification as 'continuous with science'. From the Quinean point of view, the ontological question that makes sense is the one that is answered by Einstein and Perrin; van Fraassen's 'higher' ontological question is as meaningless for Quine as it is for Carnap.[1]

So far, we've seen that Quine treats ontological questions as scientific questions, but the same goes for epistemology. Here the traditional philosophical goal was to found science on some secure, extra-scientific cornerstone: philosophers from Descartes on have made the attempt.

---

[1] An aside to readers of Quine (1969a) and related writings: I read ontological relativity as the observation that meaningful ontological enquiry must be carried out within our best science, that there is no higher, prior sense in which these questions can be asked or answered. Even within science, we see that other ontologies are possible, consistent with evidence, but this does not mean that we 'repudiate the ontology in terms of which the recognition took place' (Quine (1981c), 21). Likewise, I take inscrutability of reference as the observation that our theory of reference is given inside our current theory, in our language, 'by acquiescing in our mother tongue and taking its words at face value' (Quine (1969a), 49). The reference of the terms in our theory is 'inscrutable' only in the sense that there is no extra-theoretical perspective from which to view it. Quine is also some sort of minimalist about truth and reference, but I don't see that this follows from these positions: within science, it could turn out that there is a robust, explanatory theory of the relations between what human beings say, as described by physiology, psychology, linguistics, etc., and things in the world, as described by physics, chemistry, astronomy, etc.

Quine traces the unrelenting failure of these efforts to a problem identified early on:

Here, Hume despaired. By his identification of bodies with impressions he did succeed in construing some singular statements about bodies as indubitable truths, yes; as truths about impressions, directly known. But general statements, also singular statements about the future, gained no increment of certainty by being construed as about impressions . . . I do not see that we are farther along today than where Hume left us. The Humean predicament is the human predicament. (Quine (1969d), 71–2)

Indeed, Quine notes that the very impulse to found science on a secure foundation is driven by a scepticism that is itself internal to science: the very notion of sensory illusion depends on a rudimentary science of common sense physical objects. Thus, 'Cartesian doubt is not the way to begin' ((1975), p. 68).

The realization that epistemology could not succeed in the traditional role 'loosed a wave . . . of epistemological nihilism' (Quine (1969d), 87), but this was not Quine's reaction. Instead, he writes:

Why not settle for psychology? Such a surrender of the epistemological burden to psychology is a move that was disallowed in earlier times as circular reasoning. If the epistemologist's goal is validation of the grounds of empirical science, he defeats his purpose by using psychology or other empirical science in the validation. However, such scruples against circularity have little point once we have stopped dreaming of deducing science from observations. If we are out simply to understand the link between observation and science, we are well advised to use any available information, including that provided by the very science whose link with observation we are seeking to understand. (Ibid. 75–6)

epistemology still goes on, though in a new setting and a clarified status. (Ibid. 82)

Thus, epistemology, too, is to be carried out within natural science: on one side, we have the human subject—as understood by psychology, physiology, chemistry, etc.—on the other side, we have the world—as understood by physics, chemistry, optics, botany, etc.—and we attempt a scientific account of how the one manages to obtain (generally) reliable beliefs about the other.

Of course, Quine admits that his epistemology is not the traditional one: 'I agree . . . that repudiation of the Cartesian dream is no minor deviation' (Quine (1990), 19). Still, it is the only reasonable move in the Quinean context: if the only questions that can be rescued from the positivists are scientific questions, if scientific evidence is what evidence is (see II. 6), then there is no other arena in which to study the phenomenon of the human knower. In perhaps another mode of epistemological nihilism, some commentators have concluded that naturalized epistemology can only aim to describe how we come to believe, that it cannot hope to describe how we should come to believe. Quine disagrees:

Our speculations about the world remain subject to norms and caveats, but these issue from science itself as we acquire it. Thus one of our scientific findings is the very fact . . . that information about the world reaches us only by forces impinging on our nerve endings; and this finding has normative force, cautioning us as it does against claims of telepathy and clairvoyance. The norms can change somewhat as science progresses. For example, we once were more chary of action at a distance than we have been since Sir Isaac Newton. (Quine (1981a), 181)

Quine cites Empiricism itself as an example of a norm originating inside science; Mechanism (as described in II. 4. i) is an example of such a norm that came and went.

The sum of all this is a position Quine calls 'naturalism', which he describes as 'the recognition that it is within science itself, and not in some prior philosophy, that reality is to be identified and described' (Quine (1981c), 21). Naturalism advocates 'abandonment of the goal of a first philosophy. It sees natural science as an inquiry into reality, fallible and corrigible but not answerable to any supra-scientific tribunal, and not in need of any justification beyond observation and the hypothetico-deductive method' (Quine (1975b), 72). On epistemology, we've seen that

Naturalism does not repudiate epistemology, but assimilates it to empirical psychology. Science itself tells us that our information about the world is limited to irritations of our surfaces, and then the epistemological question is in turn a question of science: the question how we human animals can have managed to arrive at science from such limited information. (Ibid.)

One of Quine's favourite images is Neurath's picture of science, which Quine, in his post-Carnapian view, extends to philosophy: 'Neurath has likened science to a boat which, if we are to rebuild it, we must rebuild plank by plank while staying afloat in it. The philosopher and the scientist are in the same boat' (Quine (1960), 3). Quine returns to this image in his summary of naturalism:

The naturalistic philosopher begins his reasoning within the inherited world theory as a going concern. He tentatively believes all of it, but believes also that some unidentified portions are wrong. He tries to improve, clarify and understand the system from within. He is the busy sailor adrift on Neurath's boat. (Quine (1975b), 72)

We are urged to give up the absolutist hope of dragging the boat into dry dock; that way lies Carnapian nonsense. We must give up the hope of founding science on something more secure; it is the best we have. Instead, we note that versions of our traditional questions can be asked within science, as scientific questions—and this time, we can ask them with some real hope of finding answers.

Once again, Putnam is a staunch ally, developing the naturalistic theme that scientific methods are our best, in need of no extra-scientific correction or support:

the very factors that make it rational to accept a theory 'for scientific purposes' also make it rational to believe it, at least in the sense in which one ever 'believes' a scientific theory—as an approximation to the truth that can probably be bettered, and not as the final truth. . . . it is silly to agree that a reason for believing that *p* warrants accepting *p* in all scientific circumstances, and then to add 'but even so it is not *good enough.*' Such a judgement could only be made if one accepted a trans-scientific method as superior to the scientific method; but this philosopher, at least, has no interest in doing *that.* (Putnam (1971), 356)

Notice how this applies directly to unnaturalistic undertakings like van Fraassen's.

Opponents of naturalism sometimes complain that the naturalistic philosopher is reduced to recording the pronouncements of scientists, that such philosophy has no critical function, that it is reduced to mere sociology of science. But we've already seen that this is not true. Natural science itself is a self-critical enterprise that develops and debates its own methodological norms. The naturalistic philosopher is free to join in this part of ongoing science, like anyone else, except that she cannot expect to use any peculiarly philosophical methods. The only available methods are the scientific ones; for the naturalist, the evaluation and assessment of scientific method must take place within science, using those very methods themselves. This is the point of Neurath's image.

Realizing this, other opponents complain that this is a meaningless exercise, that it is a foregone conclusion that natural science will ratify its own methods. Of course, this isn't true: we've seen that natural science first adopted, then rejected Mechanism, all for good scientific reasons. Retreating, the opponent may then object that even if we were to succeed in providing a scientific justification of science, this would not show that our science is the only possible science. This the naturalist admits:

Might another culture, another species, take a radically different line of scientific development, guided by norms that differ sharply from ours but that are justified by their scientific findings as ours are by ours? And might these people predict as successfully and thrive as well as we? Yes, I think that we must admit this as a possibility in principle; that we must admit it even from the point of our own science, which is the only point of view I can offer. I should be surprised to see this possibility realized, but I cannot picture a disproof. (Quine (1981a), 181)

But the fact that there could be other successful scientific practices gives us no reason to reject our own, especially given that it *is* our own, that is, 'the only point of view [we] can offer'.[2]

This, then, is Quinean naturalism: scientific methods are fundamental. But we have already seen (in II. 6) that the understanding of scientific methods underlying the Quinean indispensability arguments does not square with the actual methods of science. That understanding does, however, square well enough with 'observation and the hypothetico-deductive method'—Quine's characterization of the scientific method in his statement of naturalism—as it does with his more developed listing of the five theoretical virtues. The trouble is that actual scientific methods are more complicated than this.

We might save the letter of Quine's position by understanding his naturalist to take scientific methods, as described by Quine, to be fundamental, and thus to take actual scientific practice to be in error in so far as it departs from that description. Such a naturalist might say, for example, that scientists were wrong to be sceptical of atoms even before Perrin, perhaps any time after Cannizzaro. Though this position is consistent with Quine's statements, I think it offends against their spirit. Quinean naturalism, as I understand it, takes actual scientific methods as fundamental, which means quite simply that there is a tension between the Quinean indispensability arguments and Quinean naturalism.

But while this tension is hidden, and perhaps unwelcome, Quine is frankly untroubled by the clash between his indispensability arguments and the actual practice of mathematics (see II. 2 and II. 7). My goal is to devise a version of naturalism that avoids this outcome, a version that incorporates the insights we've gained from Wittgenstein and Gödel.

---

[2] With the sociologists of science, Quine admits, speaking of Neurath's boat, that 'The ship may owe its structure partly to blundering predecessors who missed scuttling it only by fools' luck. But we are not in a position to jettison any part of it, except as we have substitute devices ready to hand that will serve the same essential purposes' (Quine (1960), 124).

4

Mathematical Naturalism

The version of naturalism to be outlined here begins, just as Quine's does, within natural science; it takes the actual methods of natural science as its own. Here already we have departed sharply from both Wittgenstein and Gödel. We've seen that Wittgenstein's attitude toward certain philosophical enquiries is quite like Carnap's toward external pseudo-questions and Quine's toward first philosophy, but when it comes to the evaluation of science, Wittgenstein's instincts take him in the opposite direction:

It isn't absurd . . . to believe that the age of science and technology is the beginning of the end for humanity; that the idea of great progress is a delusion . . . that there is nothing good or desirable about scientific knowledge and that mankind, in seeking it, is falling into a trap. It is by no means obvious that this is not how things are. (Wittgenstein (1914/51), 56e)[1]

With no background science to provide context for her questions, the Wittgensteinian anti-philosopher elects to 'cure' them instead. Gödel, on the other hand, stands in sharp contrast to all three of these philosophers: he is an unabashed practitioner of first philosophy.

In any case, our naturalist begins within natural science—that is, with both the methods and the theories of science ready to hand—and she sets out to explain how human beings, as they are characterized by science, come to knowledge of the world, as it is characterized by science. At the outset of this investigation, it quickly becomes obvious that mathematics is central to our scientific study of the world and that the methods of mathematics differ markedly from those of natural science. The reaction of the Quinean naturalist is to insist, nevertheless, that the true justification for the various mathematical existence claims derives from the role of mathematics in science, that (most of) what mathematicians actually

---

[1] Wittgenstein's antipathy towards natural science is well set out in Monk's excellent biography (1990). Following Spengler, Wittgenstein took the rise of science as a sign of cultural decay.

say in defence of their existence claims, their axioms, and their methodological decisions is beside the point; as we've seen, the Quinean naturalist goes so far as to advocate a set theoretic axiom that set theorists overwhelmingly reject (i.e. $V = L$). Histories of nineteenth-century mathematics[2] tell a compelling story of how mathematics gradually separated itself from physical science and undertook pursuits of its own—motivated by its own goals and interests, as well as those of science—but the Quinean naturalist persists in subordinating mathematics to science, on identifying the proper methods of mathematics with the methods of science.

To judge mathematical methods from any vantage-point outside mathematics, say from the vantage-point of physics, seems to me to run counter to the fundamental spirit that underlies all naturalism: the conviction that a successful enterprise, be it science or mathematics, should be understood and evaluated on its own terms, that such an enterprise should not be subject to criticism from, and does not stand in need of support from, some external, supposedly higher point of view. What I propose here is a mathematical naturalism that extends the same respect to mathematical practice that the Quinean naturalist extends to scientific practice. It is, after all, those methods—the actual methods of mathematics—not the Quinean replacements, that have led to the remarkable successes of modern mathematics. Where Quine holds that science is 'not answerable to any supra-scientific tribunal, and not in need of any justification beyond observation and the hypothetico-deductive method' (Quine (1975b), 72), the mathematical naturalist adds that mathematics is not answerable to any extra-mathematical tribunal and not in need of any justification beyond proof and the axiomatic method.[3] Where Quine takes science to be independent of first philosophy, my naturalist takes mathematics to be independent of both first philosophy and natural science (including the naturalized philosophy that is continuous with science)—in short, from any external standard.

The aim of this section is to fill in the outlines of this mathematical naturalism, and to assess its consequences for the assessment of mathematical methods—like decision on new axioms candidates—and for the philosophy of mathematics. I begin (in (i)) with a look at the issues

---

[2] Kline (1972) gives an overview.
[3] Here I take both 'observation and the hypothetico-deductive method' and 'proof and the axiomatic method' to be short-hand for the actual methods of science and mathematics, respectively.

involved in evaluating mathematical ontology from the naturalist's point of view. (ii) takes up the 'boundary problem': where does mathematics end and external philosophy and science begin? The implementation of naturalism in the assessment of methodology is the subject of (iii), and (iv) concludes with a glance at the remaining philosophical issues.

(i) *Naturalism and Ontology*. As mathematical naturalists, then, we approach mathematics on its own terms. Quine has shown us how the methods of science can be understood as answering various questions Carnap once took to be external; we now ask what mathematical practice can tell us about the ontology of mathematics.

Like science, mathematics begins in common sense, in our ordinary practices of counting, measuring, assessing chances, and so on. As Quine notes, common sense ratifies an ontology of medium-sized physical objects, and it tells us something about those objects: that they are located in space and time, that they exist even when we aren't looking at them, that they have the properties they do independently of our thoughts and wishes. These beliefs are so fundamental that they are scarcely learned in any ordinary sense; coming to hold them seems part of the original tuning of our perceptual and cognitive apparatus. So strong is our faith in the objectivity and spatio-temporality of physical objects that nothing short of the anomalies of quantum mechanics has shaken it, and even there, the question is as yet unresolved.

In the case of mathematics, common sense also tells us a wide range of things: that there are two houses of Congress, that $2 + 2 = 4$, that a triangle has three sides, that I'm more likely to win a raffle that sells two tickets than one that sells a hundred and two. But does common sense hold that 2 exists? A subject unspoiled by philosophy will most likely affirm the existence of ordinary physical objects (unless she finds the question so odd as to suggest some trick), but even the least suspicious is as likely to be baffled by a question like: does 2 exist? And the uncertainty will only be exacerbated by follow-ups on the nature of that existence: does it exist in space and time? Does it exist objectively?, and so on. It seems common sense is more forthcoming on physical than mathematical ontology.[4]

Moving to the level of refined and extended mathematical theories,

---

[4] Readers of my (1990a) will detect some discrepancy between this conclusion and its opening pages. Some (but not all) of this discrepancy can be explained by the emphasis there on what makes mathematical claims true.

we find many unequivocal existence claims: there are infinitely many primes; there is a one-to-one correspondence between the natural numbers and the rationals; there is a Hilbert space, a group, a probability metric of such-and-such a description. From these theories, we gain a wealth of information about these mathematical things, but for all that, we never learn whether or not they are spatio-temporal, whether or not they exist objectively. So, for example, though ZFC and its consequences present a wonderfully rich picture of the universe of sets, it is mum on the nature of their existence. In contrast, claims of the objectivity and spatio-temporality of its objects are fundamental to physical science, from its most theoretical reaches to the very design of its experiments.

But there is more to mathematics than its explicit theories: there is the level of discussion at which theories are formed, at which choices between theoretical alternatives are made. This, of course, is the level of primary interest to the overall theme of this book, as it is the level at which independent questions are debated and new axiom candidates assessed. For now, though, our question is: can this level of mathematical practice give us the ontological guidance we did not gain from common sense or our official theories? Again, Quine has shown us how ontological questions about physical objects are internal to science after all; we want to know if the same can be said of mathematics.

As we've noted (e.g. in III. 1 and 2), the discourse of actual mathematicians includes a fair amount of talk on traditional philosophical themes. The version of Gödel's thinking on the legitimacy of CH outlined in II. 1 is a conspicuous example: mathematical realism implies that CH has a determinate truth-value. He strikes much the same tone at some points in the course of his defence of impredicative definitions. First he characterizes the Constructivistic philosophy he takes to motivate the ban on such definitions:

it seems that the vicious circle principle [which rules out impredicative definitions] applies only if the entities involved are constructed by ourselves. In this case there must clearly exist a definition (namely the description of the construction) which does not refer to a totality to which the object defined belongs, because the construction of a thing can certainly not be based on a totality of things to which the thing to be constructed itself belongs. (Gödel (1944), 127)

With this, he contrasts his Realism: 'If, however, it is a question of objects that exist independently of our constructions, there is nothing in the least absurd in the existence of totalities containing members which can be described (i.e., uniquely characterized) only by reference to this totality' (ibid. 127–8). (As we've seen, this line of objection to the philosophy that underlies the VCP coexists in Gödel's paper with the more directly mathematical objection that it derails the classical theory of real numbers (see III. 2).) Similarly, Zermelo includes in his reply to critics of impredicative definitions the assertion that 'an object is not created' by a definition (Zermelo (1908a), 191), though he does not present an explicit realistic alternative to the constructivist metaphysics.

Versions of the idea that mathematical things are 'constructed by ourselves' underlie some early Definabilist objections to the Axiom of Choice as well. So, for example,—while he grants that Zermelo's proof of the Well-Ordering Theorem does not tell us how the well-ordering can actually be carried out, and that 'it remains doubtful that anyone will be able to supply such a method in the future' (Baire *et al.* (1905), 312), Hadamard nevertheless insists that its existence is 'a fact like any other' (ibid. 317). To confuse the question of existence of a well-ordering with the question of our ability to execute a well-ordering is to confuse this fact with '[a]n altogether subjective question' (ibid. 318). Later, Bernays sees his Combinatorialism as motivated by 'platonism', a 'tendency' that 'consists in viewing the objects as cut off from all links with the reflecting subject' (Bernays (1934), 259). By Bernays's day, the vague constructivism of the Definabilists had matured into the Intuitionistic school, which espoused an explicit subjectivism:

mathematics is a production of the human mind. . . . we do not attribute an existence independent of our thought . . . to the integers or any other mathematical objects. . . . mathematical objects are by their very nature dependent on human thought. Their existence is guaranteed only insofar as they can be determined by thought. They have properties only insofar as these can be discerned in them by thought. (Heyting (1931), 52–3)

In addition to modern versions of Heyting's Intuitionism, various forms of philosophical constructivism are still espoused today (e.g. Chihara (1990), Dummett (1977), Kitcher (1983)).

Given this heavy admixture of ontological discussion in these mathematical debates, the naturalist has some cause to hope that ontological guidance might be found here, that some traditional philosophical questions can be naturalized in mathematics as they were in natural science. Though this naturalization would come at a much higher level of theorizing than it does in science, perhaps various mathematical outcomes— the success of impredicative definitions, of the Axiom of Choice, and perhaps ultimately, of the search for new axioms to settle CH—could be

taken to support Realism over Constructivism. But before any such conclusion can be drawn, we must determine whether or not these philosophical debates are integral parts of the practice, whether or not they
are 'continuous with mathematics', whether or not they are external,
extra-mathematical, what Wittgenstein would call 'mere prose'. This
question—the boundary problem—is perhaps the most difficult our
mathematical naturalist will face.

(ii) *The Boundary Problem.* Let me begin with a look at a couple of illustrative examples from physics, where the naturalist also must separate
science (and the naturalistic philosophy continuous with it) from first
philosophy. Consider, for example, Mechanism (discussed in II. 4. i), the
admonition to produce mechanistic explanations of all phenomena.
Introducing this methodological maxim, Einstein and Infeld speak of
'problems which extend far beyond the restricted domain of science
itself. What is the aim of science? What is demanded of a theory which
attempts to describe nature?' (Einstein and Infeld (1938), 51). These
questions call for a 'philosophical view' (ibid.), of which Mechanism is
one example. As naturalists, we wonder if this is first philosophy or
naturalized philosophy, continuous with science. Einstein and Infeld
reply: 'Philosophical generalizations must be founded on scientific
results. Once formed and widely accepted . . . they very often influence
the further development of scientific thought by indicating one of the
many possible lines of procedure' (ibid.). We've seen that Mechanism
did arise out of successful science of the past, and that it did influence
highly successful science thereafter, so it seems the methods that supported the introduction and application of Mechanism, as well as those
that eventually overthrew it, are ordinary scientific methods. So Mechanism itself should be classified as naturalistically acceptable philosophy, as
philosophy continuous with science, if it is classified as philosophy at all.

As a second example, consider Verificationism, the view that the
meaning of a term is given by the conditions under which its application
could be verified. Einstein employs this notion in his discussion of
simultaneity:

The concept does not exist for the physicist until he has the possibility of discovering whether or not it is fulfilled in an actual case. We thus require a definition of
simultaneity such that this definition supplies us with the method by means of
which . . . he can decide by experiment whether or not both the lightning strokes
occurred simultaneously. As long as this requirement is not satisfied, I allow myself to be deceived as a physicist (and of course the same applies if I am not a

physicist), when I imagine that I am able to attach a meaning to the statement of simultaneity. (Einstein (1917), 22)

This idea is so central to the exposition that Einstein adds: 'I would ask the reader not to proceed farther until he is fully convinced on this point' (ibid.). In later autobiographical notes, Einstein relates that he was inspired 'by the reading of David Hume's and Ernst Mach's philosophical writings' (Einstein (1949), 53). The result was the special theory of relativity.

The Verificationist Bridgman praises Einstein for this work: 'Einstein's revolutionary contribution consisted in his self-conscious use of [Verificationism] in new situations and in the way in which he applied it' (Bridgman (1949), 336). He speaks of 'the new vision given to physicists by Einstein' (ibid.). But Bridgman goes on to complain that Einstein betrayed this vision in his general theory of relativity: 'Einstein did not carry over into his general theory of relativity the lessons and insights he himself has taught us in his special theory' (ibid. 335). Of course, Einstein doesn't see the matter this way. He doesn't see his effective use of Verificationism in one context as a reason to cleave to it in another.

On the general issue of the proper relations between philosophy and science, Einstein writes:

The reciprocal relationship of epistemology and science is of noteworthy kind. They are dependent upon each other. Epistemology without contact with science becomes an empty scheme. Science without epistemology is—insofar as it is thinkable at all—primitive and muddled. However, no sooner has the epistemologist, who is seeking a clear system, fought his way through to such a system, than he is inclined to interpret the thought-content of science in the sense of his system and to reject whatever does not fit into his system. The scientist, however, cannot afford to carry his striving for epistemological systematic that far. He accepts gratefully the epistemological conceptual analysis; but external conditions, which are set for him by the facts of experience, do not permit him to let himself be too much restricted in the construction of his conceptual world by the adherence to an epistemological system. He therefore must appear to the systematic epistemologist as a type of unscrupulous opportunist: he appears as *realist* insofar as he seeks to describe a world independent of the acts of perception; as *idealist* insofar as he looks upon the concepts and theories as the free inventions of the human spirit (not logically derivable from what is empirically given); as *positivist* insofar as he considers his concepts and theories justified *only* to the extent to which they furnish a logical representation of relations among sensory experiences. He may even appear as *Platonist* or *Pythagorean* insofar as he considers the viewpoint of logical simplicity as indispensable and effective tools of his research. (Einstein (1949b), 683–4)

Each of these philosophical positions can be used to the physicist's advantage in one situation or another—as perspectives or inspirations—but this does not mean they should be adhered to in the next situation. Reichenbach draws the distinction this way, speaking of another of Einstein's philosophical inspirations:

> When I, on a certain occasion, asked Professor Einstein how he found his theory of relativity, he answered that he found it because he was so strongly convinced of the harmony of the universe. No doubt his theory supplies a most successful demonstration of the usefulness of such a conviction. But . . . [t]he philosopher of science is not much interested in the thought processes which lead to scientific discoveries; he looks for a logical analysis of the completed theory, including the relationships establishing its validity. That is, he is not interested in the context of discovery, but in the context of justification. (Reichenbach (1949), 292)

Philosophy, in the sense Einstein uses it here, is not part of scientific method. A seventeenth-century physicist may have thought she was writing down the thoughts in the mind of God, but this belief is not arrived at by scientific means, not subjected to scientific test, and does not guide successful research programmes.

Einstein's own application of Verificationism more closely resembles the theology of the seventeenth-century physicist, or the realism, idealism, positivism, etc. of Einstein's own analysis, than it does the scientific role of Mechanism. Though the boundary between science and naturalized philosophy, on the one hand, and first philosophy, on the other, is no doubt vague in places, these two examples seem to lie unproblematically on opposite sides. The contrast is stark, both in genesis and in influence: Mechanism was generated by established scientific methods—by generalization from successful practice—and its application produced a long-lived, immensely fruitful research programme; Verificationism arose in philosophical contexts, and it was used once by Einstein and abandoned. While we should not belittle the inspirational role of extra-scientific principles like Verificationism, we should not mistake them for products of a truly naturalistic philosophizing that is continuous with scientific practice.

With these contrasting examples as background, let's return to the mathematical debates that concern us. On the one hand, we have a variety of ordinary methodological issues: should impredicative definitions be allowed? Must all existence proofs somehow define or construct the entities asserted to exist? Should the Axiom of Choice be adopted? Is CH a legitimate mathematical question despite its independence of ZFC?

Should we try to choose between various extensions of ZFC? On the other hand, we have a debate between Realism—mathematical things exist objectively, independently of our mathematical activity—and Constructivism—mathematical things are created by our mathematical activity. We want to know how much of this can be regarded as continuous with the practice itself.

At this point, I propose the following simple-minded historical analysis. Many of the methodological debates in question have been settled: impredicative definitions are allowed; existence proofs are not required to define or construct the entity asserted to exist; the Axiom of Choice has been adopted. (The last two questions—about CH and about new axioms—are the two we are concerned with in this book.) On the other hand, the philosophical questions remain open: various more recent versions of Constructivism are consistent with the use of impredicative definitions and the Axiom of Choice (e.g. Chihara (1990) and Kitcher (1983)), and many other alternatives to Realism also remain live options (e.g. versions of Formalism and Fictionalism, see (iv)). My point is simply that the methodological debates have been settled, but the philosophical debates have not, from which it follows that the methodological debates have not been settled on the basis of the philosophical considerations.

In fact, I think the historical record gives a fairly clear indication of what did finally resolve the methodological debates: impredicative definitions are needed for a classical theory of real numbers (among other things) (see I. 1. i and III. 2); the Axiom of Choice is so fruitful in so many branches of mathematics that mathematicians refused to give it up (see I. 3. vii). In other words, these debates were decided on straightforwardly mathematical grounds. With the philosophical questions floating free, neither deciding nor decided by the methodological conclusions of the practice, our mathematical naturalist relinquishes her last hope of ontological guidance from the practice of mathematics. Furthermore, our pursuit of mathematical naturalism has led us to the same suggestion that tempted us at the end of III. 2: if you want to answer a question of mathematical methodology, look not to traditionally philosophical matters about the nature of mathematical entities, but to the needs and goals of mathematics itself.[5] But this is the subject of (iii).

---

[5] A passing *mea culpa*. Set theoretic realism was intended to be a 'naturalistic' theory: e.g. it steadfastly refuses to recommend reform of mathematics on philosophical grounds; it scrupulously adheres to epistemology naturalized. We've already seen that it failed in this

For now, what we've learned is that mathematical practice itself gives us little ontological guidance. The methods of natural science—the very methods used to construct its theories, design its experiments, determine its research directions—also tell us that ordinary physical objects and many unobservables exist, that they do so objectively and spatio-temporally; but the methods of mathematics—the methods used to select its axiom systems, structure its proofs, determine its research directions—tell us no more than that certain mathematical objects exist. They tell us nothing about the nature of that existence—is it objective? Is it spatio-temporal?—indeed, nothing seems to preclude even Fiction-alist or Formalist interpretations. And what goes for ontology goes for epistemology: no part of mathematical practice tells of human cognizers and their acquisition of mathematical beliefs. While some traditional epistemological and ontological questions about natural science can be naturalized as scientific questions, it seems no traditional epistemological questions about mathematics and only the barest ontological questions about mathematics can be naturalized as mathematical questions.

But even if typically philosophical considerations are not part of the justificatory structure of mathematical practice, we must still insist on their importance as inspirations. In correspondence with Wang, Gödel describes how 'my objectivistic conception of mathematics and meta-mathematics in general, and of transfinite reasoning in particular, was fundamental . . . to my . . . work in logic' (Wang (1974b), 9). Gödel ar-gues persuasively that his philosophical views made it much easier for him to discover his metamathematical theorems and that the opposing views of Skolem and Hilbert made it very difficult for them to do so (Wang (1974b), 8–12). But even Gödel refers to the role of his 'objectiv-ism' in these discoveries as that of a 'heuristic principle' (ibid.). What the mathematical naturalist denies is that philosophical realism justifies Gödel's use of infinitary methods in metamathematics—this was the methodological issue in his letters to Wang—rather, the justification comes from the mathematical fruits of those methods, beginning with Gödel's own theorems. In the same way, though Bernays characterizes his Combinatorialist methods as 'platonistically inspired mathematical

goal by relying on an indispensability argument that is at odds with scientific and mathe-matical practice. But now another failing comes into view: though it recommends no re-forms, it does attempt to defend mathematical practice on the basis of a philosophical realism about sets. It took me a very long time to realize that if philosophy cannot criticize, it cannot defend, either.

conceptions' (Bernays (1934), 259), it is the success of those methods, not their platonistic inspiration, that justifies their adoption.

Conversely, some might argue that the success of the various 'platonistically inspired' methods counts as evidence for mathematical realism, but our naturalistic analysis does not support this view. It is true that many opponents of the particular methods in question have couched their objections in various anti-realist modes—Constructivism, Subjectivism—a strategy which inspires their defenders to realistic metaphysics in reaction: I think this phenomenon accounts for the traces of philosophical realism in Zermelo ('an object is not created' by our definitions), Hadamard ('a fact like any other', not 'an altogether subjective question') and Bernays ('objects . . . cut off from . . . the reflecting subject'). But, in fact, the success of these methods amounts to an intra-mathematical argument that they should not be banned from mathematics, and thus to an intra-mathematical argument that anti-realisms recommending such bans are not good heuristics. The moral is not that mathematical objects are objective and non-spatio-temporal, but that it is a bad idea to place constraints on fruitful developments of mathematics.

(iii) *Naturalized Methodology.* Our historical analysis has given us a suggestive picture of mathematical practice, but now we face the difficult task of implementing these lessons in the evaluation of our central methodological problem: the status of CH and the independent questions of descriptive set theory. It might seem that the recipe is simple: strip away the philosophical accretions and study the remaining mathematical considerations. But we have drawn no principled distinction between the philosophical and the mathematical. Our historical examples suggest that certain questions traditionally classified as philosophical—do mathematical things exist objectively? Are they spatio-temporal? etc.—are external to practice, but this, in itself, does not amount to a principle of demarcation.

Disappointing as this may be, I think there is no principled distinction to draw between mathematics and philosophy, between mathematics and science. At least, this isn't the course I take; instead, I propose a somewhat trickier approach. In outline, the plan is to construct a naturalized model of practice. Following the lead of our historical examples, this model will not include considerations that seem, by extrapolation, to be methodologically irrelevant, and it will include more detailed analysis and development of the considerations that remain. The claim is that this purified and amplified model provides an accurate picture of the actual justificatory structure of contemporary set theory and that this justificatory structure is fully rational. This is the plan. I have more to say on the status of the undertaking, but let me begin by illustrating it.

First, we return to the historical cases, where we find both negative and positive counsel. The negative counsel we've already traced: it advises us that certain typically philosophical issues are ultimately irrelevant to the defence or criticism of mathematical methods. To apply this negative counsel to the cases that interest us will require us to extrapolate from the historical cases by identifying elements and themes in contemporary discussions that seem analogous to the historically irrelevant elements and themes.

But the historical cases also provide positive counsel. There is a pattern in what remains after the extraneous is eliminated, a pattern in the considerations that *are* relevant, in the considerations that *are* ultimately decisive. In the cases we've surveyed, the community eventually reached a consensus that the controversial method was admissible because it led to certain varieties of mathematics, that is, because it was an effective means to particular desirable ends. Thus the positive counsel of history is to frame a defence or critique of a given method in two parts: first, identify a goal (or goals) of the relevant practice, and second, argue that the method in question either is or isn't an effective means toward that goal. In detail, we should expect that some goals will take the shape of means toward higher goals, and that goals at various levels may conflict, requiring a subtle assessment of weights and balances. But the simple counsel remains: identify the goals and evaluate the methods by their relations to those goals.

Let's try this out. Are CH and the open questions of set theory legitimate mathematical questions, despite their independence of ZFC? If we reflect back on the origins of Cantorian set theory (see I. 1), it is easy to identify one of Cantor's leading goals: he wanted to give as complete as possible an account of sets of real numbers (or 'point sets', as he called them). For Cantor, this goal arose out of his interest in sets of 'exceptional points', while for the French analysts, a similar goal arose from their interest in classifying functions (see I. 4). Either way, I think it is fair to identify this as one of the aims of set theory: a complete theory of sets of real numbers. Given that overarching goal, set theorists have prima facie reason to pursue CH and the questions of descriptive set theory.

But are these questions legitimate? Do they have answers? Here arises the temptation to philosophize. If we resist that urge, if we follow the counsel of our historical examples and turn our attention away from debates about an objective reality of sets, we are not left speechless; recall (from III. 2) that Gödel also raises mathematical considerations, though these tend to be overshadowed by his more dramatic philosophical pronouncements. He says, as noted above, that 'it is possible to point out ways in which a decision of the question [CH], even if it is undecidable from the axioms in their present form, might nevertheless be obtained' (Gödel (1964), 181). If these ways are mathematically defensible, then CH has a mathematical answer, and *ipso facto* is a legitimate mathematical question. The same should go for the open questions of descriptive set theory.

So, what are these ways? Gödel continues:

first of all the axioms of set theory by no means form a system closed in itself, but, quite the contrary, the very concept of set on which they are based suggests their extension by new axioms which assert the existence of still further iterations of the operation 'set of'. These axioms can also be formulated as asserting the existence of very great cardinal numbers . . . The simplest of these strong 'axioms of infinity' assert the existence of inaccessible numbers. (Ibid. 181–2)

Gödel entertains no illusion that such small large cardinals will be effective in settling CH: 'As for the continuum problem, there is little hope of solving it by means of those axioms of infinity which can be set up on the basis of principles known today (the above-mentioned proof for the undisprovability of the CH, e.g., goes through for all of them without change)' (ibid.). As we've seen (in I. 5), the hope that large cardinals of any kind might do this job was subsequently dashed by Levy and Solovay (1967), but larger large cardinals—measurables and supercompacts— have been shown to have a powerful effect on the open questions of descriptive set theory. Gödel goes on to suggest that 'hitherto unknown' axioms that might settle CH as well. Some may be implied by 'the very concept of set' (intrinsically justified); others may be 'so abundant' and fruitful in their consequences that 'they would have to be assumed at least in the same sense as any well-established physical theory' (extrinsically justified).

On this approach, the case for the legitimacy of an independent question is as strong as the case that there will eventually be a mathematically defensible new axiom candidate that decides it. For the open questions of descriptive set theory, we've seen that there are two such axiom candidates: $V = L$ and SC. So our naturalistic case for the legitimacy of those questions is at least as strong as our case for one or the other of these candidates. As a start on this project, III. 6 contains a sketch of what I hope to be the beginnings of a cogent naturalistic case against $V = L$.

The current situation is less promising for CH. Even if the argument of III. 6 is a complete success, neither the goals identified there, nor the general methods defended on their behalf, seem to provide any guidance on the size of the continuum. Furthermore, nothing I've seen in the recent literature or heard from contemporary practitioners is particularly encouraging. There is no general consensus on CH[6]—as there is against $V = L$ and for SC—and the methods on which there is general consensus are all inadequate for its solution.

Under these circumstances, one sometimes hears a contemporary set theorist opine that 'CH may turn out not to have a determinate truth-value', or 'CH may be inherently ambiguous', or some other remark in this general tone, and it is not unusual to hear such comments explicated in familiar philosophical terms. So, for example, our Realist might suggest that we could discover there are two or more different kinds of sets—sets$_1$, which satisfy CH, and sets$_2$, which don't—just as chemists discovered that water consists of both H_2O and D_2O (heavy water). Going further along this line, the Plentiful Platonist holds that there is a universe of sets corresponding to every consistent extension of ZFC.[7] Writers of both sorts could hold that the truth-value of CH depends on which sets or which universe we are talking about, that CH is ambiguous. The Formalist, on the other hand, might understand 'CH is true' to mean 'CH follows from our current formal theory of sets', and 'CH is false' to mean 'not-CH follows from our current formal theory of sets'. Neither of these is the case, so CH has no truth-value. The Fictionalist could say something very similar, speaking of 'our current story about sets' in place of 'our current formal theory of sets'.

Once again, the counsel of our historical examples advises us to resist these philosophical accounts, in so far as we are interested in the justification of actual methodological decisions. In fact, I think there are some sound mathematical considerations underlying remarks like these of the set theorist—as described in III. 5. ii, below—considerations that merit full inclusion in the naturalist's purified and amplified model. But before we attempt any further elaboration of the model, we should pause a moment to clarify its status.

Suppose our naturalist has studied the historical cases, examined the

---

[6] For an array of opinions, see my (1988), § II. 3.

[7] Balaguer (1995) presents a closely related position.

contemporary discussion, and produced a naturalized model of the practice, a model that is purified—by leaving out considerations that the historical record suggests are methodologically irrelevant—and amplified—by highlighting the goals that remain behind and by elaborating means–ends defences or criticisms of particular methodological decisions. Our naturalist then claims that this model accurately reflects the underlying justificatory structure of the practice, that is, that the material excised is truly irrelevant, that the goals identified are among the actual goals of the practice (and that the various goals interact as portrayed), and that the means–ends reasoning employed is sound. If these claims are true, then the practice, in so far as it approximates the naturalist's model, is rational. So, how are these claims to be tested?

First, the procedures for constructing the naturalized model can be tested against other historical cases, other cases in which methodological decisions were debated and resolved. Secondly, the means–ends arguments produced can be tested for plausibility in the eyes of contemporary practitioners. Thirdly, the naturalist's model can be taken as a prediction—that these controversies will eventually be settled in these ways on these grounds—and the progress of mathematics will ultimately determine the fate of these predictions. So the claim that the model reflects the underlying justificatory structure of the practice is subject to confirmation and disconfirmation from a number of different quarters. Finally, the judgement that the arguments depicted in the model are rational is based on a simple fundamental of practical reason: the soundness of means–ends reasoning.[8]

Notice that the second in our list of tests takes us back to the old question addressed to Quinean naturalism: is the word of the practitioner to be taken as gospel? We saw (in III. 3) that the answer is no, that the views of any particular practitioner or group of practitioners are subject to criticism, as long as that criticism uses scientific, not extra-scientific, methods. Perhaps the Quinean intends to demarcate the one from the

---

[8] Here the rationality of mathematical methods is being assessed in terms of some minimal theory of the rationality of simple instrumental reasoning. Two remarks are in order. First, such instrumental reasoning is not external to mathematics; it is used in mathematics as it is in all human undertakings (e.g. 'I want to prove that P is false, so I'll assume P and derive a contradiction'). Second, the naturalist is not holding mathematics accountable to an external standard of 'rationality', not e.g. recommending that mathematics be reformed if it does not meet this standard; rather she is noting, as a descriptive claim, that when the underlying justificatory structures of mathematics are laid bare, they are, in fact, rational (by this minimal standard).

other explicitly: science is the realm of observation and the hypothetico-deductive method. We've seen (in II. 6) that this version is too simple; perhaps something better can be offered. But however the scientific case is resolved, I've renounced the corresponding task of providing a principled distinction between mathematics and the rest. So this old question becomes more difficult.

The question of practitioner authority is easier for some parts of the naturalist's central claim than for others. For example, it is easy to see that practitioners could be mistaken about their goals, for failure of self-analysis. This is the type of error a sociologist might find in any human practice: by careful analysis, we see that the practice is directed towards achieving goals A and B, while practitioners give lip service to goal C. Nothing mysterious here. Similarly, the evaluation of particular bits of means–ends reasoning, carried out against our everyday principles of instrumental rationality, is something a practitioner could be wrong about. The second type of error would seem less likely than the first, though both are conceptually possible. On the other hand, the naturalist has no independent grounds on which to criticize or defend the actual goals of the practice; the possibility of practitioner error is in the identification of goals, not in the choice of goals.

It is the remaining part of the naturalist's claim that raises subtle questions, the claim the material excised is truly irrelevant. Sometimes, the irrelevance of certain types of considerations will turn up in the resolution of the debate, as it did in our historical cases. Sometimes, a particular style of justification is idiosyncratic or special to a certain segment of the community, so that the naturalist is only excising what fails of stable consensus. But if our model is formed and evaluated as described here, the naturalist has no independent grounds on which to rule against a conclusion of the entire community; if the community in fact comes to a stable decision on a methodological issue on the basis of consideration X, which the naturalist thought worthy of excision, this would simply count as disconfirmation of the naturalist's evaluation of X.[9] So the nat-

---

[9] This conclusion is less alarming for typically 'philosophical' considerations (our focus here) than for typically 'sociological' considerations. To take a wild example, suppose mathematicians decided to reject the old maxim against inconsistency—so that both '2 + 2 = 4' and '2 + 2 = 5' could be accepted—on the grounds that this would have a sociological benefit for the self-esteem of school children. This would seem a blatant invasion of mathematics by non-mathematical considerations, but if mathematicians themselves insisted that this was not so, that they were pursuing a legitimate mathematical goal, that this goal overrides the various traditional goals, I find nothing in the mathematical naturalism presented here that provides grounds for protest.

uralist should not be viewed as protecting the practice from outside inter-
ference; if any 'outside' influence leads to methodological consensus, it
wasn't 'outside', after all. What the naturalist can do is encourage
progress towards consensus by proposing to ignore considerations that
seem likely to be mere distractions, and by highlighting considerations
that seem likely to be decisive.

To make the implicit explicit, let me break the naturalist's undertaking into a series of steps: (1) construction of a naturalized model of
practice, (2) amplification and enhancement of this model to address contemporary debates, (3) testing of the model and its enhancements, and
(4) evaluation of the rationality of the arguments involved. Notice that
much of this process employs familiar methods of natural science. The
first step—construction of the naturalized model—takes place in a more-
or-less sociological spirit: the historical record is examined and contemporary discourse analysed in light of those findings. Granted, the
practitioner's utterances are not taken as gospel in this process, but working sociologists certainly allow that the testimony of subjects can be less
than fully trustworthy, that accurate description of a practice sometimes
requires a discounting of some participants's reports. The third step is a
matter of empirical testing like any other, and the final step—the certifi-
cation of the rationality of the practice—also takes place on familiar turf,
within some minimal theory of practical reasoning.

The only exception is at the second stage, when the mathematical
naturalist attempts to enhance and extend various arguments implicit in
the practice (e.g., when I try, in III. 6, to present a case against $V = L$).
At this point, the naturalist is not doing sociology or natural science of
any kind; she is using the methods of mathematics, not those of science,
and she is doing so exactly as a mathematician might, except that her
choices among the available styles of argument are guided by the results
of the previous historical analysis. In other words, she is functioning
within mathematics, just as a mathematician might, except that she uses
only those styles of argument that her previous analysis suggests are the
relevant, effective ones. It is important to notice that the arguments
themselves are not sociological; the naturalist does not argue 'this method
is preferable because it conforms to previous practice', but 'this method
is preferable because it is the most effective method available for achieving this goal'. At this stage, the naturalist is doing what the sociologist
might call 'going native'. Going native is something the sociologist
avoids, as detrimental to scientific objectivity, but for the naturalistic
methodologist, it marks one desired payoff of the analysis.

Finally, notice that mathematical naturalism, as described here, is more a method than a thesis.[10] As a naturalistic methodologist, I do not assert that philosophy is irrelevant to the assessment of mathematical methodology; I could hardly do so without a principled distinction between philosophy and mathematics. What I do assert, on the basis of the historical analysis, is that certain types of typically philosophical considerations have turned out to be irrelevant in the past. I then propose, guided by this fact, a naturalized model of the underlying justificatory structure of the practice that can then be tested empirically. If this method is successful, we will have learned a lot about the nature of mathematics, and more particularly, of set theory. The (admittedly faint) hope is that our elaboration of the model could eliminate irrelevant distractions from the practice and draw out sound and persuasive arguments already implicit there, and in so doing, illuminate contemporary methodological debates.

(iv) *Naturalized Philosophy.* While typically philosophical questions may well be irrelevant to methodology, as the naturalistic methodologist suspects, it follows neither that they are without interest nor that they are pseudo-questions. Recall (from (i) above) that our mathematical naturalist began within natural science; it was only after noting that mathematics seems to be carried out using methods of its own that she elected to study and evaluate those methods on their own terms. Nothing in this precludes a scientific study of mathematics. Just as scientific naturalists have always found room for a scientific study of science, a scientific study of scientific language, scientific truth, and scientific methods, there is room for a scientific study of mathematical language, mathematical truth, and mathematical methods. As we've seen (in (iii)), part of our naturalized approach to mathematical methodology belongs to such a study.

There is an important difference, however, between a scientific study of science and a scientific study of mathematics, namely, that the former study uses the same methods and has the same goals as its object, while a scientific study of mathematics uses scientific, rather than mathematical, methods and has scientific, rather than mathematical, goals. It is conceivable, if only barely, that a cracker-jack scientific study of scientific language or scientific truth might influence the practice of science itself, given that the study and the practice have the same methods and goals. But the mathematical naturalist notes that mathematical methods and

---

[10] One might say its conclusions are shown rather than said.

goals are not those of science, that the scientific study of mathematics is extra-mathematical and, for that reason, is not relevant to the evaluation of mathematical methods.

Notice, once again, that the naturalist is not relying on a principled distinction between mathematics and the rest. Rather, approaching the scientific study of human discourse, she notes that mathematics seems to be operating on different routines from science. Using the techniques outlined in (iii), she attempts to isolate the underlying structure of mathematical practice, and she notes as an afterthought that typically scientific and typically philosophical considerations do not intrude. In other words, a rough-and-ready sense of what is mathematical and what is extra-mathematical emerges out of the analysis itself, and is confirmed to the extent that the resulting naturalistic model is confirmed.

Now suppose that we've generated a well-confirmed naturalized model of mathematical practice. If our experience so far is any guide, we can expect (from (i)) that it will tell us little about the metaphysical nature of mathematical things. So when we undertake our scientific study of mathematics, there will be large areas to be filled in, areas in which the naturalized model will provide no direct guidance. But—and here's the important point—if we are to adhere to our fundamental naturalistic impulse, the conviction that a successful practice should be understood and evaluated on its own terms, then what we say as we fill in those blank areas using our scientific methods should neither conflict with nor attempt to justify the content of the well-confirmed naturalistic model. In this way, our scientific study of mathematics differs from our scientific study of science: respect for the distinctive mathematical methods requires the naturalistic philosopher of mathematics to refrain from criticizing or defending those methods from an extra-mathematical standpoint, and our analysis suggests that science is such an extra-mathematical standpoint.[11]

---

[11] To draw a crude comparison: for Carnap, theoretical questions are internal, pseudo-questions are external; pragmatic questions are meaningful, but not theoretical. For Quine, Carnap's theoretical and pragmatic questions are all scientific questions, and first philosophy is pseudo. My mathematical naturalist agrees with Quine on science (except for disagreements about the actual details of scientific method and the relations between science and mathematics); on mathematics, she takes ordinary theorems and some higher-level discussions all to be mathematical questions, some questions about mathematics to be scientific and not mathematical, and some questions about mathematics to be first philosophy and hence psuedo. To be a tad less crude, I don't see that the mathematical naturalist, or the Quinean scientific naturalist, need actually declare anything pseudo: from the naturalist's position inside science, there is no way of discussing first philosophical questions (like

So naturalistic philosophy of mathematics takes place within natural science, like naturalistic philosophy of science, but unlike naturalistic philosophy of science, it takes a hands-off attitude towards the naturalized model of mathematical practice. Let me give a few crude examples of how this might affect our philosophizing. Suppose, for the sake of argument, that the mathematical considerations put forth in III. 5. ii do show that set theoretic practice could reasonably end up declaring CH to be a question without an answer. Suppose, also, that we have been tempted by a form of mathematical realism that rules this out, for example, a form of realism that posits a single world of sets in which CH is either true or false, and somehow precludes that discovery that there are, in fact, different varieties of sets. Then this form of realism conflicts with our naturalized model of practice—it rules out a possibility that the practice takes to be open—and is thus unacceptable to our naturalistic philosopher of mathematics.

On the other hand, consider Glib versions of our various other sample philosophies: the Glib Formalist holds that every (relatively consistent) extension of ZFC is as good as any other; the Glib Fictionalist holds that every (consistent?) extension of our current story about sets is as good as any other; the Glib Plentiful Platonist holds that there is an equally good set theoretic universe corresponding to every consistent extension of ZFC. From the point of view of these Glib philosophies, there are no mathematical grounds on which to prefer one extension of ZFC to another. If our preliminary impression that mathematicians do have good reason to prefer one new axiom candidate to another should pan out in the well-confirmed naturalistic model of practice, then these philosophies are also naturalistically unacceptable.

In contrast, consider Subtle versions of these same views: for example, the Subtle Formalist holds that mathematics is the study of which conclusions follow from which hypotheses, and that all consistent axiom systems are on a metaphysical par, but also that there are rational reasons, springing from the goals of mathematics itself, that justify the choice of one axiom system over another for extensive study. When the Subtle Formalist turns to a study of mathematical methodology, her work may well coincide with that of our mathematical naturalist. The same goes for Subtle versions of Fictionalism and Plentiful Platonism.[12]

---

van Fraassen's), so she need only refrain from such discussions until they are given sense, from her point of view, which means, from the point of view of science.

[12] Some who find Formalism or Fictionalism attractive as accounts of higher set theory

As my focus in this book is on methodological issues, I won't pursue the question of which of these naturalized philosophies of mathematics is preferable, but I should recall in passing that philosophizing about mathematics can be motivated by a variety of impulses. Here, we have been investigating the prospects for a scientific study of mathematical practice that respects a well-confirmed naturalistic model of that practice and is guided by standard scientific methods and goals. But we've also seen (in (ii)) that extra-mathematical philosophy, even unnaturalized first philosophy, is capable of playing an important inspirational role, and some writers, especially mathematicians, philosophize about mathematics from this second perspective. We can hardly expect that an excellent inspirational or heuristic philosophy will also be a scientifically adequate philosophy, or vice versa: for example, as Einstein's comments on philosophy and natural science suggest, the best inspirational philosophy might change from problem to problem, while the best scientific philosophy would be adopted consistently. We must be clear, in each instance, of the motivations for the philosophical view put forward, so as to judge it by the appropriate standards.

Let me conclude with a look at one last potential worry about mathematical naturalism. We have pictured the situation like this: the scientific naturalist begins her study of human cognition within natural science, where she quickly notices that mathematics is conducted by methods other than those of science; the mathematical naturalist reacts to this situation by extending the fundamental naturalistic respect for successful practice to include mathematics as well as natural science, and thus sets out to judge mathematics by its own standards, not by extra-mathematical standards, be they scientific or philosophical. The question arises: why does mathematics merit this special treatment? Should we also move, for example, to an astrological naturalism, which holds that astrological methods should not be subject to scientific criticism?

A move like this might be welcome to the pluralist or the relativist, but it is unlikely to sit well with the scientific naturalist. The trick, then,

may still be tempted to insist that the identities of elementary arithmetic are robustly true, and the brief survey of II. 6. iii may seem to support this point of view. As my focus here is on set theory, I won't pursue this point except to note (as an aside to readers of Hilbert (1926) and related writings) that even if we admit '2 + 2 = 4' to be true in a sense that the Axiom of Choice is not, this need not commit us to a Hilbert-style programme of justifying the contentless in terms of the contentful. To be motivated in that direction, one would presumably hold that investigation of the contentful is the overriding goal of mathematics, a claim that hardly squares with the practice of modern mathematics.

is to explain what singles out mathematics from the rest. In fact, I think there are good reasons, from the scientific naturalist's point of view— that is, from the point of view of natural science—to treat mathematics differently from other non-scientific disciplines. One of these gives the scientific naturalist reason to refrain from criticizing mathematical methods; the other gives her reason to want to account for mathematics nevertheless. The combination leads to mathematical naturalism, but not to astrological naturalism.

To see the first point, notice that the domain of science includes all of spatio-temporal reality, the entire causal order, but that pure mathematics has nothing to say about this domain. Philosophical accounts of mathematics may have something to say about it—e.g. that it does or doesn't include mathematical things—but mathematics itself, on the naturalist's model, does not. Astrology, on the other hand, is a different story. Webster's defines it as 'a pseudo-science claiming to foretell the future by studying the supposed influence of the relative positions of the moon, sun, and stars on human affairs'.[13] In this sense,[14] astrology posits new causal powers and makes new predictions about spatio-temporal events. From the scientific naturalist's point of view, these are ordinary scientific claims, subject to the usual scientific scrutiny. Thus astrology, on this interpretation, is subject to scientific correction in a way that pure mathematics is not.

To see the second point, suppose we give another interpretation of astrology, one that runs more directly parallel to pure mathematics; suppose we understand it to treat of certain supernatural vibrations that don't interact causally with ordinary physical phenomena. Then astrological claims will no longer come into conflict with the pronouncements of science. Should we then move to astrological naturalism?

Again, I think the answer is no. The reason is simple: mathematics is staggeringly useful, seemingly indispensable, to the practice of natural

---

[13] *Webster's New World Dictionary of the American Language*, 2nd college edn. (Cleveland, Ohio: William Collins Publishers, 1979).

[14] There are other interpretations of the goals and methods of astrology. For example, discussions of an astrological chart between the astrologer and the subject are expressed in terms of archetypes that seem to go deep into human psychology; some astrologers hold that this process allows the subject to tap into a deeper level of understanding of his/her life and actions, which can be beneficial. On this interpretation, the astrologer is engaged in psychological counselling, not in describing causal mechanisms or making predictions. There remains room for debate within psychology about the effectiveness of this therapeutic technique, and on this interpretation of astrology, these are the relevant scientific standards.

science, while astrology is not. As a result, one part of understanding science, within science, is understanding what mathematics is, what it does for science when it is used in application, and why it does this job so well.[15] Thus, there is a strong motivation for the scientific naturalist to give an acceptable account of mathematics with no parallel in the case of astrology, however the latter is interpreted.[16]

In sum, then, I've suggested that the scientific naturalist has good reasons to move to mathematical (but not astrological) naturalism, and I've tried to outline the structure of this position. Given the demise of realism, my recommendation is that we return to our original methodological problem and view it this time in a naturalistic spirit. Though naturalism is not a metaphysical rival to realism, it does provide a practical approach to the open questions of set theory and the evaluation of new axiom candidates.

---

[15] A naturalist with lingering Quinean sentiments might conclude that we have reason to study that part of mathematics that is actually or potentially applied, not that we have reason to study all of contemporary mathematics. In contrast, my mathematical naturalist sees mathematics as a unified undertaking which we have reason to study as it is, and the study of the actual methods of mathematics, which includes pure mathematics, quickly reveals that modern mathematics also has goals of its own, apart from its role in science.

[16] Notice that the naturalistic philosopher of mathematics also stands to gain from a scientific account of the role of mathematics in science: some of the goals of mathematics undoubtedly arise from these interconnections.

5

The Problem Revisited

My goal at this point is to apply the naturalistic approach (as described in III. 4) to our original questions of set theoretic methodology. This section draws together some preliminary observations, beginning (in (i)) with a re-evaluation of the realist's argument against $V = L$ from our new perspective. This review points the way towards a naturalistic defence of two general set theoretic maxims introduced in (ii). Finally, in (iii), I show how the naturalistic approach affects our evaluation of an embryonic debate over $V = L$. A more detailed argument against $V = L$, the best I have to offer, is outlined in the concluding III. 6.

(i) *Another Look at the Realist's Case.* Recall (from II. 4. ii) the realist's parallel: Combinatorialism replaced the troubled Definabilism much as Field Theories replaced the troubled Mechanism; $V = L$ then presents itself as a throwback to the discredited Definabilism. The poor track record of the Definabilist approach was displayed in a series of anomalies. In each case, Definabilist sentiment counselled against a mathematical innovation that was eventually incorporated into standard mathematical practice. Thus the Definabilist is pictured as opposing the fruitful expansion of mathematics.

This line of thought is realistic in the sense that it plays on the realist's analogy between mathematics and natural science. But notice that some of the 'hints of trouble' sketched in II.5 cast doubt on the realist's right to this approach: even if it is beyond debate that the innovations opposed by the Definabilist lead to mathematical theories we like, this is not enough to show that these theories are true in the realist's sense, not enough to show that they are true in the objective world of mathematical entities. Here, as elsewhere, the realist seems to owe more than she has delivered.

However, the situation looks very different from the perspective of the mathematical naturalist. Our naturalist hypothesizes, on the basis of historical evidence, that consideration of an 'objective world of mathematical entities' is beside the point, methodologically. Instead, she focuses on isolation of the particular goals of the practice, and on the evaluation of the means employed to achieve them. In other words, she focuses on the very sorts of considerations that are actually featured in the historical survey of II. 4. ii. Let's re-examine these with the naturalist's eye.

The first anomaly for Definabilism came in the debate between Euler and d'Alembert over the scope of allowable functions. In this case, the goal that motivated Euler's anti-Definabilism is easily identified: he wanted mathematics to provide tools for physics, for mechanics, and to achieve this goal, he argued that a wider range of functions should be admitted.[1] The counsel of history suggests that many mathematicians shared this goal, enough to guide the practice towards acceptance of Euler's position over d'Alembert's. Here the naturalist sees the practice engaged in the perfectly rational process of adopting an effective means toward its acknowledged end.

The second anomaly arose in Riemann's defence of 'pathological' functions. Here helpfulness to physical science is explicitly not the goal in question; Riemann does not doubt that functions covered by Dirichlet's theorem include 'all cases which present themselves in nature' (Bottazzini (1986), 242). Riemann appeals instead to two purely intra-mathematical goals—providing a foundation for the calculus,[2] and solving problems of number theory—and he argues that his 'pathological' functions play an important role in both undertakings. Again, subsequent practice has borne him out: his functions have played the roles predicted, and practitioners, sharing his goals, have admitted them.

Finally, the third anomaly was produced by Zermelo's proof of the Well-Ordering Theorem: both the Axiom of Choice and impredicative definitions came under Definabilist fire in the ensuing controversy. And, once again, we've seen that these innovations were eventually accepted

---

[1] Notice that this is not a case of holding mathematics to scientific standards, as the Quinean indispensability theorist would urge. Euler is not arguing that functions exist when and only when they are used in well-confirmed science. Rather, he notes that Definabilist restrictions on mathematics will limit the range of tools it makes available for scientific purposes. Science is not the arbiter of what mathematical things there are, but providing a generous store of models for scientific use is among the goals of mathematical activity.

[2] Frege himself provided an intra-mathematical justification for the search for foundations: 'if, by examining the simplest cases, we can bring to light what mankind has there done by instinct, and can extract from such procedures what is universally valid in them, may we not thus arrive at general methods for forming concepts and establishing principles which will be applicable also in more complicated cases?' (Frege (1884), § 2). In the present case, it is hard to see how the higher flights of modern analysis could have been achieved if the basics of the calculus had not been made rigorous.

because of their mathematical consequences: a classical theory of real numbers, the final link in the project of founding the calculus; a rich theory of transfinite numbers, which grew out of Cantor's interest in sets of real numbers; various fundamental results in algebra, topology, and mathematical logic; etc. The moral is that the naturalist, unlike the realist, has a clear path to explicating all three anomalies and their resolutions, and thus, that the case against Definabilism is actually more cogent from the naturalist's than from the realist's point of view.

Now consider Combinatorialism, the maxim that eventually replaced Definabilism. One aspect of Combinatorialism is the bare rejection of Definabilism: it 'abstracts from the possibility of giving definitions' (Bernays (1934), 259). The other aspect of Combinatorialism is the 'analogy of the infinite to the finite' (ibid.), according to which 'one views a set of integers as the result of infinitely many independent acts of deciding for each number whether it should be included or excluded' (ibid. 260). Another way of putting the point is to insist that at each stage of the cumulative hierarchy, we include 'all possible collections' (e.g. Boolos (1971), 491–2) of previously-formed entities. Yes, we reject the requirement that all collections be definable, but we also add a maximizing idea that every collection that can be formed at a given stage, will be formed at that stage.

An extremely general form of this admonition to maximize seems fundamental to set theoretic practice. Let's turn our naturalistic attention to this maxim and another at a similar level of generality and centrality.

(ii) *Maximize and Unify*. Both these maxims can be understood as effective means towards a single one among the various goals of set theory: the goal of providing a foundation for mathematics (in the sense of I. 2). As has been noted, set theorists could freely adopt this goal without insisting that no other mathematical theory provides a viable alternative; that is, set theorists could aim to found mathematics even if category theorists do likewise. Furthermore, set theorists could freely adopt this goal even if mathematicians in other branches of mathematics tend to reject set theoretic foundations with one or another degree of vehemence. For the foundational goal to have legitimate methodological consequences inside set theory, all that matters is that it is, in fact, a goal of set theoretic practice. And I have argued that it is.

One methodological consequence of adopting the foundational goal is immediate: if your aim is to provide a single system in which all objects and structures of mathematics can be modelled or instantiated, then you must aim for a single, fundamental theory of sets. This methodological moral is just the flip-side to one of the common objections to set theoretic foundations; for example, Mostowski remarks: 'if there are a multitude of set-theories then none of them can claim the central place in mathematics' (Mostowski (1972), 94). And MacLane elaborates at greater length:

the Zermelo–Fraenkel axioms do not settle the famous continuum hypothesis—there are models of ZF for which the hypothesis holds and models for which it fails. The demonstration of the latter fact by Cohen's method of forcing suggests other 'independence' results and leads to the construction of many alternative models of set theory. Another result is the introduction of a considerable variety of axioms meant to supplement ZF . . . For these reasons 'set' turns out to have many meanings, so that the purported foundation of all Mathematics upon set theory totters. (MacLane (1986), 358–9)

We arrive at the methodological maxim UNIFY by running this argument in reverse.[3] If set theorists were not motivated by a maxim of this sort, there would be no pressure to settle CH, to decide the questions of descriptive set theory, or to choose between alternative new axiom candidates; it would be enough to consider a multitude of alternative set theories.

To see how another methodological maxim can be traced to the foundational goal, we should pause a moment to consider the evolution of modern mathematics. There was a time when mathematics and physical science were quite closely intertwined; in Kline's words:

the Greeks, Descartes, Newton, Euler and many others believed mathematics to be the accurate description of real phenomena. . . . they regarded their work as the uncovering of the mathematical design of the universe. Mathematics did deal with abstractions, but these were no more than the ideal forms of physical things or happenings. Even such concepts as functions and derivatives were demanded by real phenomena and served to describe them. (Kline (1972), 1028)

Thus, Euler is inspired to expand his range of functions by the need to represent initial conditions of the vibrating string; Gauss investigates non-Euclidean geometry out of concern with the actual geometry of space; Fourier develops his trigonometric expansions to handle problems of heat flow. In short, the development of mathematics was guided by

---

[3] Riskin makes this point in his (1994). He is quite right that in earlier work I failed to appreciate the fundamental role of the foundational goal.

the needs of natural science; mathematical theories were chosen for their physical effectiveness.

This situation changed dramatically during the course of the nineteenth century: 'gradually and unwittingly mathematicians began to introduce concepts that had little or no direct physical meaning' (ibid. 1029). Kline cites negative and complex numbers, which troubled some consciences until they were given geometric interpretations. Non-Euclidean geometry, as it developed, led first to the realization that physical space is not known a priori to be Euclidean, and later to the conviction that it is best represented by an alternative geometry as mathematically cogent as Euclidean. Similarly, the consideration of n-dimensional spaces, once dismissed as laughable, gradually became the norm; a note from a 1845 discussion describes n-dimensional geometry as 'free of all spatial intuition . . . a pure mathematical science'.[4] Meanwhile, non-commutative algebras arose as purely mathematical alternatives to ordinary number theory, and Cantor extended the notion of number into the transfinite, remarking that 'Mathematics is entirely free in its development'.[5] Abstract algebra and the axiomatic method encouraged this liberation of mathematics from the demands of physical science.

As a result of this development, contemporary pure mathematics is pursued on the assumption that mathematicians should be free to investigate any and all objects, structures, and theories that capture their mathematical interest. This is not to say, with the Glib Formalist, that all theories are of equal interest—mathematicians, for all their freedom, do concentrate on particular lines of development—but it is to say that some of that concentration is determined by purely mathematical, as opposed to scientific, goals. As my focus here is on set theory (to which my meagre expertise is limited), I won't attempt a full naturalistic accounting of this aspect of mathematics as a whole, but I don't doubt that such an accounting could be given by persons of sufficient mathematical and historical sensitivity.

The pay-off of these observations for set theoretic methodology is simple. If mathematics is to be allowed to expand freely in this way, and if set theory is to play the hoped-for foundational role, then set theory should not impose any limitations of its own: the set theoretic arena in which mathematics is to be modelled should be as generous as possible;

---

[4] As quoted by Kline (1972), 1030.
[5] As quoted ibid. 1031.

the set theoretic axioms from which mathematical theorems are to be proved should be as powerful and fruitful as possible. Thus, the goal of founding mathematics without encumbering it generates the methodological admonition to MAXIMIZE.[6] And, given that set theory is out to provide models for all mathematical objects and instantiations for all mathematical structures, one way in which it should MAXIMIZE is in the range of available isomorphism types.[7] I hope to clarify this admonition as I apply it (first crudely in (iii), then, somewhat more carefully, in III. 6).

But before turning to applications, let me return to a point left dangling in III. 4. iii, namely, the discouraged set theorist's lament that 'CH may turn out not to have a determinate truth-value' or 'CH may be inherently ambiguous'. We noted there how these remarks can be given a range of typically philosophical explications, but that these explications are of the sort that our naturalistic analysis projects as ultimately irrelevant. But we now have access to a reading that is more to the methodological point.

Notice that there is a tension between MAXIMIZE and UNIFY: faced with alternatives like $V = L$ and MC, the easiest way to MAXIMIZE would be to adopt both theories, to use whichever happens to be most useful in a given situation. But UNIFY counsels against this course. The subtlety of applying MAXIMIZE and UNIFY will come in the effort to satisfy both admonitions at once. In the case against $V = L$, I argue (in III. 6) that this is possible, but the case of CH is more difficult. I suggest that the methodologically relevant worry that lies behind the discouraged set theorist's remark is precisely this: in this case, it might turn out not to be possible to MAXIMIZE and UNIFY simultaneously. It might turn out, for example, that ZFC can be extended in a number of incompatible ways—each with different consequences for the size of the continuum—and that no mathematically defensible considerations allow

---

[6] This is perhaps not the only goal served by MAXIMIZE. After all, set theory itself, as a branch of mathematics, shares the contemporary charge to pursue whatever is of mathematical interest, and much of the MAXIMIZing in higher set theory serves this goal as well.

[7] After all, one of set theory's greatest achievements was providing a set to model continuous structure (see I. 2). (Two structures are 'isomorphic' iff they are structurally similar; e.g. if A and B are sets and R and S are binary relations on A and B, respectively, then the structure of A with R is isomorphic to the structure of B with S iff there is a function f that maps A one-to-one onto B, such that for all $a,a' \in A$, $a\,R\,a'$ iff $f(a)\,S\,f(a')$. Two structures belong to the same 'isomorphism type' iff they are isomorphic.)

us to choose between them. If this were to happen, the pressure to MAX-IMIZE[8] might well lead the community to sacrifice UNIFY, that is, to embrace a range of theories, all with different values for the size of the continuum.[9] In the naturalistic model of the practice, the set theorist's worry is rendered in this way.

(iii) *An Example.* Let's now take a moment to explore the general outlines of the naturalistic model. As we move closer to our test case—the status of $V = L$—my goal in this subsection is to present an example of how the naturalistic approach might effect our analysis of particular modes of argumentation in fairly subtle ways. A full-dress naturalistic case against $V = L$ is postponed until III. 6.

In our naturalistic model, set theoretic discussion takes place in a natural language, for our purposes, in English. Natural language versions of the axioms of Zermelo–Fraenkel are asserted,[10] and theorems derived from them using informal logic. Among these theorems are set-theoretic surrogates for the theorems of the various branches of classical mathematics. This much constitutes the core of naturalized set theoretic activity.

As we've seen, in addition to this bare proving activity, actual set theoretic practice includes a wide range of metaconsiderations: arguments for or against axiom candidates, debates about the legitimacy of various innovative methods, discussions of the status of various independent questions, and so on. We've also seen that some of this material seems (by extrapolation from the historical cases) to merit inclusion in the naturalist's model; for example, I've suggested that Combinatorialism and the methodological maxims MAXIMIZE and UNIFY belong here. In the model, the naturalistic portion of this meta-talk forms a penumbra around the object-talk of the core.

It is important to distinguish this penumbra from what's standardly called 'metamathematics'. Strictly speaking, metamathematics is identified with a certain area in the core practice: a series of theorems about particular sets called 'formulas', 'proofs', 'theorems', and so on (the set theoretic version of proof theory); a series of theorems about particular

---

⁸ Perhaps on the grounds suggested in n. 6 above.

⁹ Of course, 'CH or not-CH' would remain a theorem within each particular theory; no threat to the law of the excluded middle is projected.

¹⁰ With the understanding that the 'properties' in the Separation Axioms and the 'functions' in the Replacement Axioms must be expressed with some care, in an austere sublanguage of English that corresponds to the limited resources of first-order logic.

sets called 'models', about a relation between models and formulas called 'satisfaction', and so on (the set theoretic version of model theory); and a series of theorems connecting the two (e.g. the Completeness Theorem, the Compactness Theorem, the Löwenheim-Skolem Theorems, Gödel's Incompleteness Theorems).

But there is more to it than that. In the penumbra, set theorists acknowledge that the concepts and theorems of metamathematics provide a good applied mathematical theory of the language and the proving activity in the core.[11] In the metamathematics of the core, we can prove 'if Con(ZFC), then Con(ZFC + CH) and Con(ZFC + ~CH)'.[12] Because we believe (in the penumbra) that first-order logic is a good representation of the natural language employed in our core set theorizing, because we think the formal notion of proof is a good representation of the modes of proof allowed there, because we think our set theory is consistent, we conclude (in the penumbra) that we most likely will not be able to prove or to disprove CH from the fundamental assumptions we've accepted so far, that we will need new axioms if we are to make further progress on this problem.

Now suppose our naturalistic set theorist is considering whether or not to add $V = L$ as a new axiom for the core theory. Sensitive to the admonition to MAXIMIZE, she begins by comparing ZFC + $V = L$ with ZFC + '$0^{\#}$ exists'. She notes that latter theory implies the existence of a non-constructible set.[13] This is not automatically maximizing, she realizes, unless that extra set realizes an isomorphism type that cannot be realized by any constructible set, but she is able to prove this, as well.[14] So adding '$0^{\#}$ exists' to our core theory would allow us to prove the existence of non-constructible isomorphism types. Should our naturalistic set theorist conclude that ZFC + '$0^{\#}$ exists' is maximizing, and hence preferable?

We'll see, in III. 6, that this line of thought is far too simple, but for

---

[11] See Burgess (1992) for a discussion of mathematical logic along these lines.

[12] Here 'Con(T)' abbreviates 'T is consistent'.

[13] For example, $0^{\#}$ itself is not constructible.

[14] For connoisseurs: Suppose $0^{\#}$ exists, and consider the structure $(V_{\omega+1}, \in)$. If $(y, S) \in L$ is isomorphic to $(V_{\omega+1}, \in)$, then S is well-founded and extensional on y. These notions are both absolute for L, so L thinks S is extensional and well-founded on y, and so (since L also thinks Mostowski's theorem on transitive collapse), L thinks there is a transitive A such that $(A, \in) \cong (y, S)$. A given function being such an isomorphism is also absolute for L, so the two structures must actually be isomorphic. Thus, $(A, \in) \cong (V_{\omega+1}, \in)$, and they are both transitive, so $A = V_{\omega+1}$. But $0^{\#} \in V_{\omega+1} = A \in L$ and L is transitive, so $0^{\#} \in L$. So L thinks $V \neq L$, which is impossible. So $(V_{\omega+1}, \in)$ is not isomorphic to any (y, S) in L.

now, let's consider a similar-sounding counter-argument, proposed by Martin as devil's advocate: ZFC + $V = L$ implies that no transitive model of the theory ZFC + '$0^{\#}$ exists' can contain all countable ordinals,[15] and thus, no transitive model of ZFC + '$0^{\#}$ exists' can contain any uncountable ordinal.[16] But ZFC + $V = L$ implies the existence of many uncountable ordinals. For reasons of pure cardinality, no countable ordinal can be isomorphic to an uncountable ordinal, so ZFC + $V = L$ implies the existence of isomorphism types not present in any transitive model of ZFC + '$0^{\#}$ exists'. The advocate concludes that ZFC + $V = L$ is actually the maximizing theory.

Of course, no one believes that $V = L$ is maximizing, but the trick here is to isolate what's wrong with this pro-$V = L$ argument. I take up these considerations in more detail in III. 6, but for now, let's imagine the naturalistic set theorist musing as follows: there is a disanalogy between the two arguments, the one for adding '$0^{\#}$ exists' and the one for adding $V = L$. The pro-'$0^{\#}$ exists' argument is direct; it tells me that if I adopt the new axiom, I can prove the existence of a non-constructible isomorphism type. The pro-$V = L$ argument, in contrast, is less direct; it tells me that if I adopt the new axiom, I can prove something about transitive models of ZFC + '$0^{\#}$ exists', that they don't contain uncountable ordinals. But, after all, ZFC + '$0^{\#}$ exists' can prove the existence of uncountable ordinals as well as ZFC + $V = L$ can! The first argument rests on a theorem, provable in the core, from the extended theory; the second argument points to a metamathematical theorem, provable in the core, from the extended theory, and asks us to draw conclusions in the penumbra from that metamathematical theorem. The style of the first argument is straightforward, but the style of the second requires some further thought.

Suppose the naturalistic set theorist continues her meditation as follows: I grant that the logical language and proof theory in the core are good representations of the natural language and proving activities of the core. I also grant that the Tarskian definition of truth in a model is a good representation of what it is for a theory to be true under a certain interpretation, of the 'semantics' of the theory. So, as I contemplate, in

---

[15] For connoisseurs: '$x = 0^{\#}$' is Π_2^1, so by Shoenfield's Absoluteness Theorem, it is absolute for transitive models containing all countable ordinals.

[16] Recall that a model is transitive iff it contains the members of its members, the members of the members of its members, and so on. If a transitive model contains any uncountable ordinal, it must contain all countable ordinals.

the penumbra, adding '$0^{\#}$ exists' to my core theory, the pro-$V = L$ argument tells me that if I adopt $V = L$, I can prove a core metamathematical theorem, from which I'm invited to draw (negative) semantic conclusions about ZFC + '$0^{\#}$ exists'. But this is odd. If I adopt $V = L$, I immediately know all I need to know about the semantics of '$0^{\#}$ exists', namely, that it is false! What more am I supposed to get from this subtle bit of metamathematics?

At this point, suppose the devil's advocate explicates the pro-$V = L$ argument like this: it isn't an argument about what would happen if we were to adopt $V = L$ as an additional axiom, it is an argument about what would happen if $V = L$ were *true*, independently of what theory we may or may not adopt. If $V = L$ were *true* in this sense, then ZFC + '$0^{\#}$ exists' is not *true* in that sense, but this is not the force of the argument. The idea is that if $V = L$ is *true*, and if we erroneously adopt '$0^{\#}$ exists', then we will be confining our discourse to a model of ZFC + '$0^{\#}$ exists'; under these circumstances, the featured metatheorem will be *true* (though unprovable in ZFC and refutable in our adopted theory ZFC + '$0^{\#}$ exists'), so the model to which our discourse is in fact confined does not in fact contain any uncountable ordinals. So ZFC + '$0^{\#}$ exists' is restrictive.

Notice that this notion of *true* is not the notion available in the core theory: truth in a set theoretic model. It is not the notion available in the penumbra, where we say 'ZFC is true' in the sense that we are willing to assert each axiom of ZFC. It is not the notion, also available in the penumbra, of truth in V, in so far as V, in the penumbra, is as described by our accepted theory of sets, the theory of the core. What's needed for this argument is a notion of *true* that is independent of our theorizing, in both the core and the penumbra. Furthermore, it requires a rather odd theory of reference, according to which the *false* theory ZFC + '$0^{\#}$ exists' comes to be interpreted in a set model that makes it true in the ordinary core sense. Whatever their merits, I suggest (extrapolating from the historical cases) that both these notions go beyond the methodologically relevant into extra-mathematical theorizing. As such, they do not appear in the naturalistic model, so this version of the second argument does not persuade our naturalistic set theorist.

I hope this example gives some sense of how the naturalistic approach can make fairly subtle distinctions in the detail of methodological argumentation. Let's now turn to $V = L$ in earnest.

6

A Naturalist's Case against $V = L$

My aim now is to argue that $V = L$ is 'restrictive' in some sense and that 'restrictiveness' in this sense is bad, and to argue these things on naturalistically acceptable grounds. The idea is to motivate the case against restrictive theories by appeal to MAXIMIZE, so the central claim will be that restrictive theories somehow restrict isomorphism types. I begin (in (i)) with an attempt to refine the crude anti-$V = L$ argument of III. 5. iii into a formal criterion of restrictiveness. In (ii) I use some fairly esoteric counterexamples due to Steel to demonstrate the shortcomings of this criterion and to show, in general, how we can expect our purely formal approach to need supplementation. A final sketch of a naturalistic case against $V = L$ appears in (iii).

(i) *A Formal Criterion.* The crude argument of III. 5. iii can be put like this: there are things like $0^{\#}$ that are not in L. And not only is $0^{\#}$ not in L, its existence implies the existence of an isomorphism type that is not realized by anything in L. These facts wouldn't carry any weight if ZFC + '$0^{\#}$ exists' were inconsistent—CONSISTENCY is an overriding maxim[1]—but accumulated evidence suggests that ZFC + '$0^{\#}$ exists' is not inconsistent.[2] So it seems that ZFC + $V = L$ is restrictive because it rules out the extra isomorphism types available from ZFC + '$0^{\#}$ exists'.

By way of contrast, recall AFA (from I. 3. ix), that is, set theory with the non-well-founded sets guaranteed by Aczel's anti-foundation axiom.[3]

---

[1] There have been episodes in the history of mathematics when CONSISTENCY has been (temporarily) sacrificed—e.g. in the development of the calculus—but given the motivating concern of axiomatic set theory with the issue of consistency, this is not a likely instance for such a sacrifice.

[2] For connoisseurs: I have in mind the relative consistency results of Jensen and Solovay (1970), the extended successful work on inner models, and the ordinary inductive evidence that no one has yet derived a contradiction from ZFC + '$0^{\#}$ exists'.

[3] Actually, 'AFA' is usually used to stand for the anti-foundation axiom itself, so my AFA is what's standardly referred to as (ZFC-Foundation) + AFA. Steel first recommended that I consider this case in connection with restrictiveness arguments against $V = L$.

It might seem that reasoning similar to what we've just rehearsed would classify ZFC as restrictive, because there are non-well-founded sets available from AFA that are not in WF (the class of well-founded sets).[4] But the supposed analogy is illusory: the new, non-well-founded sets do not realize any isomorphism types that are not realized in WF.[5]

The further merits of this argument can be appreciated if we consider another abortive pro-$V = L$ argument: $V = L$ is good because it produces a deep and rich theory of sets;[6] we can say a lot about constructible sets, much less about sets in general. Similarly, in abstract algebra, the study of groups is richer and more productive that the study of arbitrary structures with one binary operation. At least one goal of mathematics, so the argument runs, is to produce these strong structure theories, and $V = L$ is well suited to this goal.

Notice, first, that this line of argument falls entirely within our naturalistic model: it is based on an assessment of the goals of mathematics and the most effective means for reaching them. In addition, it seems likely that a strong case could be made in favour of a preference for strong structure theories; let's assume so, for the sake of argument. Would this additional maxim then count against ZFC + '$0^{\#}$ exists'? The answer, I think, is no, because the new isomorphism types gained by ZFC + '$0^{\#}$ exists' are gained, as it were, for free. In moving from ZFC + $V = L$ to ZFC + '$0^{\#}$ exists', we aren't losing anything, because L can still be constructed from ZFC + '$0^{\#}$ exists', we still have L itself. In this case, it seems we can maximize isomorphism types—by moving to ZFC + '$0^{\#}$ exists'—without sacrificing the strong structure theory of L.

This observation shows how the underlying tension between our two methodological maxims—UNIFY and MAXIMIZE—is resolved in this case. Faced with alternatives like ZFC + $V = L$ and ZFC + '$0^{\#}$ exists', the worry was that the easiest way to MAXIMIZE would be to allow both theories, but that this runs afoul of UNIFY (see III. 5. ii). The beauty of

---

[4] In the familiar context of ZFC, $V = $ WF. To leave room for AFA in what follows, I use 'V' for the class of all sets, well-founded or not, which may or may not be identical to WF.

[5] For connoisseurs: if A is a set (possibly non-well-founded) and R is a relation on A, then in ZFC-Foundation, it can be shown that A is equinumerous with some ordinal α; let f be a one-to-one correspondence between them. Let S be $\{\langle f(x), f(y)\rangle \mid \langle x, y\rangle \in R\}$. Then $(A,R) \cong (\alpha, S)$, which is in WF. So AFA adds no new isomorphism types. See McLarty (1993) for a related discussion.

[6] Jensen began developing what's called the 'fine structure theory' of L in the mid-1960s. See Devlin (1984) for a textbook treatment.

this case is that it seems possible to UNIFY—that is, to choose between ZFC + $V = L$ and ZFC + '$0^\#$ exists'—while still MAXIMIZING, because the choice of ZFC + '$0^\#$ exists' doesn't require the sacrifice of any of the content of ZFC + $V = L$.

So far, then, this approach to the case against $V = L$ seems promising, but there is a serious problem with the crude version we've been considering. We're looking for a criterion of restrictiveness that applies to theories, like ZFC + $V = L$, but our discussions so far have centred on a model, namely L. The same switch appears in the AFA case, when we move from talk of the theory ZFC to talk of the model WF. In fact, some such switch is almost unavoidable, because we are investigating the realization of isomorphism types, which happens in models, not in theories.

To shift the comparison from models to theories, we replace talk of models with talk of interpretations of one theory in another: instead of saying that L is still available from ZFC + '$0^\#$ exists', we say that ZFC + $V = L$ can be interpreted in ZFC + '$0^\#$ exists'. Our interpretation[7] of ZFC + $V = L$ in ZFC + '$0^\#$ exists' sends a formula ϕ to the formula ϕL (that is, ϕ with its quantifiers relativized[8] to the condition '$x \in L$'); our interpretation of ZFC in AFA sends a formula ϕ to the formula ϕ^{WF} (quantifiers relativized to the condition '$x \in WF$'). Our naturalistic argument then comes to the observation that ZFC + '$0^\#$ exists' implies the existence of an isomorphism type not realized by anything satisfying '$x \in L$', while AFA does not imply the existence of an isomorphism type not realized by anything satisfying '$x \in WF$'.[9]

Unfortunately, without some further explication, this line of thought is subject to a more refined version of Martin's devil's advocate argument from III. 5. Consider the theory

ZFC + $V = L$ + 'there is a transitive model of ZFC + "$0^\#$ exists"'.

Call this theory T. Obviously, T implies that there is a transitive model of ZFC + '$0^\#$ exists'. Now because of the way L is constructed, the Well-

---

[7] This counts as an interpretation of ZFC + $V = L$ in ZFC + '$0^\#$ exists' because: if ZFC + $V = L$ implies ϕ, then ZFC + '$0^\#$ exists' implies ϕ^L.

[8] To relativize ϕ to a condition ψ, replace $\forall x(\ldots)$ with $\forall x(\psi(x) \to \ldots)$ and replace $\exists x(\ldots)$ with $\exists x(\psi(x) \wedge \ldots)$.

[9] That is, ZFC + '$0^\#$ exists' proves $\exists x \exists R \subseteq x^2 \forall y \forall S \subseteq y^2(y \in L \wedge S \in L \to (x,R) \not\cong (y,S))$, while AFA does not prove $\exists x \exists R \subseteq x^2 \forall y \forall S \subseteq y^2(y \in WF \wedge S \in WF \to (x,R) \not\cong (y,S))$. In fact, AFA proves $\forall x \forall R \subseteq x^2 \exists y \exists S \subseteq y^2(y \in WF \wedge S \in WF \wedge (x,R) \cong (y,S))$. This is the upshot of n. 14 of III. 5 and n. 5, above.

Ordering Theorem is true there in an especially strong form:[10] there is a formula with two free variables, usually written $x <_L y$, that well-orders all of L. Let $\psi(x)$ say that x is in the $<_L$-least transitive model of ZFC + '$0^\#$ exists'. Then the replacement of ϕ by ϕ^ψ is an interpretation of ZFC + '$0^\#$ exists' in T. But T also proves that any transitive model of ZFC + '$0^\#$ exists' is missing some countable ordinals,[11] and hence that there are isomorphism types not realized by anything satisfying ψ. Does it follow that ZFC + '$0^\#$ exists' is restrictive?

Intuitively, what's wrong with this line of reasoning is that an interpretation of ZFC + '$0^\#$ exists' using ψ is not comparable to the interpretation of ZFC + $V = L$ in L or the interpretation of ZFC in WF. L is just the right interpretation for ZFC + $V = L$, WF is just the right interpretation of ZFC, but $\{x \mid \psi(x)\}$ is a paltry interpretation of ZFC + '$0^\#$ exists'; to begin with, it's countable! The claim that we can UNIFY while MAXIMIZING in fact rests on the idea that interpreting ZFC + $V = L$ in L somehow 'preserves' that theory, in a way that the proposed interpretation of ZFC + '$0^\#$ exists' does not seem to preserve it. To make any progress here, we need some notion of a satisfying or fair interpretation of one theory in another.

To get at the idea of 'preserving' or 'fairly interpreting' a theory T, consider for a moment the point of view of the T-theorist. Obviously, her intention is to give a theory of V itself. In the cases that interest us, the interpreting theorist will not agree to this; she thinks that T is false in V. But it seems that sometimes the two can agree on an interpretation in something less than V, as they do in the case of L or WF. Even if $V \neq L$ or $V \neq$ WF, L and WF are substantial approximations to V. Perhaps the T-theorist and her opponent can agree if the proposed interpretation is sufficiently robust in this way.

In the history of set theory, two robust approximations to V stand out. The first is Zermelo's series of models V_κ, for κ inaccessible (introduced in Zermelo (1930)). Zermelo's idea (see I. 5) is that the full cumulative hierarchy is a 'boundless progression' of these approximations. Each

---

[10] The general point is not mysterious: at each stage, we add a set for each formula (there are only countably many of these, so they can be ordered first, second, third, fourth, etc.) and each assignment of finitely many previously-formed sets to the free variables of the formula. If the previously-formed sets have already been well-ordered, we can well-order the stage; so we can well-order the whole thing recursively. For a textbook treatment, see Drake (1974), 135–6, or Kunen (1980), 173–4.

[11] By the argument of n. 15 of III. 5.

satisfies not only the first-order, but also the full second-order axioms of Zermelo–Fraenkel, which contributes to the impression that they match the intuitive idea of the full cumulative hierarchy. Current textbooks refer to them by such honorific titles as 'natural models' or 'standard complete models' (e.g. Drake (1974), 110, 122).

The second conspicuous style of approximation to V is the proper class inner models, beginning with Gödel's L. So, for example, L contains all the ordinals, and thus, as many stages as V, but (e.g. on sufficiently large large cardinal hypotheses) it may fail to contain the full power set of every set it contains (e.g. in those circumstances, it does not contain $0^{\#}$, a subset of ω). During the 1960s and early 1970s, shortly after Scott's proof that the existence of a measurable cardinal implies the existence of non-constructible sets, Solovay, Silver, and Kunen used the notion of relative constructibility[12] to describe inner models with measurable cardinals;[13] these contain some sets missing in L, but perhaps not all present in V. Since then, the development of inner models for ever stronger large cardinal hypotheses has been among the liveliest research programmes in set theory.[14] Crudely put, while natural models compromise on the 'tallness' of V, the proper class inner models compromise on its 'thickness'; while the natural models for larger and larger inaccessibles are ever higher, and thus, improving approximations to V, the proper class inner models of larger and larger large cardinals are ever broadening, and thus, improving approximations to V.

I propose to use these two salient notions of approximation to V to formulate a rough stab at the notion of a 'fair interpretation' of one theory in another. First, we need the interpreting theory to guarantee the existence of one of our robust approximations. Working in the formal language of set theory (that is, first-order logic with '∈' as the only non-logical symbol), suppose α is a variable ranging over ordinals,[15] and ϕ is a formula with one free variable. Then,

> *definition*: 'T shows ϕ is an inner model' iff
>   (i) for all σ in ZFC, T proves σ^{ϕ}, and

---

[12] If A is a set, $L[A]$—the sets constructible relative to A—is the smallest proper class inner model M of ZFC such that, for every $x \in M$, $x \cap A \in M$. For textbook treatment, see Drake (1974), 150–1; for historical discussion, see Kanamori (1994), 34–5.

[13] See Kanamori (1994), § 20.

[14] Martin and Steel (1994) begins with an overview. See also Mitchell (1994), Mitchell and Steel (1994), and Steel (1993).

[15] That is, '∀α(. . .)' is '∀x(x is an ordinal → . . .)' and '∃α(. . .)' is '∃x(x is an ordinal ∧ . . .)'.

(ii) T proves $\forall\alpha\phi(\alpha)$ or T proves $\exists\kappa(\text{Inacc}(\kappa) \wedge \forall\alpha(\alpha < \kappa \rightarrow \phi(\alpha)))$, and

(iii) T proves $\forall x \forall y((x \in y \wedge \phi(y)) \rightarrow \phi(x))$.

I'm using 'inner model' here as a blanket term for natural models, proper class inner models, and truncations of proper class inner models at inaccessible levels (a simultaneous compromise on 'tallness' and 'thickness'). Now we can express the idea that a theory T' interprets a theory T in such an inner model:

> *definition*: ϕ is a *fair interpretation* of T in T' (where T extends ZFC) iff
> (i) T' shows ϕ is an inner model, and
> (ii) for all $\sigma \in T$, T' proves σ^ϕ.

I require that the interpreted theory T extend ZFC because all our robust interpretations—natural models, proper class inner models, and inaccessible truncations thereof—start out as models of ZFC.

This definition ratifies our informal thinking. ZFC + '$0^\#$ exists' shows '$x \in L$' is an inner model, and it proves every axiom of ZFC + $V = L$ relativized to L, so '$x \in L$' is a fair interpretation of ZFC + $V = L$ in ZFC + '$0^\#$ exists'. On the other hand, there is no fair interpretation of ZFC + '$0^\#$ exists' in ZFC + $V = L$.[16] Finally, AFA implies that '$x \in$ WF' is an inner model, and that the axioms of ZFC hold relativized to WF, so there is a fair interpretation of ZFC in AFA.

The next step towards an account of restrictiveness is to get at the notion of providing new isomorphism types. Our informal idea was that ZFC + '$0^\#$ exists' delivers a new isomorphism type because it proves the existence of a structure that is not isomorphic to anything constructible, that is, to anything in L. Here L (or really '$x \in L$') is the fair interpretation of ZFC + $V = L$ in ZFC + '$0^\#$ exists'. In general form, this is

> *definition*: T' *maximizes* over T iff there is a ϕ such that
> (i) ϕ is a fair interpretation of T in T', and
> (ii) T' proves $\exists x \exists R \subseteq x^2 \forall y \forall S \subseteq y^2(\phi(y) \wedge \phi(S) \rightarrow (x,R) \not\cong (y,S))$.[17]

---

[16] If there were, call it $\psi(x)$, then ZFC + $V = L$ would prove '$0^\#$ exists' relativized to ψ. But 'being $0^\#$' is absolute for inner models, so ZFC + $V = L$ would prove '$0^\#$ exists' outright. So ZFC + $V = L$ would prove $V \neq L$, which is impossible (assuming ZFC is consistent).

[17] For connoisseurs: notice that if T', as well as T, extends ZFC, then clause (ii) can be

For good measure, let's add:

> *definition*: T' *properly maximizes* over T iff T' maximizes over T
> and T does not maximize over T'.

Using this definition, our informal argument can be rephrased as: ZFC + '$0^{\#}$ exists' properly maximizes over ZFC + $V = L$, but AFA doesn't even maximize over ZFC.[18]

At this point, given the structure of our informal argument, it is tempting to call a theory 'restrictive' if there is a (probably consistent) theory that properly maximizes over it. But this can't be quite right. To see this, consider the theory $T' =$ ZFC + 'there is an inaccessible cardinal'. Arguing in T', we can show that '$x \in V_{\kappa}$' is a fair interpretation of ZFC (where κ is the inaccessible), and that there are isomorphism types not realized in V_{κ}, so T' maximizes over ZFC. But ZFC cannot maximize over T': if ZFC proved the existence of an inner model with an inaccessible, it would prove the existence of an inner model of its own consistency, but the consistency of ZFC is absolute[19] for inner models, so ZFC would prove its own consistency outright, which it can't.[20] So T' properly maximizes over ZFC. But, it seems wrong to say that ZFC is restrictive simply because it doesn't assert the existence of an inaccessible cardinal. It may not be as forthcoming as it might, but it doesn't actually restrict (assuming T' is consistent). This suggests that for a theory

---

replaced by the simpler (ii') T' proves $\exists x(\sim\phi(x))$. In the presence of Foundation, an extra set is an extra isomorphism type. (Arguing in T': if A is the set such that $\sim\psi(A)$, let B be the transitive closure of A, and suppose there are y and $S \subseteq y^2$ such that $\psi(y)$ and $\psi(S)$ and $(B,\in) \cong (y,S)$. Use Mostowski's Collapse relativized to ψ to get a C such that $\psi(C)$ and $(y,S) \cong (C,\in)$ relativized to ψ. But being an isomorphism is absolute for inner models, so $(C,\in)$ really is isomorphic to (y,S). So is $(B,\in)$. So $(B,\in) \cong (C,\in)$, and they are both transitive; thus $B = C$. It follows that $\psi(B)$, and hence that $\psi(A)$. Contradiction.) I retain the more complicated (ii) of the text so that the definition will apply to AFA, which doesn't extend ZFC precisely because it doesn't include Foundation.

[18] For connoisseurs: our previous informal argument is not quite enough to establish this second claim, as the definition of fair interpretation now allows for AFA to interpret ZFC in models other than WF. Given that Con(ZFC-Foundation) $\to$ Con(AFA) (see Moschovakis (1994), 259–62, recalling that my AFA is Moschovakis's (ZFC-Foundation) + AFA), AFA cannot prove the existence of an inaccessible. Now suppose AFA interprets ZFC in L rather than WF. The argument of n. 5 then shows that (A,R) is isomorphic to a set in WF. If AFA could prove that this set is not in L, it could prove the existence of a non-constructible, well-founded set. To see that AFA cannot do this, modify Moschovakis's construction by beginning from L rather than WF; the result will be a model of AFA + WF = L.

[19] Recall that σ is absolute for M iff (σ is true in M iff σ is true in V).

[20] Assuming, as always, that ZFC itself is consistent.

T to be genuinely restrictive, the maximizing theory T' must actually contradict T:

> definition: T' *inconsistently maximizes* over T iff T' properly maximizes over T and T' is inconsistent with T.

Of course, ZFC + '$0^{\#}$ exists' inconsistently maximizes over ZFC + $V = L$.

But even this isn't quite enough. To see why, consider the supposition that there are arbitrarily large measurable cardinals:

$$T = \text{ZFC} + \forall\alpha\exists x(\text{MC}(x) \wedge x > \alpha)$$

(where '$\text{MC}(x)$' abbreviates 'x is a measurable cardinal'). This surely seems a generous theory, one whose fair interpretations ought to realize lots of isomorphism types. But now consider another theory that asserts the existence of many measurable cardinals, but which also asserts that the sequence of measurable cardinals eventually comes to an end:[21]

$$T' = \text{ZFC} + \exists x(\text{Inacc}(x) \wedge \sim\text{MC}(x) \wedge x = \sup\{y \,|\, \text{MC}(y)\})$$

(where '$\text{Inacc}(x)$' abbreviates 'x is an inaccessible cardinal' and '$\sup A$' is the supremum[22] of a set of ordinals A). So T' says there is an inaccessible above all the measurables. Though T' seems restrictive—it says there are no more measurables past a certain point—it is easy to see that T' maximizes over T. Surely it would be counterintuitive to classify T as restrictive on the grounds of T'!

I think we need not go very far afield to see what's gone wrong here. We must grant that T' provides something that T cannot prove to exist, namely, a set of measurable cardinals with an inaccessible, but not measurable, supremum; in that sense, T' is richer than T. But nothing in T precludes what T' provides; that is, T can be extended to say that there is such a set of measurables:

$$T'' = T + \exists x(\forall y(y \in x \rightarrow \text{MC}(y) \wedge \text{Inacc}(\sup(x)) \wedge$$
$$\sim\text{MC}(\sup(x))))$$

This new theory T'' maximizes over T', which suggests, once again, that though T doesn't go as far as it might, it doesn't actually restrict. The

---

[21] This example is also due to Martin.

[22] If A is a set of ordinals, then $\sup A$ is the smallest ordinal β such that $\beta \geq \alpha$, for all $\alpha \in A$.

term 'restrictive' ought to be reserved for theories that actually rule out a certain line of development. So,

> *definition*: T' *strongly maximizes* over T iff
> (i) T' inconsistently maximizes over T, and
> (ii) there is no consistent[23] T'' extending T that properly maximizes over T'.

(In most interesting cases, we won't be able to prove the consistency of a candidate for T'', so the conclusion to be drawn will be that whatever evidence we have for the consistency of a candidate T'' is also evidence that T' doesn't strongly maximize over T.) Since 'being $0^\#$' is absolute for inner models, no extension of ZFC + $V = L$ can provide a fair interpretation of ZFC + '$0^\#$ exists'. Thus ZFC + '$0^\#$ exists' strongly maximizes over ZFC + $V = L$.

Finally, the proposal is:

> *definition*: T is *restrictive* iff there is a consistent T' that strongly maximizes over T.

(Once again, we will often be unable to prove the consistency of a candidate T', but evidence for its consistency will be evidence for the restrictiveness of T.) Given that ZFC + '$0^\#$ exists' strongly maximizes over ZFC + $V = L$, we can be as confident that ZFC + $V = L$ is restrictive as we are of the consistency of ZFC + '$0^\#$ exists', and we are fairly confident of the latter. In fact, we can do even better than this by observing that ZFC + $V \neq L$ also strongly maximizes over ZFC + $V = L$,[24] and that we have the best possible evidence that ZFC + $V \neq L$ is consistent (it is consistent if ZFC is).

In these terms, we have clear grounds for claiming that ZFC + $V = L$ is restrictive. Furthermore, MAXIMIZE tells us that we should maximize isomorphism types, and thus, presumably, that we should reject restrictive theories, so we also have clear grounds for the consensus against $V = L$. We are left with a wide range of theories that strongly maximize over ZFC + $V = L$, including ZFC + '$0^\#$ exists', ZFC + MC, ZFC + $V \neq L$, and for that matter, such duds as ZFC + $V \neq L$ + ~Con(ZFC).[25] The next step would be to examine the rational grounds for a choice between these.

---

[23] Notice that an inconsistent T'' would properly maximize over any consistent T'.

[24] This follows using the argument of n. 17 and the fact that 'x is constructible' is also absolute.

[25] Thanks to Steel for bringing up this last example.

(ii) *False Negative and False Positives*.[26] I think the argument of (i) has some promise as forerunner to a complete and cogent naturalistic argument against $V = L$, but it will not do precisely as stated. The first symptom of trouble is that the proposed criterion of restrictiveness admits both false positives and false negatives, that is, it classifies as restrictive certain theories that don't seem restrictive and it fails to classify as restrictive certain theories that do seem restrictive. In both cases, the structure of the counterexamples suggests that the formal criterion will need supplementation by informal considerations of a broader character. To see this, let's begin with the false negatives.

$V = L$, as we know, is the claim that the universe, V, is identical with the smallest proper class inner model, L. Given the development of 'wider' proper class inner models that include various large cardinals, beginning with measurables, the next test case would be to ask what the criterion has to say about various theories of the form ZFC + '$V =$ the canonical inner model with such-and-such large cardinals'. A theory like this seems restrictive because it rules out the existence of additional large cardinals; the expectation is that it would be strongly maximized over by a theory of the form ZFC + 'the next larger large cardinal exists'. In fact, this pattern is satisfied for a considerable distance. So, for example, ZFC + 'there are two measurable cardinals' (ZFC + 2MC) provides a fair interpretation of ZFC + '$V =$ the canonical inner model with one measurable cardinal' (ZFC + $V = L[U]$).[27] Furthermore, ZFC + $V = L[U]$ implies that there is no inner model of ZFC + 2MC, so neither it nor any extension of it can fairly interpret ZFC + 2MC. Thus, ZFC + 2MC strongly maximizes over ZFC + $V = L[U]$, and the latter is restrictive, as seems right.

The trouble comes later. Recall (from I. 5) that various central determinacy hypotheses can be derived from the existence of large cardinals; the culminating result in this development was the proof by Woodin, Martin and Steel that the determinacy of every set of reals constructible from the reals (that is, every set of reals in $L(\mathbb{R})$)[28] follows from ZFC +

---

[26] The examples in this section are due to Steel. Without the help of those much more knowledgeable than myself—particularly, Martin, Steel, and Resnikoff—I wouldn't have even the weak understanding of these matters that I now enjoy.

[27] The 'canonical inner model with one measurable cardinal' is $L[U]$, the sets constructible relative to U, where U is the measure on the first measurable cardinal κ.

[28] Recall (from I. 5) that $L(\mathbb{R})$, the sets constructible from $\mathbb{R}$, is the result of starting with the reals, and proceeding as in the construction of L. This is not the same as $L[\mathbb{R}]$, the sets constructible relative to the $\mathbb{R}$, as described in n. 12: to cite just one difference, $L[\mathbb{R}]$ is

SC, where SC asserts the existence of a supercompact cardinal. Now, in fact, this result can be obtained from a hypothesis much weaker than the assumption of a full supercompact.[29] The central notion here is that of a Woodin cardinal, a 'technical hypothesis' of which Kanamori writes, 'its full significance can only be appreciated after an extended exegesis' (Kanamori (1994, 360).[30] I refer the interested reader to Kanamori's book for that exegesis. For our purposes, it is enough to note that Martin and Steel (1988, 1989) proved: if there are *n* Woodin cardinals with a measurable cardinal above them, then all Π^1_{n+1} sets of reals are determined. It follows that: if there are $\aleph_0$ Woodin cardinals, then all projective sets of reals are determined (that is, projective determinacy (PD) holds). Using a key result of Woodin's, Martin and Steel improved this result to: if there are $\aleph_0$ Woodins and a measurable above them, then every set of reals in $L(\mathbb{R})$ is determined; in other words, the full axiom of determinacy (AD) is true in $L(\mathbb{R})$ (written $AD^{L(\mathbb{R})}$). This last is a particularly natural hypothesis, stating that AD is true in the smallest model of ZF containing all ordinals and all reals.

So Woodin cardinals are central to the theory of sets of real numbers provided by the large cardinal alternative to ZFC + $V = L$, and thus a most important step in the hierarchy of large cardinal axioms.[31] After the development of inner models for measurable cardinals and other intermediate large cardinals, Mitchell and Steel (1994) and Steel (1993) developed inner models with Woodin cardinals, and it is here that the criterion generates its false negatives. Consider the theory ZFC + $V = L[E]$, where $L[E]$ is the canonical inner model with two Woodin cardinals; this theory rules out the existence of a third Woodin cardinal, which surely seems restrictive. But, surprisingly, ZFC + $V = L[E]$ can be extended to provide proper class inner models for such theories as ZFC + 'there are

a model of ZFC; $L(\mathbb{R})$ is a model of ZF, but need not satisfy the Axiom of Choice, because the reals themselves may not be well-ordered. See Drake (1974), 149–52 for the contrast.

[29] Recall (from I. 5) that κ is λ-supercompact (for $\lambda \geq \kappa$) iff it is the critical point of an elementary embedding j of V into an inner model M such that $j(\kappa) > \lambda$ and M is closed under λ sequences; κ is supercompact iff it is λ-supercompact for all $\lambda \geq \kappa$. Then for a cardinal κ, being Woodin is considerably weaker than being κ^+-supercompact (where κ^+ is the next cardinal number after κ).

[30] Cf. Mitchell (1994), 164: 'The definition of a Woodin cardinal has been included to satisfy the reader's curiosity, but it was probably more puzzling than satisfying.' Martin and Steel (1994), 4–5, make the opposite choice: 'The rather involved definition of a Woodin cardinal would not illuminate this discussion.'

[31] Mitchell (1994), 164–5, makes a more complete case for the importance of Woodin cardinals.

five Woodins', ZFC + 'there is a supercompact', and so on.[32] This means that none of these theories strongly maximizes over ZFC + $V = L[E]$, so it cannot be shown to be restrictive in the usual way. Our definitions produce a false negative.

I think the diagnosis of what's going wrong here is not too difficult. Though the relevant extensions of ZFC + $V = L[E]$ undeniably provide proper class inner models for theories like ZFC + 'there is a supercompact', those inner models lack various mathematically desirable features of 'canonical' inner models.[33] In cases like this, there will be more than one way to provide an inner model for a given theory T—what we've defined as a 'fair interpretation' of T—and there may also be clear and legitimate mathematical reasons to judge some to be 'optimal' and others not. Naturally, the T theorist, in agreeing to a fair interpretation, will want an optimal interpretation; to interpret T in a sub-optimal model is not to 'preserve' it, to interpret it 'without loss'. This phenomenon is masked in the case of ZFC + $V = L$, our focus case, because the only possible inner models are L and inaccessible truncations thereof: we've seen that L is the smallest proper class inner model of ZFC (if a proper class inner model M is such that $M \subseteq L$, then $M = L$) and it is also the largest proper class inner model of $V = L$ (if $L \subseteq M$, and M thinks $V = L$, then $M = L$). In this case, the only available proper class inner model is also optimal, but in more complex cases, we can't count on this welcome simplification.

This suggests that the definition of 'fair interpretation' should be modified to require that the inner model be 'optimal'. The trouble with this suggestion is that we have no formal criterion for optimality, and the current prospects are dim. For comparison, notice that some of the central notions of contemporary inner model theory—for example, 'core model'[34]—have not been formally defined:

---

[32] For connoisseurs: the trick, as it's been explained to me, is that the canonical inner model with two Woodins is Σ_4^1-correct, and inner models of the larger large cardinals can be coded by Δ_4^1 reals. The relevant extension of ZFC + $V = L[E]$ simply adds the claim that the larger large cardinal axiom is true relativized to the formula defining the appropriate inner model.

[33] e.g. they are not iterable. See Martin and Steel (1994), Mitchell and Steel (1994), and Steel (1996).

[34] On the importance of core models, Martin and Steel write: 'Among the multitude of . . . models of ZFC . . . the class of core models stands out. The models in this class have a high degree of resemblance to one another, and there are powerful methods which produce a detailed account of their structure. On the other hand, the class seems rich enough to contain models for all the known large cardinal hypotheses. Moreover, the core models are arranged in a natural well-ordered hierarchy that corresponds to the consistency-

we should warn the reader that there is no precise general definition of 'core model' . . ., just as there is no such definition of 'large cardinal hypothesis'. One can only point to instances. The preceding paragraphs only describe the pattern of existing theory in these instances, although, as we said, we expect that one day this pattern will extend much further. (Martin and Steel (1994), 2–3)

Even figuring out what counts as extending the pattern is itself part of the problem:

Suppose that we are given a model: how do we recognize it as the core model? There is only a limited sense in which we can give an answer to this question—as we consider larger and larger cardinals the core model will look less and less like L, and a good part of the interest in the investigation of large cardinals, including core model theory, is in the discovery of these necessary differences. (Mitchell (1994), 160)

Perhaps, with the development of inner model theory, it will one day be possible to define notions like 'core model' in formal terms, but these definitions will come at the end of the analysis rather than the beginning. And there is no reason to suppose that the required notion of 'optimality' will be any more tractable.

The lesson of the false negative, then, is this. The notion of 'fair interpretation', as defined here, is too weak to deal justly with these more complex cases. When a theory T admits a range of inner model interpretations, there can be mathematically defensible reasons for preferring some of these to others, and the T theorist will justifiably regard any suboptimal interpretation as less than fair. If we had a formal criterion for 'optimality', we could modify the formal definition of 'fair interpretation' accordingly, but we don't, and given the current state of inner model theory, the immediate prospects are not good. The fact remains, however, that we can recognize L as an optimal interpretation of ZFC + $V = L$, and the inner model of ZFC + 'there are five Woodin cardinals' provided by the proposed extension of ZFC + $V = L[E]$ as suboptimal.[35]

strength hierarchy on the large cardinal hypotheses they satisfy' (Martin and Steel (1994), 1–2). According to Mitchell, these results 'show that large cardinals, which once seemed an amorphous contrast to the order of the constructible sets, can in fact be gathered into a similarly rigid and powerful structure' (Mitchell (1994), 173–4).

[35] Compare Mitchell on core models: 'One possible way around this question [how to define "core model"] is to simply assert that we will recognize the core model when we see it. This answer is not entirely frivolous: part of the strength of core model theory so far has been that the core models defined have been clearly and unambiguously recognizable as such' (Mitchell (1994), 160).

Let's turn now to the false positives. Here again, the example is due to Steel, and it involves a new notion: $0^{\dagger}$. It is perhaps not too misleading to say that $0^{\dagger}$ is a set of natural numbers that bears the same relation to the canonical inner model with one measurable cardinal that $0^{\#}$ bears to L.[36] Just as the existence of $0^{\#}$ follows from the existence of (at least) one measurable cardinal, the existence of $0^{\dagger}$ follows from the existence of (at least) two measurable cardinals. For the example, then, we start with ZFC + 'there is a measurable cardinal' (ZFC + MC) and consider the following theory:

$$\text{ZFC} + \text{`}0^{\dagger}\text{ exists'} + \forall \alpha < \omega_1 (L_\alpha[0^{\dagger}] \text{ does not satisfy ZFC}).$$

(Call this ZFC + σ.) Now '$0^{\dagger}$ exists' implies the existence of the canonical inner model of ZFC + MC, so ZFC + σ provides an (optimal) fair interpretation of ZFC + MC, and thus, ZFC + σ maximizes over ZFC + MC. On the other hand, ZFC + MC implies that if $0^{\dagger}$ exists, then there is a countable α such that $L_\alpha[0^{\dagger}]$ satisfies ZFC,[37] that is, ZFC + MC proves ~σ. To show that ZFC + σ strongly maximizes over ZFC + MC, suppose ZFC + MC has an extension, T', with a fair interpretation of ZFC + σ. Then T' proves there is an inner model M of ZFC + σ. Because of its structure,[38] σ is absolute upwards for models like M, so the fact that M satisfies σ implies that V satisfies σ. We've been arguing inside T', so T' proves σ. But T' is an extension of ZFC + MC, so T' proves ~σ, too. Thus, T' is inconsistent. It follows that T strongly maximizes over ZFC + MC, and thus, that ZFC + MC is restrictive. But asserting the existence of a measurable cardinal certainly doesn't seem to restrict! Here our definitions produce a false positive.

To diagnose what's gone wrong in this case, we need to take a careful look at the theory ZFC + σ. Essentially, σ is a way of saying that $0^{\dagger}$ exists, but is not contained in any transitive set model of ZFC.[39] To say that $0^{\dagger}$ does not appear in any transitive set model of ZFC isn't as strong as saying that ZFC + '$0^{\dagger}$ exists' is inconsistent, but leans hard in that direction. From Gödel's second incompleteness theorem, we know that a

---

[36] For more, see Kanamori (1994), § 21.

[37] For connoisseurs: if κ is a measurable cardinal and $0^{\dagger}$ exists, then V_κ is a model of ZFC to which $0^{\dagger}$ belongs. This model has a submodel of the form $L_\kappa[0^{\dagger}]$, which is also a model of ZFC. $L_\kappa[0^{\dagger}]$, in turn, has a countable, transitive, elementary submodel containing $0^{\dagger}$. This last must be of the form $L_\alpha[0^{\dagger}]$ for some countable α.

[38] It is Σ^1_3.

[39] By essentially the argument of n. 37, if $0^{\dagger}$ is contained in some transitive set model of ZFC, it is contained in one of the form $L_\alpha[0^{\dagger}]$ for some countable α.

theory like ZFC + ~Con(ZFC) is consistent if ZFC itself is consistent, but given CONSISTENCY—our legitimate preference for consistent theories—and given that a metamathematical theorem like ~Con(T) provides good evidence for the inconsistency of T, it is hard to see how ZFC + ~Con(ZFC) could ever present itself as a serious candidate for adoption. And ZFC + σ is similarly flawed.

Looking back, we realize that among the theories listed (at the end of (i)) as strongly maximizing over ZFC + $V = L$ was ZFC + $V \neq L$ + ~Con(ZFC). (Of course, ~Con(ZFC) implies ~Con(ZFC + $V \neq L$).) This didn't cause any discomfort in the case of $V = L$ because there were also other, more attractive theories strongly maximizing over it; at the time, I simply referred to ZFC + $V \neq L$ + ~Con(ZFC) as a 'dud' that appears among the range of these theories, presumably one that would not be in the running (for good reasons) when we set out to chose between them. But in the current example, the only known theory that strongly maximizes over ZFC + MC is such a dud. It seems unreasonable to count ZFC + MC as restrictive on that account; it doesn't restrict set theory from developing in any direction we might be inclined to take.

Along this same line of thought, notice that another of the theories that strongly maximizes over ZFC + $V = L$ is the simple ZFC + $V \neq L$. This isn't a dud in the same sense as theories like ZFC + ~Con(ZFC), but it is an unattractive theory, nevertheless. It is too weak to settle any of the outstanding open questions, and though it does, strictly speaking, provide a new isomorphism type, it tells us nothing about that type, which makes it pretty much unusable. It is as if a physicist were to conclude that the known elementary particles—A, B, and C—do not exhaust the range of such particles, and then propose as a new physical theory the claim 'There are particles that are not of types A, B, or C'. This would not be a good physical theory, and likewise, ZFC + $V \neq L$ is not a good set theory. If the only theory strongly maximizing over T is a non-starter like ZFC + $V \neq L$, it again seems that T is not restricting set theory from developing in any direction we might be inclined to take.

This suggests that the moral of the false positive is this: a given set theory should be counted as restrictive only if it is strongly maximized over by a theory that has some merits of its own, only if it restricts set theory from developing in a direction that has identifiable attractions. None of the odd theories we've been considering—ZFC + σ, ZFC + ~Con(ZFC), ZFC + $V \neq L$—has such virtues; to make the case against ZFC + $V = L$, we must argue that ZFC + '$0^{\#}$ exists' or ZFC + MC does. Obviously, we can entertain no reasonable hope of giving a formal criterion for 'attractiveness', but we can argue directly for the attractions (or lack thereof) of individual theories.

Thus, Steel's ingenious examples show that the formal criterion for restrictiveness is not enough by itself; it must be supplemented by useful but nevertheless imprecise notions of the 'optimality' of inner model interpretations and 'attractiveness' of alternative theories. (iii) contains a sketch of how this might be done for the case of $V = L$.

(iii) *An Overview of the Naturalist's Case against V = L.* We've already seen (in (i)) that ZFC + $V = L$ is strongly maximized over by both ZFC + '$0^\#$ exists' and ZFC + MC. We've also seen (in (ii)) that the fair interpretations of ZFC + $V = L$ involved in these strong maximizations qualify as optimal. All that's left, then, is to argue that one or the other or both of ZFC + '$0^\#$ exists' and ZFC + MC are attractive theories in their own right, so that adopting ZFC + $V = L$ would restrict the development of set theory from avenues that it might otherwise legitimately value.

As the more technical of the two additional hypothesis, '$0^\#$ exists' is the more difficult to discuss in accessible terms. Nevertheless, I have little doubt that a careful and sophisticated analysis would uncover mathematically reasonable goals at various levels of generality that are served by the existence of $0^\#$ and its generalizations—$0^{\#\#}$, $0^{\#\#\#}$, etc. I leave it to my betters to determine how this story is best told. But notice, for the record, that the present argument does not require a conclusive justification of ZFC + '$0^\#$ exists' or a direct comparison of the virtues of ZFC + '$0^\#$ exists' with those of ZFC + $V = L$. To classify $V = L$ as restrictive, we need only establish that ZFC + '$0^\#$ exists' has merits of its own, that it is not a dud or a non-starter like ZFC + ~Con(ZFC) or ZFC + $V \neq L$. The point is that ZFC + $V = L$ will be classified as restrictive, not because the theories that maximize over it are shown to be 'better' in a direct comparison, but because they provide some identifiable benefits of their own while preserving all the benefits of ZFC + $V = L$.

The case of ZFC + MC is a bit easier than that of ZFC + '$0^\#$ exists'. We've seen (in I. 5) that the existence of a measurable cardinal settles a few of the open questions of descriptive set theory; given that providing a complete theory of sets of reals in one of the original goals of set theory, we can see that this is a welcome consequence.[40] It is also significant that

---

[40] Again, we know that ZFC + $V = L$ provides a more complete theory of sets of reals, and thus, achieves this goal better than ZFC + MC does, but what's at issue here is an

the existence of a measurable cardinal can be viewed as a generalization of Cantor's original positing of the completed infinite at ω; the vivid success of Cantor's hypothesis lends promise to large cardinal axioms, which generalize it. Along the same lines, the way measurability can itself be generalized—on the basis of its elementary embedding formulation—to a rich array of further large cardinals, including Woodins and supercompacts, is further evidence of its fruitfulness. (Not to mention that it implies the existence of $0^{\#}$!)

Obviously, this story can and should be elaborated, but I hope this is enough to suggest that there is ample material for the project. The point is that theories like ZFC + '$0^{\#}$ exists' and ZFC + MC have welcome consequences of various sorts, that either can be adopted without loss of the welcome consequences of ZFC + $V = L$, but that adopting ZFC + $V = L$ would foreclose the welcome consequences of ZFC + '$0^{\#}$ exists' and ZFC + MC. And we can make this case against $V = L$ without asking whether the welcome consequences of ZFC + MC are more welcome than those of ZFC + $V = L$. I offer this as a naturalistic attempt to spell out (at least some of) the grounds underlying the common intuition that $V = L$ is to be rejected because it is restrictive.

assessment of whether or not ZFC + MC has anything of interest to offer, not a direct comparison between ZFC + $V = L$ and ZFC + MC as means to various ends.

CONCLUSION

This book has been a prolonged meditation on a profound methodological problem in the foundations of contemporary set theory: how are the independent questions to be understood and resolved? My attention has focused on the practice of those set theorists, beginning with Gödel, who believe that the independent questions remain legitimate mathematical questions despite their independence from the standard axioms, and that new axioms should be investigated with an eye to settling them. My goal has been to explicate this practice in such a way as to lay bare its underlying rationality.

Along the way, I have described an approach to these problems based on mathematical realism, and argued that it is ultimately unsatisfying. In its place, I propose a very different approach—a largely non-philosophical (but not anti-philosophical) approach—that turns away from metaphysics and toward mathematics. This is the naturalism of my title. While the realist undertakes to determine the truth or falsity of independent set theoretic statements in the objective world of sets, the naturalistic methodologist ignores these issues to focus instead on the advantages and disadvantages of these statements as means towards particular mathematical goals. If and when the naturalistic philosopher does turn to metaphysical questions, she is constrained by the conclusions of her naturalistic methodological enquiries.

Finally, I hope to have demonstrated the viability of naturalism by mounting a naturalistic case against a particular new axiom candidate, the Axiom of Constructibility. In the end, I think the full naturalistic case against $V = L$ is broader than that sketched in my final section. It begins with the Definabilist vs. Combinatorialist considerations of II. 4, as understood in III. 5 ; these give us good reason to be wary of hypotheses like $V = L$. It continues through the case in III. 6, based on the notion that set theory aims to MAXIMIZE and UNIFY because of its foundational role. But it must also include an analysis of the purely set theoretic goals that motivate the development of set theory on its own terms, an additional level of means/ends reasoning only hinted at in footnotes to III. 5. All this is a long and fascinating story, though not an easy one for non-specialists (like me) to trace. My hope is that the beginnings sketched here are compelling enough to inspire those cleverer and more knowledgeable than myself—to correct my errors, to fill in what's been passed over in the case against $V = L$, and to extend naturalistic methods to the evaluation of higher and more controversial hypotheses.

BIBLIOGRAPHY

ACZEL, PETER (1988), *Non-Well-Founded Sets*, CSLI Lecture Notes, No. 14 (Stanford, Calif.: CSLI).

ADDISON, JOHN (1959), 'Some consequences of the axiom of constructibility', *Fundamenta Mathematicae*, 46, pp. 337–57.

AYER, A. J. (1946), 'The a priori', ch. VI of *Language, Truth and Logic*, 2nd edn. (New York: Dover, 1952), repr. in Benacerraf and Putnam (1983), 315–28. (Page references are to the reprinting.)

BAIRE, RENÉ, BOREL, EMILE, HADAMARD, JACQUES, and LEBESGUE, HENRI (1905), 'Five letters on set theory', transl. and repr. in Moore (1982), 311–20.

BALAGUER, MARK (1994), 'Against (Maddian) naturalized platonism', *Philosophia Mathematica*, 2, pp. 97–108.

—— (1995), 'A platonist epistemology', *Synthese*, 103, pp. 303–25.

BARWISE, JON (ed.) (1977), *Handbook of Mathematical Logic* (Amsterdam: North Holland).

BENACERRAF, PAUL (1965), 'What numbers could not be', repr. in Benacerraf and Putnam (1983), 272–94.

—— (1973), 'Mathematical truth', repr. in Benacerraf and Putnam (1983), 403–20.

—— (1981), 'The last logicist', *Midwest Studies in Philosophy*, 6, pp. 17–35, repr. in Demopoulos (1995), 41–67.

—— and PUTNAM, HILARY (eds.) (1983), *Philosophy of Mathematics*, 2nd edn. (Cambridge: Cambridge University Press).

BERKELEY, GEORGE (1734), *The Analyst*, repr. in *'De Motu' and 'The Analyst'*, ed. and trans. D. Jesseph (Dordrecht: Kluwer, 1992), 157–221.

BERNAYS, PAUL (1934), 'On platonism in mathematics', repr. in Benacerraf and Putnam (1983), 258–71.

BERNSTEIN, JEREMY (1983/4), 'Out of my mind . . . Ernst Mach and the quarks', *The American Scholar*, repr. as the introduction to Mach (1898).

BOOLOS, GEORGE (1971), 'The iterative conception of set', *Journal of Philosophy*, 68, pp. 215–32, repr. in Benacerraf and Putnam (1983), 486–502. (Page references are to the reprinting.)

—— (1987), 'The consistency of Frege's "Foundations of Arithmetic"', in J. J. Thompson (ed.), *On Being and Saying* (Cambridge, Mass.: MIT Press), 3–20, repr. in Demopoulos (1995), 211–33.

BOOLOS, GEORGE (1990), 'The standard of equality of numbers', in G. Boolos (ed.), *Meaning and Method* (Cambridge: Cambridge University Press), 261–77, repr. in Demopoulos (1995), 234–54.

—— (1995), Introduction to Gödel (1951), in Gödel (1995), 290–304.

BORN, MAX (1949), 'Einstein's statistical theories', in Schilpp (1949), 161–77.

BOS, H. J. M. (1974/5), 'Differentials, higher-order differentials, and the derivative in Leibnizian calculus', *Archive for the History of the Exact Sciences*, 14, pp. 1–90.

BOTTAZZINI, UMBERTO (1986), *The Higher Calculus: A History of Real and Complex Analysis from Euler to Weierstrass*, trans. W. van Egmond (New York: Springer).

BOYER, CARL (1949), *The History of the Calculus and its Conceptual Development* (New York: Dover, 1959).

BRIDGMAN, P. W. (1949), 'Einstein's theories and the operational point of view', in Schilpp (1949), 333–54.

BURALI-FORTI, CESARE (1897), 'A question on transfinite numbers', repr. in van Heijenoort (1967), 105–12.

BURGE, TYLER (1984), 'Frege on extensions of concepts, from 1884 to 1903', *Philosophical Rview*, 93, pp. 3–34.

BURGESS, JOHN (1984), Review of Wright (1983), *Philosophical Review*, 93, pp. 638–40.

—— (1990), 'Epistemology and nominalism', in Irvine (1990), 1–15.

—— (1992), 'Proofs about proofs', in M. Detlefsen (ed.), *Proof, Logic and Formalization* (London: Routledge), 8–23.

—— (199?), 'Occam's razor and scientific method', in Schirn (199?) (forthcoming).

—— and ROSEN, GIDEON (1997), *A Subject with no Object* (Oxford: Oxford University Press).

CANTOR, GEORG (1878), 'Ein Beitrag zur Mannigfaltigkeitslehre', *Journal für die reine und angewandte Mathematik*, 84, pp. 242–58.

—— (1883), 'Über unendliche, lineare Punktmannichfaltigkeiten, V', *Mathematische Annalen*, 21, pp. 545–86.

—— (1884a), 'An unpublished paper by Georg Cantor', ed. I. Grattan-Guinness, *Acta Mathematica*, 124 (1970), 65–107.

—— (1884b), 'Über unendliche, lineare Punktmannichfaltigkeiten, VI', *Mathematische Annalen*, 23, pp. 453–88.

—— (1895/7), *Contributions to the Founding of the Theory of Transfinite Numbers*, trans. P. E. B. Jourdain (La Salle, Ill: Open Court, 1952).

—— (1899), 'Letter to Dedekind', repr. in van Heijenoort (1967), 113–17.

CARNAP, RUDOLF (1950), 'Empiricism, semantics and ontology', repr. in Benacerraf and Putnam (1983), 241–57.

CARSON, EMILY (1996), 'On realism in set theory', *Philosophia Mathematica*, 4, pp. 3–17.

CARTWRIGHT, NANCY (1989), *Nature's Capacities and their Measurement* (Oxford: Oxford University Press).

CHIHARA, CHARLES (1973), *Ontology and the Vicious Circle Principle* (Ithaca, NY: Cornell University Press).

—— (1982), 'A Gödelian thesis regarding mathematical objects: Do they exist? Can we perceive them?', *Philosophical Review*, 91, pp. 211–27.

—— (1990), *Constructivism and Mathematical Existence* (Oxford: Oxford University Press).

COHEN, PAUL (1963/4), 'The independence of the continuum hypothesis, I and II', *Proceedings of the National Academy of Sciences, USA*, 50–1, pp. 1143–8, 105–10.

DALES, GARTH, and OLIVERI, GIANLUIGI (eds.) (199?), *Truth in Mathematics* (Oxford: Oxford University Press) (forthcoming).

DAUBEN, JOSEPH (1979), *Georg Cantor: His Mathematics and Philosophy of the Infinite* (Cambridge, Mass: Harvard University Press).

DAVIES, PAUL (1989a), 'The new physics: a synthesis', in his (1989b), pp. 1–6.

—— (ed.) (1989b), *The New Physics* (Cambridge: Cambridge University Press).

DE BROGLIE, LOUIS (1954), Foreword to Duhem (1906), v–xiii.

DEDEKIND, RICHARD (1872), 'Continuity and irrational numbers', repr. in Dedekind (1901), 1–27.

—— (1888), 'The nature and meaning of numbers', repr. in Dedekind (1901), 31–115.

—— (1901), *Essays on the Theory of Numbers*, trans. W. W. Beman (La Salle, Ill: Open Court, 1948).

DEMOPOULOS, WILLIAM (1994), 'Frege and the rigorization of analysis', *Journal of Philosophical Logic*, 23, pp. 235–46, repr. in Demopoulos (1995), 68–88.

—— (ed.) (1995), *Frege's Philosophy of Mathematics* (Cambridge, Mass.: Harvard University Press).

DETLEFSEN, MICHAEL (1986), *Hilbert's Program* (Dordrecht: Reidel).

DEVLIN, KEITH (1977), *The Axiom of Constructibility*, Lecture Notes in Mathematics No. 617 (Berlin: Springer).

—— (1984), *Constructibility* (Berlin: Springer).

DRAKE, FRANK (1974), *Set Theory: An Introduction to Large Cardinals* (Amsterdam: North Holland).

DUHEM, PIERRE (1906), *The Aim and Structure of Physical Theory* (Princeton, NJ: Princeton University Press, 1954).

DUMMETT, MICHAEL (1967), 'Platonism', repr. in *Truth and Other Enigmas* (Cambridge, Mass.: Harvard University Press, 1978), 202–14.

—— (1977), *Elements of Intuitionism* (Oxford: Oxford University Press).

EINSTEIN, ALBERT (1905), 'On the movement of small particles suspended in a stationary liquid demanded by the molecular-kinetic theory of heat', repr. in Einstein (1926), 1–18.

—— (1917), *Relativity: The Special and the General Theory*, trans. R. W. Lawson (New York: Crown, 1961).

—— (1926), *Investigations on the Theory of Brownian Movement*, ed. R. Furth, trans. A. Cowper (London: Methuen).

238 *Bibliography*

EINSTEIN, ALBERT (1949a), 'Autobiographical notes', in Schilpp (1949), 1–94.

—— (1949b), 'Reply to criticisms', in Schilpp (1949), 663–88.

—— and INFELD, LEOPOLD (1938), *The Evolution of Physics* (New York: Simon & Schuster).

EKLOF, PAUL (1976), 'Whitehead's problem is undecidable', *American Mathematical Monthly*, 83, pp. 775–88.

ENDERTON, HERBERT (1972), *A Mathematical Introduction to Logic* (New York: Academic Press).

—— (1977), *Elements of Set Theory* (New York: Academic Press).

FEFERMAN, SOLOMON (1964), 'Systems of predicative analysis', *Journal of Symbolic Logic*, 29, pp. 1–30.

—— (1995), Introduction to Gödel (1933), in Gödel (1995), 36–44.

FEYNMAN, RICHARD (1967), *The Character of Physical Law* (Cambridge, Mass.: MIT Press).

—— (1985), *QED: The Strange Theory of Light and Matter* (Princeton, NJ: Princeton University Press).

——, LEIGHTON, ROBERT, and SANDS, MATTHEW (1963), *The Feynman Lectures on Physics*, vol. i (Reading, Mass.: Addison-Wesley).

—— —— —— (1964), *The Feynman Lectures on Physics*, vol. ii (Reading, Mass.: Addison-Wesley).

FIELD, HARTRY (1980), *Science without Numbers* (Princeton, NJ: Princeton University Press).

—— (1985), 'Can we dispense with space-time?', repr. in Field (1989), 171–226.

—— (1989), *Realism, Mathematics, and Modality* (Oxford: Basil Blackwell).

FØLLESDAL, DAGFINN (1995), Introduction to Gödel (1961/?), in Gödel (1995), 364–73.

FRAENKEL, ABRAHAM (1922), 'Zu den Grundlagen der Cantor–Zermeloschen Mengenlehre', *Mathematische Annalen*, 86, pp. 230–7.

——, BAR-HILLEL, YEHOSHUA, and LEVY, AZRIEL (1973), *Foundations of Set Theory*, 2nd rev. edn. (Amsterdam: North Holland).

FREGE, GOTTLOB (1879), 'Begriffsschrift', repr. in van Heijenoort (1967), 5–82.

—— (1884), *Die Grundlagen der Arithmetic*, trans. J. L. Austin as *The Foundations of Arithmetic* (Evanston, Ill: Northwestern University Press, 1968).

—— (1893), *Grundgesetze der Arithmetik*, vol. i (Jena: Hermann Pohle). Partially trans. M. Furth as *The Basic Laws of Arithmetic* (Berkeley, Calif.: University of California Press, 1967).

—— (1902), 'Letter to Russell', trans. and repr. in van Heijenoort (1967), 127–8.

—— (1903), *Grundgesetze der Arithmetik*, vol. ii (Jena: Hermann Pohle). Excerpts trans. in P. Geach and M. Black (eds.), *Translations from the Philosophical Writings of Gottlob Frege* (Oxford: Basil Blackwell, 1970), 159–244.

—— (1924/5), 'A new attempt at a foundation for arithmetic', in *Posthumous Writings*, ed. H. Hermes *et al.* (Chicago, Ill.: University of Chicago Press, 1979), 278–81.

FRIEDMAN, HARVEY (1971), 'Higher set theory and mathematical practice', *Annals of Mathematical Logic*, 2, pp. 325–57.

FRIEDMAN, MICHAEL (1988), 'Logical truth and analyticity in Carnap', in W. Aspray and P. Kitcher (eds.), *History and Philosophy of Modern Mathematics* (Minneapolis, Minn.: University of Minnesota Press), 82–94.

GEACH, PETER (1956), 'On Frege's way out', repr. in Klemke (1968), 502–4.

GLYMOUR, CLARK (1980), *Theory and Evidence* (Princeton, NJ: Princeton University Press).

GÖDEL, KURT (1930), 'The completeness of the axioms of the functional calculus of logic', repr. in van Heijenoort (1967), 583–91, and in Gödel (1986), 102–23.

—— (1931), 'On formally undecidable propositions of *Principia Mathematica* and related systems', repr. in van Heijenoort (1967), 596–616, and in Gödel (1986), 144–95.

—— (1933), 'The present situation in the foundations of mathematics', in Gödel (1995), 45–53.

—— (1938), 'The consistency of the axiom of choice and of the generalized continuum hypothesis', repr. in Gödel (1990), 26–7.

—— (1939), 'Consistency proof for the generalized continuum hypothesis', repr. in Gödel (1990), 28–32.

—— (1944), 'Russell's mathematical logic', repr. in Gödel (1990), 119–41, and in Benacerraf and Putnam (1983), 447–69. (Page references are to the first of these reprintings.)

—— (1946), 'Remarks before the Princeton bicentennial conference on problems in mathematics', repr. in Gödel (1990), 150–3.

—— (1946/9), 'Some observations about the relationship between the theory of relativity and Kantian philosophy', in Gödel (1995), 230–59.

—— (1947), 'What is Cantor's continuum problem?', repr. in Gödel (1990), 176–87.

—— (1951), 'Some basic theorems on the foundations of mathematics and their implications' (the Gibbs lecture), in Gödel (1995), 304–23.

—— (1953/9), 'Is mathematics syntax of language?', in Gödel (1995), 334–62.

—— (1961/?), 'The modern development of the foundations of mathematics in the light of philosophy', in Gödel (1995), 374–87.

—— (1964), 'What is Cantor's continuum problem?', rev. version of Gödel (1947), repr. in Gödel (1990), 254–70, and in Benacerraf and Putnam (1983), 470–85. (Page references are to the first of these reprintings.)

—— (1986), *Collected Works*, vol. i, ed. S. Feferman *et al.* (New York: Oxford University Press).

—— (1990), *Collected Works*, vol. ii, ed. S. Feferman *et al.* (New York: Oxford University Press).

—— (1995), *Collected Works*, vol. iii, ed. S. Feferman *et al.* (New York: Oxford University Press).

GOLDFARB, WARREN (1995), Introduction to Gödel (1953/9), in Gödel (1995), 324–34.

GOODMAN, NELSON, and QUINE, W. V. (1947), 'Steps toward a constructive nominalism', *Journal of Symbolic Logic*, 12, pp. 105–22.

HACKING, IAN (1983), *Representing and Intervening* (Cambridge: Cambridge University Press).

HAHN, LEWIS, and SCHILPP, PAUL ARTHUR (eds.) (1986), *The Philosophy of W. V. Quine* (La Salle, Ill.: Open Court).

HALLETT, MICHAEL (1984), *Cantorian Set Theory and Limitation of Size* (Oxford: Oxford University Press).

HALLIDAY, DAVID, and RESNICK, ROBERT (1974), *Fundamentals of Physics*, 3rd edn. (New York: Wiley).

HARRINGTON, LEO (1978), 'Analytic determinacy and $0^\#$', *Journal of Symbolic Logic*, 43, pp. 685–93.

HAWKINS, THOMAS (1970), *Lebesgue's Theory of Integration: Its Origins and Development*, 2nd edn. (New York: Chelsea).

HECK, RICHARD, JR. (1993), 'The development of arithmetic in Frege's *Grundgesetze der Arithmetik*', *Journal of Symbolic Logic*, 58, pp. 579–601, repr. (with postscript) in Demopoulos (1995), 257–94.

HELLMAN, GEOFFREY (199?), 'Some ins and outs of indispensability: a modal-structuralist perspective', in A. Cantini, E. Casari, and P. Minari (eds.), *Logic in Florence* (Kluwer) (forthcoming).

HEYTING, AREND (1931), 'The intuitionist foundations of mathematics', repr. in Benacerraf and Putnam (1983), 52–61.

HILBERT, DAVID (1926), 'On the infinite', repr. in Benacerraf and Putnam (1983), 183–201.

HODES, HAROLD (1984), 'Logicism and the ontological commitments of arithmetic', *Journal of Philosophy*, 81, pp. 123–49.

IHDE, AARON (1964), *The Development of Modern Chemistry* (New York: Harper & Row).

IRVINE, ANDREW (ed.) (1990), *Physicalism in Mathematics* (Dordrecht: Kluwer).

ISHAM, CHRIS (1989), 'Quantum gravity', in Davies (1989b), 70–93.

JECH, THOMAS (1977), 'About the axiom of choice', in Barwise (1977), 345–70.

JENSEN, RONALD, and SOLOVAY, ROBERT M. (1970), 'Some applications of almost disjoint sets', in Y. Bar-Hillel (ed.), *Mathematical Logic and Foundations of Set Theory* (Amsterdam: North Holland), 84–104.

JOURDAIN, PHILIP E. B. (1904), 'On the transfinite cardinal numbers of well-ordered aggregates', *Philosophical Magazine*, 7, pp. 61–75.

—— (1952), Introduction to Cantor (1895/7).

KANAMORI, AKIHIRO (1994), *The Higher Infinite* (Berlin: Springer).

KITCHER, PHILIP (1983), *The Nature of Mathematical Knowledge* (New York: Oxford University Press).

—— (1989), 'Innovation and understanding in mathematics', *Journal of Philosophy*, 86, pp. 563–4.

KLEMKE, E. D. (ed.) (1968), *Essays on Frege* (Urbana, Ill.: University of Illinois Press).

KLINE, MORRIS (1972), *Mathematical Thought from Ancient to Modern Times* (New York: Oxford University Press).

KUNEN, KENNETH (1980), *Set Theory: An Introduction to Independence Proofs* (Amsterdam: North Holland).

LAKATOS, IMRE (ed.) (1972), *Problems in the Philosophy of Mathematics* (Amsterdam: North Holland).

LAVINE, SHAUGHN (1992), Review of Maddy (1990), *Journal of Philosophy*, 89, pp. 321–6.

LEVY, AZRIEL (1979), *Basic Set Theory* (Berlin: Springer).

—— and SOLOVAY, ROBERT M. (1967), 'Measurable cardinals and the continuum hypothesis', *Israel Journal of Mathematics*, 5, pp. 234–48.

MCALOON, KENNETH (1966), 'Consistency results about ordinal definability', *Annals of Mathematical Logic*, 2 (1971), 449–67.

MACH, ERNST (1898), *Popular Scientific Lectures*, trans. T. J. McCormack (La Salle, Ill.: Open Court, 1986).

MACLANE, SAUNDERS (1986), *Mathematics: Form and Function* (New York: Springer).

—— (1992), 'Is Mathias an ontologist?', in H. Judah, W. Just, and H. Woodin (eds.), *Set Theory of the Continuum* (Berlin: Springer), 119–22.

MCLARTY, COLIN (1993), 'Anti-foundation and self-reference', *Journal of Philosophical Logic*, 22, pp. 19–28.

MCMULLIN, ERNAN (1985), 'Galilean idealization', *Studies in the History and Philosophy of Science*, 16, pp. 247–73.

MADDY, PENELOPE (1983), 'Proper classes', *Journal of Symbolic Logic*, 48, pp. 113–39.

—— (1988), 'Believing the axioms', *Journal of Symbolic Logic*, 53, pp. 481–511, 736–64.

—— (1990a), *Realism in Mathematics* (Oxford: Oxford University Press).

—— (1990b), 'Physicalistic platonism', in Irvine (1990), 259–89.

—— (1990c), 'Mathematics and Oliver Twist', *Pacific Philosophical Quarterly*, 71, pp. 189–205.

—— (1992), 'Indispensability and practice', *Journal of Philosophy*, 89, pp. 275–89.

—— (1993a), 'Does *V* = *L*?', *Journal of Symbolic Logic*, 58, pp. 15–41.

—— (1993b), 'Wittgenstein's anti-philosophy of mathematics', in K. Puhl (ed.), *Wittgenstein's Philosophy of Mathematics*, Proceedings of the 15th Annual International Wittgenstein Symposium, Pt. 2 (Vienna: Hölder–Pichler–Tempsky), 52–72.

—— (1994), 'Taking naturalism seriously', in Prawitz, Skyrms, and Westerståhl (1994), 383–407.

—— (1995), 'Naturalism and ontology', *Philosophia Mathematica*, 3, pp. 248–70.

—— (1996a), 'The Legacy of "Mathematical Truth"', in A. Morton and S. Stich (eds.), *Benacerraf and his Critics* (Oxford: Basil Blackwell), 60–72.

242 *Bibliography*

MADDY, PENELOPE (1996b), 'Set theoretic naturalism', *Journal of Symbolic Logic*, 61, pp. 490–514.

—— (199?a), 'Ontological commitment: between Quine and Duhem', in J. Tomberlin (ed.), *Philosophical Topics* (forthcoming).

—— (199?b), 'Naturalizing mathematical methodology', in Schirn (199?) (forthcoming).

—— (199?c), 'How to be a naturalist about mathematics', in Dales and Oliveri (199?) (forthcoming).

—— (199?d), '$V = L$ and maximize', in V. Harnik and J. Makowsky (eds.), *Logic Colloquium 1995* (Berlin: Springer) (forthcoming).

—— (199?e), 'Mathematical progress', in E. Grosholz and H. Breger (eds.), *Mathematical Progress* (forthcoming).

MALAMENT, DAVID (1982), Review of Field (1980), *Journal of Philosophy*, 79, pp. 523–34.

MARTIN, DONALD A. (SVC), 'Sets versus classes', unpublished ms.

—— (1970), 'Measurable cardinals and analytic games', *Fundamenta Mathematicae*, 66, pp. 287–91.

—— (1975), 'Borel determinacy', *Annals of Mathematics*, 102, pp. 363–71.

—— (1976), 'Hilbert's first problem: the continuum hypothesis', in F. Browder (ed.), *Mathematical Developments Arising from Hilbert's Problems*, Proceedings of Symposia in Pure Mathematics, vol. xxviii (Providence, RI: American Mathematical Society), 81–92.

—— (1977), 'Descriptive set theory: projective sets', in Barwise (1977), 783–815.

—— (1978), 'Infinite games', in O. Lehto (ed.), *Proceedings of the International Congress of Mathematicians, 1978* (Helsinki: Academia Scientiarum Fennica, 1980), 269–73.

—— (199?), 'Mathematical evidence', in Dales and Oliveri (199?) (forthcoming).

—— and SOLOVAY, ROBERT M. (1970), 'Internal Cohen extensions', *Annals of Mathematical Logic*, 2, pp. 143–78.

—— and STEEL, JOHN (1988), 'Projective determinacy', *Proceedings of the National Academy of Sciences, USA*, 85, pp. 6582–6.

—— (1989), 'A proof of projective determinacy', *Journal of the American Mathematical Society*, 2, pp. 71–125.

—— (1994), 'Iteration trees', *Journal of the American Mathematical Society*, 7, pp. 1–73.

MATHIAS, ADRIAN R. D. (1992), 'What is MacLane missing?', in H. Judah, W. Just, and H. Woodin (eds.), *Set Theory of the Continuum* (Berlin: Springer), 113–18.

MILL, JOHN STUART (1843), *A System of Logic* (London: Longman, Green).

MILLER, RICHARD (1987), *Fact and Method* (Princeton, NJ: Princeton University Press).

MIRIMANOFF, DIMITRY (1917), 'Les antinomies de Russell et de Burali-Forti et le problème fondamental de la théorie des ensembles' and 'Remarques sur la théorie des ensembles et les antinomies cantoriennes', *L'Enseignement mathématique*, 19, pp. 37–52, 209–17.

MITCHELL, WILLIAM (1994), 'The core model up to a Woodin cardinal', in Prawitz, Skyrms, and Westerståhl (1994), 157–75.

—— and STEEL, JOHN (1994), *Fine Structure and Iteration Trees*, Lecture Notes in Logic No. 3 (Berlin: Springer).

MONK, RAY (1990), *Ludwig Wittgenstein* (New York: Penguin Books).

MONNA, A. F. (1972), 'The concept of function in the 19th and 20th centuries, in particular with regard to the discussions between Baire, Borel and Lebesgue', *Archive for History of the Exact Sciences*, 9, pp. 57–84.

MOORE, GREGORY H. (1982), *Zermelo's Axiom of Choice* (New York: Springer).

—— (1988), 'The roots of Russell's paradox', *Russell*, 8, pp. 46–56.

—— (1989), 'Toward a history of Cantor's continuum problem', in D. Rowe and J. McCleary (eds.), *The History of Modern Mathematics*, vol. i: *Ideas and their Reception* (Boston, Mass.: Academic Press), 79–121.

—— (1990), Introduction to Gödel (1947) and (1964), in Gödel (1990), 144–75.

MOSCHOVAKIS, YIANNIS (1980), *Descriptive Set Theory* (Amsterdam: North Holland).

—— (1994), *Notes on Set Theory* (New York: Springer).

MOSTOWSKI, ANDRZEJ (1972), 'Recent results in set theory', in Lakatos (1972), 82–96.

MYCIELSKI, JAN, and STEINHAUS, HUGO (1962), 'A mathematical axiom contradicting the axiom of choice', *Bulletin de l'Académie Polonaise des Sciences*, 10, pp. 1–3.

NYE, MARY JO (1972), *Molecular Reality* (New York: Elsevier).

PARSONS, CHARLES (1965), 'Frege's theory of number', in M. Black (ed.), *Philosophy in America* (Ithaca, NY: Cornell University Press), 180–203, repr. (with postscript) in Parsons (1983), 150–75, and in Demopoulos (1995), 182–210.

—— (1974), 'Sets and classes', repr. in Parsons (1983), 209–20.

—— (1977), 'What is the iterative conception of set?', repr. in Parsons (1983), 268–97, and in Benacerraf and Putnam (1983), 503–29. (Page references are to the second reprinting.)

—— (1980), 'Mathematical intuition', *Proceedings of the Aristotelian Society*, 80, pp. 145–68.

—— (1983), *Mathematics in Philosophy* (Ithaca, NY: Cornell University Press).

—— (1990), Introduction to Gödel (1944), in Gödel (1990), 102–18.

—— (1995), 'Platonism and mathematical intuition in Kurt Gödel's thought', *Bulletin of Symbolic Logic*, 1, pp. 44–74.

PERRIN, JEAN (1913), *Atoms*, trans. D. Hammick (New York: Van Nostrand, 1923).

POINCARÉ, HENRI (1909), 'The Logic of Infinity', repr. in Poincaré (1913), 45–64.

—— (1913), *Mathematics and Science: Last Essays*, trans. John Bolduc (New York: Dover, 1963).

PRAWITZ, DAG, SKYRMS, BRIAN, and WESTERSTÅHL, DAG (eds.) (1994), *Logic, Methodology and Philosophy of Science IX* (Amsterdam: Elsevier).

PUTNAM, HILARY (1971), 'Philosophy of logic', repr. in Putnam (1979), 323–57.

—— (1975), 'What is mathematical truth?', repr. in Putnam (1979), 60–78.

—— (1979), *Mathematics, Matter and Method: Philosophical Papers*, vol. i, 2nd edn. (Cambridge: Cambridge University Press).

QUINE, W. V. (1937), 'New foundations for mathematical logic', repr. (and expanded) in Quine (1980), 80–101.

—— (1940), *Mathematical Logic* (New York: Norton), rev. edn. (Cambridge, Mass.: Harvard University Press, 1951).

—— (1941), 'Whitehead and the rise of modern logic', repr. in Quine (1966), 3–36.

—— (1948), 'On what there is', repr. in Quine (1980), 1–19.

—— (1951), 'Two dogmas of empiricism', repr. in Quine (1980), 20–46.

—— (1954), 'Carnap and logical truth', repr. in Quine (1976), 107–32, and in Benacerraf and Putnam (1983), 355–76. (Page references are to the second reprinting.)

—— (1955a), 'On Frege's way out', repr. in Quine (1966), 146–58, and in Klemke (1968), 485–501.

—— (1955b), 'Posits and reality', repr. in Quine (1976), 246–54.

—— (1960), *Word and Object* (Cambridge, Mass.: MIT Press).

—— (1964), 'Ontological reduction and the world of numbers', repr. in Quine (1976), 212–20.

—— (1966), *Selected Logic Papers* (New York: Random House).

—— (1967), Introduction to Russell's 'The theory of types', in van Heijenoort (1967), 150–2.

—— (1969a), 'Ontological relativity', repr. in Quine (1969b), 26–68.

—— (1969b), *Ontological Relativity and Other Essays* (New York: Columbia University Press).

—— (1969c), *Set Theory and Its Logic*, rev. edn. (Cambridge, Mass.: Harvard University Press).

—— (1969d), 'Epistemology naturalized', in Quine (1969b), 69–90.

—— (1975a), 'The nature of natural knowledge', in S. Guttenplan (ed.), *Mind and Language* (Oxford: Oxford University Press), 67–81.

—— (1975b), 'Five milestones of empiricism', repr. in Quine (1981b), 67–72.

—— (1976), *The Ways of Paradox and Other Essays*, rev. edn. (Cambridge, Mass.: Harvard University Press).

—— (1980), *From a Logical Point of View*, 2nd edn. (Cambridge, Mass.: Harvard University Press).

—— (1981a), 'Response to Creswell', repr. in Quine (1981b), 179–81.

—— (1981b), *Theories and Things* (Cambridge, Mass.: Harvard University Press).

—— (1981c), 'Things and their place in theories', in Quine (1981b), 1–23.

—— (1984), Review of Parsons (1983), *Journal of Philosophy*, 81, pp. 783–94.

—— (1986), 'Reply to Parsons', in Hahn and Schilpp (1986), 396–403.

—— (1990), *Pursuit of Truth* (Cambridge, Mass.: Harvard University Press).

RAMSEY, FRANK PLUMPTON (1925), 'The foundations of mathematics', repr. in his *The Foundations of Mathematics and Other Logical Essays*, ed. R. Braithwaite (Totowa, NJ: Littlefield, Adams & Co., 1965), 1–61.

REICHENBACH, HANS (1949), 'The philosophical significance of the theory of relativity', in Schilpp (1949), 287–311.

RESNIK, MICHAEL (1985a), 'How nominalist is Hartry Field's nominalism?', *Philosophical Studies*, 47, pp. 163–81.

—— (1985b), 'Ontology and logic: remarks on Hartry Field's anti-platonist philosophy of mathematics', *History and Philosophy of Logic*, 6, pp. 191–209.

—— (1995), 'Scientific and mathematical realism: the indispensability argument', *Philosophia Mathematica*, 3, pp. 166–74.

RISKIN, ADRIAN (1994), 'On the most open questions in the history of mathematics: a discussion of Maddy', *Philosophia Mathematica*, 2, pp. 109–21.

RUSSELL, BERTRAND (1902), 'Letter to Frege', trans. and repr. in van Heijenoort (1967), 124–5.

—— (1903), *Principles of Mathematics* (New York: Norton).

—— (1906), 'On some difficulties in the theory of transfinite numbers and order types', repr. in Russell (1973), 135–64.

—— (1907), 'The regressive method of discovering the premises of mathematics', repr. in Russell (1973), 272–83.

—— (1920), *Introduction to Mathematical Philosophy* (New York: Simon & Schuster).

—— (1973), *Essays in Analysis*, ed. D. Lackey (New York: George Braziller).

—— and WHITEHEAD, ALFRED NORTH (1910), *Principia Mathematica to *56* (Cambridge: Cambridge University Press, 1967).

SCHILPP, PAUL ARTHUR (ed.) (1949), *Albert Einstein: Philosopher-Scientist* (La Salle, Ill.: Open Court).

SCHIRN, MATTHIAS (ed.) (199?), *Philosophy of Mathematics Today* (Oxford: Oxford University Press) (forthcoming).

SCOTT, DANA (1974), 'Axiomatizing set theory', in T. Jech (ed.), *Axiomatic Set Theory, Proceedings of Symposia in Pure Mathematics*, 13, Pt. 2 (Providence, RI: American Mathematical Society), 207–14.

—— (1977), Foreword to J. Bell, *Boolean-Valued Models and Independence Proofs in Set Theory* (Oxford: Oxford University Press), pp. xi–xviii.

SHAPIRO, STEWART (1983), 'Conservativeness and incompleteness', *Journal of Philosophy*, 80, pp. 521–31.

—— (1994), 'Mathematics and the philosophy of mathematics', *Philosophia Mathematica*, 2, pp. 148–60.

SHELAH, SHARON (1974), 'Infinite abelian groups, Whitehead problem and some constructions', *Israel Journal of Mathematics*, 18, pp. 243–56.

SHELAH, SHARON (1984), 'Can you take Solovay's inaccessible away?', *Israel Journal of Mathematics*, 48, pp. 1–47.

SHOENFIELD, J. R. (1967), *Mathematical Logic* (Reading, Mass.: Addison-Wesley).

—— (1977), 'Axioms of set theory,' in Barwise (1977), 321–44.

SKOLEM, THORALF (1922), 'Some remarks on axiomatized set theory', repr. in van Heijenoort (1967), 291–301.

SOBER, ELLIOTT (1993), 'Mathematics and indispensability', *Philosophical Review*, 102, pp. 35–57.

SOLOVAY, ROBERT M. (1965), 'The measure problem (abstract)', *Notices of the American Mathematical Society*, 12, p. 217.

—— (1969), 'The cardinality of Σ_2^1 sets of reals', in J. Bulloff *et al.* (eds.), *Foundations of Mathematics*, Symposium papers commemorating the 60th birthday of Kurt Gödel (Berlin: Springer), 58–73.

—— (1970), 'A model of set theory in which every set of reals is Lebesgue measurable', *Annals of Mathematics*, 92, pp. 1–56.

—— (1990), Introduction to Gödel (1938) and (1939), in Gödel (1990), 1–25.

—— (1995a), Introduction to Gödel's lectures on the consistency of the continuum hypothesis, in Gödel (1995), 114–27.

—— (1995b), Introduction to Gödel's unpublished material on the continuum hypothesis, in Gödel (1995), 405–20.

STEEL, JOHN (1993), 'Inner models with many Woodin cardinals', *Annals of Pure and Applied Logic*, 65, pp. 185–209.

—— (1996), *The Core Model Iterability Problem*, Lecture Notes in Logic, No. 8 (Berlin: Springer).

STEIN, HOWARD (1995), Introduction to Gödel (1946/9), in Gödel (1995), 202–29.

STEINER, MARK (1975a), *Mathematical Knowledge* (Ithaca, NY: Cornell University Press).

—— (1975b), Review of Chihara (1973), *Journal of Philosophy*, 72, pp. 184–96.

TILES, MARY (1989), *The Philosophy of Set Theory* (Oxford: Basil Blackwell).

TRUESDELL, C. A. (1960), *The Rational Mechanics of Flexible or Elastic Bodies, 1638-1788*, his introduction to Euler's *Opera Omnia*, ser. 2, vols. x and xi (Leipzig: Turici).

ULAM, STANISŁAW (1930), 'Zur Masstheorie in der allgemeinen Mengenlehre', *Fundamenta Mathematicae*, 16, pp. 140–50.

VAN FRAASSEN, BAS (1980), *The Scientific Image* (Oxford: Oxford University Press).

VAN HEIJENOORT, JEAN (ed.) (1967), *From Frege to Gödel* (Cambridge, Mass.: Harvard University Press).

VON NEUMANN, JOHN (1923), 'On the introduction of transfinite numbers', repr. in van Heijenoort (1967), 346–54.

—— (1925), 'An axiomatization of set theory', repr. in van Heijenoort (1967), 393–413.

WANG, HAO (1974a), 'The concept of set', from Wang (1974b), 181–223, repr. in Benacerraf and Putnam (1983), 530–70. (Page references are to the reprinting.)

—— (1974b), *From Mathematics to Philosophy* (London: Routledge & Kegan Paul).

WEYL, Hermann (1918), *Das Kontinuum* (Leipzig: Veit).

WILSON, MARK (1992), 'Frege: the royal road from geometry', *Nous*, 26, pp. 149–80, repr. (with postscript) in Demopoulos (1995), 108–59.

WITTGENSTEIN, LUDWIG (1914/51), *Culture and Value*, ed. G. H. von Wright, trans. P. Winch (Chicago: University of Chicago Press, 1980).

—— (1929/32), *Wittgenstein and the Vienna Circle*, ed. B. McGuinness (Oxford: Basil Blackwell, 1979).

—— (1932/4), *Philosophical Grammar*, ed. R. Rhees, trans. A. Kenny (Berkeley, Calif.: University of California Press, 1974).

—— (1933/44), *Remarks on the Foundations of Mathematics*, rev. edn., ed. G. H. von Wright, R. Rhees, and G. E. M. Anscombe, trans. G. E. M. Anscombe (Cambridge, Mass.: MIT Press, 1978).

—— (1938/46), *Lectures and Conversations*, ed. C. Barrett (Berkeley, Calif.: University of California Press, 1967).

—— (1939), *Lectures on the Foundations of Mathematics*, ed. C. Diamond (Ithaca, NY: Cornell University Press, 1976).

—— (1953), *Philosophical Investigations* (New York: Macmillan).

WOODIN, W. HUGH (1988), 'Supercompact cardinals, sets of reals, and weakly homogeneous trees', *Proceedings of the National Academy of Sciences, USA*, 85, pp. 6587–91.

WRIGHT, CRISPIN (1983), *Frege's Conception of Numbers as Objects* (Aberdeen: Aberdeen University Press).

YOUSCHKEVITCH, A. P. (1976), 'The concept of function up to the middle of the 19th century', *Archive for the History of the Exact Sciences*, 16, pp. 37–85.

ZERMELO, ERNST (1904), 'Proof that every set can be well-ordered', repr. in van Heijenoort (1967), 139–41.

—— (1908a), 'A new proof of the possibility of a well-ordering', repr. in van Heijenoort (1967), 183–98.

—— (1908b), 'Investigations in the foundations of set theory I', repr. in van Heijenoort (1967), 200–15.

—— (1930), 'Über Grenzzahlen und Mengenbereiche: Neue Untersuchungen über die Grundlagen der Mengenlehre', *Fundamenta Mathematicae*, 16, pp. 29–47.

INDEX